THE MYTHICAL ZOO

THE MYTHICAL ZOO

AN ENCYCLOPEDIA OF ANIMALS IN
WORLD MYTH, LEGEND, & LITERATURE

Boria Sax

A B C  C L I O

Santa Barbara, California   Denver, Colorado   Oxford, England

Library of Congress Cataloging-in-Publication Data

Sax, Boria.
    The mythical zoo : an encyclopedia of animals in world myth, legend,
and literature / Boria Sax.
        p. cm.
Includes index.
Summary: An encyclopedia of animals as they have appeared in myth and
legend throughout history.
ISBN 1-57607-612-1 (hardcover : alk. paper); 1-57607-613-X (e-book)
    1. Animals—Folklore—Encyclopedias. 2. Animals—Mythology—
Encyclopedias. 3. Animals, Mythical—Encyclopedias. 4. Animals in
literature—Encyclopedias. [1. Animals—Folklore—Encyclopedias. 2. Animals—
Mythology—Encyclopedias. 3. Animals, Mythical—Encyclopedias.] I. Title.
GR705 .S344 2001
398.24'5'03—dc21
                                    2001004422

06 05 04 03 02 01   10 9 8 7 6 5 4 3 2 1

This book is also available on the World Wide Web as an e-book.
Visit abc-clio.com for details.

ABC-CLIO, Inc.
130 Cremona Drive, P.O. Box 1911
Santa Barbara, California 93116-1911

This book is printed on acid-free paper ∞.

Manufactured in the United States of America

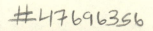

CONTENTS

Preface, vii
Introduction, ix

The Mythical Zoo

PREFACE

Now as at all times I can see in the mind's eye,
In their stiff, painted clothes, the pale unsatisfied ones
Appear and disappear in the blue depth of the sky
With their ancient faces like rain-beaten stones,
And all their helms of silver hovering side by side,
And all their eyes still fixed, hoping to find once more,
Being by Calvary's turbulence unsatisfied,
The uncontrollable mystery on the bestial floor.
　　　　　　　—W. B. Yeats, "The Magi"

I would like to thank my wife, Linda Sax, who read parts of this manuscript at various stages of composition and made numerous corrections and offered many useful suggestions. My thanks go also to Dianne Littwin, my agent, who did an excellent job of selling the manuscript. Several of the illustrations are taken from the Pictorial Archive Series from Dover Books. All biblical quotations are from the Jerusalem Bible.

Both animals and their symbolism are overwhelming in their variety, and this book could theoretically become as endless as the subject itself. In a similar way, the sources of this book are so many and varied that it would be very cumbersome, and perhaps impossible, to list them all. I have tried, in the selected references following each entry, to give either those that had special importance for the preceding text or would be particularly useful to the reader who wishes to investigate further. Citations have been confined to direct quotations. In a few retellings of stories, I have taken the liberty of inventing bits of dialogue to make the story more vivid, and these, of course, are not cited. In doing this, I have never changed the plot, and this mild license certainly follows in the tradition of the legendary Aesop, whose stories exist in several variants but not in any definitive edition.

In a project such as this one, finding material is never a problem, but deciding what to leave out can be a very big one indeed. My policy has been to emphasize depth rather than breadth. I wished to convey the ideas underlying the treatment of animals in myth, legend, and related aspects of human culture, rather than simply give bits of disconnected information. This book is intended not only for use as a reference but also to document how profoundly animals and their symbolism are integrated into human values. It is important for us to be aware of this today, as we confront the massive extinction of familiar varieties and the genetic engineering of new ones.

INTRODUCTION

There are more things in heaven and earth, Horatio,
Than are dreamt of in your philosophy.
  —William Shakespeare, *Hamlet* (act 1, scene 5)

You are sitting in the park and your eyes meet those of a squirrel. What do you see? The Vikings saw a messenger that moved back and forth between the underworld and the abodes of humans and gods. The Ainu saw the worn, discarded sandals of the god Aioina. For late medieval people, the squirrel was sometimes a form taken by a witch. Simply by saying the name "squirrel," however, we dissipate part of the mystery.

In the second biblical tale of creation, Adam gains dominance over the animals by naming them (Gen. 2:20). Did he give them names as species such as "Elephant"? Did he give them individual names such as "Babar"? In the language of God, words fit reality so perfectly that there was no need for such distinctions. Since human beings were scattered after Babel, we have lost that perfect language. A single creature is "Rover," "dog," "pet," "canid," "mammal," and many other things besides.

Without the primal language of Adam, the act of naming the animals is a continuous process. Aristotle first systematized the classification of animals. In the modern era, the Aristotelian system of classification was greatly refined by Carolus Linnaeus. Before the eighteenth century, bats were usually considered winged mice. After looking carefully at their anatomy, Linnaeus decided that bats were really primates. Reconsidering, he finally placed them in a separate family, and that is where they have stayed ever since. The classifications we use in everyday life are usually rough, informal versions of those that have been worked out by scientists over the centuries.

Scientists generally regard animals as belonging to different species when they do not habitually mate together. Although dogs, wolves, jackals, and coyotes are capable of mating together, they generally do not do so in the wild, so each of these is considered a distinct species. In contexts of domestication, however, such a definition becomes problematic. A horse and an ass not only can mate but also are often induced to do so to produce a mule, which retains useful qualities of both species. Today, with food animals the genetic manipulation is so intense that sometimes one can no longer speak of species at all. The turkeys that are sold for Thanksgiving have such large breasts that they cannot reach one another to mate but must be reproduced through artificial insemination.

With gene splicing, it is now possible to cross divisions not only of species and genus but even between plants and animals. Scientists have produced a cross between a sheep and a goat, known as a "geep." They have inserted genes from flounder into the genetic code of tomatoes to increase resistance to frost, and they have inserted genes from chickens into tomatoes to make the plants more resistant to disease. They have placed human genetic material in pigs to produce organs that will not be rejected when transplanted into human beings. These creatures are like the monsters of folklore, and it may well be that in the future we will see crosses between human beings and chimpanzees or gorillas. Contemporary genetic theory views animals, including human beings, less as individuals or representatives of species than as repositories of hereditary information. As we examine new ways of thinking about animals, it is best not to forget the older ones. These traditional perspectives are intimately linked to cultural values and practices that we have developed over millennia.

When it comes to establishing the identity of an animal, biology is not nearly enough. Often we are so impressed with the success of science that we forget it is merely one aspect of a larger tradition. Every name places an animal in a tradition that is constantly developing. It surrounds the animal with ideas and associations. My dictionary defines "tradition" as "an inherited pattern of thought and action." It comes from "trade," which originally meant "track." To study a tradition is to track a creature, as though one were a hunter, back through time. The names we give animals carry intricate expectations and assumptions. As we learn of the traditions that have grown up around animals, they regain something of the magical quality that they had in cave paintings of prehistoric times.

Tradition does not mean uncritically following precedents but simply retaining continuity with the values of the past. Some people are suspicious of tradition because they associate it with cruelty and injustice—as in the Inquisition, for example. Yet it is the values embedded in tradition that enable us to protest such abuses. The Christian value of love, for example, proved more basic than injunctions against heresy, and so the Inquisition was ended. Traditions develop in an organic way, which is a bit like the evolution of living organisms. Like many species of animals and plants, traditions are vanishing.

To define a kind of animal strictly in terms of biology is too narrow, too technical, and too restrictive. It is not even very meaningful under conditions of domestication, whether on a farm or in a zoo, where animals do not necessarily choose the partners with which they breed. It becomes almost meaningless with genetic engineering, where breeders exchange genes across lines of species. Suppose we work to preserve either a species in the wild or a breed in domesticity. What exactly are we preserving? A collection of physical characteristics? A piece of genetic code? A part of a habitat?

If we define each sort of animal as a tradition, our definition includes all of these and more. It also includes stories from myth, legend, and literature. All of these, with the love and fear they may engender, are part of an intimate relationship with human beings that has been built up over millennia. To regard each sort of animal as a tradition also encourages respect. Why should we care about species extinction? Why should we care about the welfare of strays? Appeals to transcendent reasons do not satisfy people in our secular society. Appeals to pragmatic reasons, such as preserving the ecosystem, are easily subject to challenge. Tradition links animals to the ideas, practices, and events that make up human culture.

Perhaps the greatest of the many ethical problems faced by human beings at the beginning of a new millennium is deciding the extent to which we are entitled to alter the natural world for our convenience. Unprecedented capabilities such as genetic engineering and the harnessing of atomic energy give us far more power than wisdom. The idea of every animal as a tradition will not give us a simple answer to our dilemmas, but it will at least provide a way in which to think of them. Traditions tend to degenerate when they are not adjusted to changing conditions, but alterations are generally made in a cautious and respectful manner. To preserve an animal as a tradition, we must know it intimately, we must be familiar with the lore that has grown up around the creature since time immemorial.

Metamorphosed Animals

Remember the Frog Prince from a famous fairy tale by the Grimm brothers, the very first in their collection? Well, he had a long and distinguished history, though it is not mentioned in books for children. Long ago in the days of the mammoths, he was a powerful totem, sacred to human beings. During the Middle Ages, he joined forces with the Devil to become the animal companion, or "familiar," of a witch. Then, probably in the eighteenth or nineteenth century, he reformed. A young woman transformed him into a human prince by—depending on which version of the story you prefer—giving him a kiss, throwing him against a wall, or chopping off his head.

In tribal societies, human form is not always important. All beings are forever changing their shapes, like waves breaking on the shore. Human beings may become ravens, while hares may turn into human beings. You become what you eat; you become what you are eaten by. Death is simply a transition, a bit like the passage from girl to woman or boy to man.

Totems are animals from which a tribe traces its ancestry. Beyond that, they are guardians of the tribe, at times revisiting the members in trances or in dreams. Among the Indo-Europeans, the tribal totem was perhaps most frequently the wolf. Going into battle, warriors would be possessed by the spirit of the wolf, and our legends of werewolves are a legacy of that archaic time. A mother wolf suckled Romulus and Remus, the legendary founders of Rome; a woodpecker fed them. Among people of the Far North, totems were most often birds. For the Native Americans of the Northwest coast, the favorite totem was frequently the raven, sometimes the bear; for tribes farther south, it might have been the coyote, beaver, or jaguar.

Legends of totemistic societies commemorate learning the arts of civilization from observation of animals. The Navaho Indians, for example, tell how women learned to weave from Spider Woman. Other stories may tell of learning to build from beavers or to hunt from wolves. Traditional dances often imitate the motions of animals, while music sometimes mimics their sounds. Observing what bears or snakes would eat has revealed many herbal medicines. Many totems from archaic societies lived on as the helpful animals in fairy tales— the cat in Charles Perrault's "Puss in Boots," for example. Today the legacy of totemism is everywhere, from the mascots of sports teams to heraldic animals on coins.

Marriages of people with animals often led to the founding of a tribe. As they hunted or went off to war, men told tales of animal brides. As they sat together and spun, women told of animal grooms.

For both men and women, the animal was that mystery in a partner
that no intimacy could fully overcome. In each other's eyes, lovers
still are "squirrel" and "dove."

Among many tribal peoples, the ability to take the form of an animal had been the sign of a great shaman, but this changed in urban
societies. In the *Metamorphoses* of the Roman poet Ovid, taking the
form of an animal was generally a punishment. The maiden Arachne
was changed into a spider for being arrogant. Zeus changed King Lycaon into a wolf for serving his guests human flesh. The goddess Diana changed the hunter Actaeon into a stag for intruding upon her
bath. Buddhists and Hindus believed that animals needed many rein-
carnations spread across millennia to become human beings.

Divine Animals

The prehistoric cave paintings of France and Spain are among the most
ancient works of art that we have. The human beings in these paintings
are usually crude stick figures that the artists must not have considered
very important. The animals are painted with far more care and passion. The first clearly identifiable religious shrines in history are at
Çatal Hüyük in Anatolia and date from around the middle of the seventh millennium A.D. They were dedicated to animals, especially bulls,

Some of the forms taken by the Egyptian cow-goddess Hathor.

but also vultures, foxes, and others. The ancient Egyptians believed their creator god Ptah was incarnated in a bull named Apis that could be recognized by specific markings. Apis was kept in a temple and honored in sacred rites. The Egyptians also worshipped their gods as incarnated in cats, ibises, and many other creatures.

Over millennia, anthropomorphic goddesses and gods slowly replaced the animal deities. The archaic divinities accompanied their more human successors, often as mascots or alternate forms. Athena, for example, was pictured with an owl, Zeus with an eagle; Odin was accompanied by ravens and by wolves; Mary, mother of Christ, was often shown with a dove. The monkey-god Hanuman, who fought alongside the hero Rama in the epic *Ramayana,* is now perhaps the most popular figure in the Hindu pantheon. There is a bit of an archaic mother-goddess in the "wicked witch" of Halloween, pictured with a faithful spider at her side.

As tribes were absorbed into kingdoms and empires, their religions were fused and local deities were combined. Archaic practices sometimes continued as local cults or customs. In Rome, people would sometimes keep snakes in their homes, believing it the spirit of an ancestor. This practice survived into modern times in parts of Italy. A few holy men and women retained the shaman's gift of speaking with creatures of the woods and fields. Saint Francis preached to the birds, while Saint Anthony evangelized the fish.

Figures that blend human and animal features became common with the transition from hunting and gathering to agriculture. The gods and goddesses of ancient Egypt often had a human torso and the head of an animal—crocodile, baboon, jackal, cat, falcon, or ibis. The

Greeks had their centaurs and satyrs, while the Hebrews had cherubim and seraphim. Garuda, the carrier of the Hindu god Vishnu, had the torso and face of a man but the wings and beak of an eagle. Yet another fantastic animal was al-Borak, the steed on which Mohammed made his flight to Heaven; she had the body of a horse and the face of a woman, and she could see the dead.

The unicorn, usually shown as a horse with the horn of a narwhal, became the most popular fantastic animal in the Middle Ages. Edward Topsell, a zoologist of Renaissance England, rebuked those who doubted the existence of the unicorn, saying that that was to doubt the power of God. In the early modern period, many sailors told of encountering mermaids, creatures that embodied the wonder and terror of the sea.

Demonic Animals

The Hebrews constantly struggled against the old animal cults. Moses killed thousands of people for introducing the Hebrews to worship of the golden calf. The old totems would not simply disappear; they often became devils. A devil will often have the horns of a bull, the teeth of a wolf, the legs of a goat, the tail of a monkey, and the tusks of a boar. One poor weaver who was convicted of sorcery in early modern Scotland described demons as being "like flies dancing around a candle" (Scott, p. 249).

In witch trials of the Renaissance, especially in Britain, people claimed that demons would visit a sorcerer as an animal companion. The demon was frequently a cat, and felines might be burned along with a convicted witch. Often, it was a snake, toad, lizard, spider, cat, or dog. A suspect was sometimes forced to sit in the middle of a room where she would be deprived of sleep and watched for twenty-four hours. Witch hunters made a hole in her door, and any creature that approached her, whether spider or cat, was considered her familiar. For the poor and vulnerable, keeping pets or even feeding animals could arouse suspicion of witchcraft.

Furthermore, witches themselves were often shape shifters. In sixteenth-century Scotland, Isobel Gowdie confessed without compulsion to being a witch. She said that witches commonly took the form of animals such as crows or cats. Once she took on the form of a hare to deliver a message for the Devil. A neighbor's hounds began to chase her; she jumped into her home and took refuge behind a chest. Finally, Isobel managed to elude the dogs long enough to say a charm that returned her to human form. A mark where a dog had nipped at her remained on her back.

Satiric Animals

In *The Epic of Gilgamesh*, from Mesopotamia early in the first millennium, the hero undertook a journey to the world below and found the plant of immortality. A snake stole the plant, shed its skin, and lived eternally. Ever since human beings have striven to be heroes, animals have deflated human pretensions. Along with the story of Gilgamesh, archeologists digging up the library of Assyrian king Assurbanipal found the first animal epic, known as *The Fable of the Fox*, where lion, dog, and wolf all boast and plead, acting as pretentious and vulnerable as human beings.

After Homer wrote of the heroes of the Trojan War, an unknown Greek wrote *Batrachyomachy*, the epic battle between frogs and mice. These mighty warriors clashed around a pond, as Zeus and all the gods looked on. The invincible mouse-hero Meridarpax seemed about to lead his men—or, rather, mice—to victory, when Zeus sent armored crabs to drive the invaders away.

According to Judeo-Christian tradition, animals spoke to Adam and Eve in the Garden of Eden. Countless tales all over the world begin with a formula like "In the days when animals talked like people . . ." The fables of Aesop, who lived on the Greek island of Sámos in the sixth century before Christ, are set in a world where all beings, from gnat to lion, can speak to one another like human beings. In epic stories of animals, such as the Hindu *Panchatantra* or the Arab *Kalila wa Dimna*, animals have a society unto themselves. They bargain, quarrel, and make friends with little regard for species.

In the folklore of the Merovingians, who ruled Germany and much of France at the beginning of the Middle Ages, the creatures of the forest have a court. The lion is king, while the bear and stag are nobles. Every year at the summer solstice they meet to hear lawsuits and dispense justice. As human rulers in Europe appeared less glamorous and more corrupt, people also took a more jaundiced view of the animal kingdom. In stories of Renard the Fox, told throughout Europe toward the end of the Middle Ages, the king of beasts was just a fool for all his pomp. The wolf and fox quarreled over chicken stolen from the coop, in the language of piety and romance.

Brer Rabbit outwitted the fox and wolf in tales told among people of African descent in the Caribbean and the South of the United States. Satirists such as J. J. Grandville drew goats and roaches parading about in formal clothes. On the editorial pages of newspapers, politicians today become newts and dogs.

Illustration by J. J. Grandville to a fable by La Fontaine, "The Frog Who Wanted to Be as Large as a Bull."

Political Animals

Animals became degraded as giant industries took agriculture over from smaller farms and private homes. Once feared and killed with ceremony, animals are now raised in cramped cells and according to rigid regimens, and then they are slaughtered on assembly lines. And yet this degradation and helplessness makes human beings identify with animals. The experimental lab where several million rats and rabbits are killed every year has often been used as a metaphor for Bolshevik Russia; the industrial abattoir has become a common metaphor for the concentration camps in Nazi Germany.

Animal Farm by George Orwell, first published in 1946, begins with the animals revolting and driving the farmers away. Gradually, however, the pigs become more and more like human beings, as they learn to sell, slaughter, imprison, and exploit the other creatures. The novella ends, "The creatures outside looked from man to pig, and from pig to man again; but already it was impossible to say which was which" (p. 128).

Animals are constantly used in propaganda. Portrayed as apes, people might be mocked. Or people might be called "pigs" or "sheep," so they could be slaughtered. They might be called "wolves" or "bears" so they could be hunted down, or "viruses" so they could be exterminated. In *Maus* (1991), a comic book telling of his father's life in Auschwitz, cartoonist Art Spiegelman made inmates into mice, the Nazis into pigs or cats. In 1988 the prime minister of Israel said he would crush the Palestinians "like grasshoppers." A sales pitch for mouthwash shows little creatures cowering in terror and tells us, "They're germs; they deserve to die." One advertisement for Orkin pest control shows the barrel of a large high-tech gun pointed by an exterminator with the caption "The last thing a bug sees." Still another, this one for Combat Roach Bait, shows a bunch of dead cockroaches lying on their backs with the caption "Tired of living with thousands of strangers"—a clear appeal to resentment against recent immigrants (Boxer, section 4, p. 2).

The Modern Period and After

People usually think that there is a big difference between animals and ourselves, but just what it is, is very hard to say. Is it our intellect? Emotion? Stupidity? Technology? Tragic destiny? Religion? Language? Success? Morality? Wickedness? Power? War? Our use of fire? Our upright stance?

Modern scientific culture began in the seventeenth century with René Descartes. He described animals as intricate machines, yet few people could believe that of a beloved dog. As pets proliferated, so did their stories: a cat had learned to open all the locks in her home; a pig could do arithmetic and spell; a nightingale gave singing lessons to other birds from inside its cage; dogs beat all comers in card games. Toward the end of the sixteenth century, Michel de Montaigne in France collected anecdotes in "Apology for Raymond Sebond" to show that human intelligence was not so special. He explained that tuna must know mathematics since they move in regular patterns; they must also know astrology, since they guide themselves by stars.

In the Romantic Movement of the late eighteenth and early nineteenth centuries, a revolt against the constraints of civilization led to the celebration of wild animals. Georges-Louis Leclerc de Buffon, the most popular naturalist of the time, believed that all animals once had a civil society with laws, before they were murdered and enslaved by human beings. The last remnants could be found in the New World, where beavers still built villages, created constitutions, and held courts of law.

In the eighteenth century, Linnaeus classed human beings as primates, placing them in the same genus as apes, monkeys, and lemurs. Then in 1859 Charles Darwin proclaimed his theory of evolution in *The Origin of Species*, suggesting (at first, he did not dare say it outright) that humanity evolved from something like an ape. There were passionate debates and embarrassed snickers; people joked about having gorillas for grandfathers. Racists depicted those from other cultures—Africans, Irish, Jews, and Japanese—as being like apes. The targeted people were drawn as slouched over with dangling arms and receding foreheads.

But modern people have feared above all the "animal" in themselves. The metaphor of "the beast within" was used in the Victorian era to explain all sorts of vices, from lechery to gluttony. Physiognomists looked for animal features in the faces of human beings. Sigmund Freud and his disciples divided human character into the "id," which represented the beast (or instinct) in human beings, and the "ego," or self—the two of which were in constant conflict.

Today anthropomorphic animals are everywhere we look: tigers sell cornflakes and gasoline; talking cows sell milk; bulls and ducks represent sports teams. Centerfolds of undressed women in *Playboy* are called "bunnies," while in *Penthouse*, a rival magazine, they are called "pets." The cartoon character Joe Camel was so effective in selling cigarettes to teenagers that massive protests forced the tobacco company to discontinue ads with him in 1997.

Hatred as well as love can still "humanize" other creatures. Demonic animals fill our horror stories, such as *Cujo* by Stephen King (1981), named after a beloved pet who goes on a rampage of lurid murders. Perhaps Cujo was infected with rabies by a bat? Perhaps Cujo is a reincarnation of a policeman who killed many women? The author leaves the reader to decide. Diabolic animals also fill the silver screen, from the shark in *Jaws* to the tyrannosaurus in *Jurassic Park* and the snake in *Anaconda*.

Over the millennia, the greatest trend in our understanding of animals has been an increasing secularization. In early human settlements, animal gods replaced the totems of tribal societies. These deities, in turn, were generally subordinated to anthropomorphic gods and goddesses. By the Middle Ages, the predominant view of animals was symbolic and allegorical, and it became increasingly naturalistic in the modern period. Today, countless species are driven to extinction, and people, who are becoming increasingly urban, have ever less contact with animals on a daily basis. This has resulted in two seemingly contradictory trends.

On the one hand, there is ruthless exploitation of animals in factory farms and in industry. In 1989, an animal was patented for the first time: a mouse genetically engineered to develop cancer. The cloning of a sheep named Dolly in 1997 has largely broken down the boundary between living organisms and manufactured objects. There are now entire varieties called "pharm animals," developed solely to produce certain chemicals.

At the same time, our current estrangement from animals seems to have revived some of the numinous qualities they had in the archaic past. They connect us with a history in which people often seemed to live on a grander and more heroic scale than they do today. Now the discipline of ecology makes animals guardians of the ecosystem, and their fate is linked with that of human beings. Ecologists count frogs or butterflies to learn about a possible apocalypse; these researchers are a bit like the ancient priests of Greece or Babylon who would foretell the future from the flight of birds. Scientists have tried to decipher the languages of animals, from bees to monkeys.

Every animal is a tradition, and together animals are a vast part of our heritage as human beings. No animal completely lacks humanity, yet no person is ever completely human. By ourselves, we people are simply balls of protoplasm. We merge with animals through magic, metaphor, or fantasy, growing their fangs and putting on their feathers. Then we become funny or tragic; we can be loved, hated, pitied, and admired. For us, animals are all the strange, beautiful, pitiable, and frightening things that they have ever been: gods, slaves, totems, sages, tricksters, devils, clowns, companions, lovers, and far more. When we contemplate the inner life of animals, myth is finally our only truth.

Selected References

Boxer, Sarah. "Look into Those Big Bug Eyes and Shoot." *New York Times* 4 (August 27, 1995): 2.

Cooper, J. C. *Symbolic and Mythological Animals.* London: Aquarian/ Thorson's, 1992.

Griffin, Donald R. *The Question of Animal Awareness: Evolutionary Continuity of Mental Experience.* New York: Rockefeller University, 1976.

King, Stephen. *Cujo.* New York: New American Library, 1981.

Le Guin, Ursula. *Buffalo Gals and Other Animal Presences.* New York: New American Library, 1987.

Montaigne, Michel de. "Apology for Raymond Sebond." In *The Complete Essays of Montaigne* (2 vols.). Trans. Donald M. Frame. Stanford: Stanford University Press, 1959, vol. 1, pp. 428–561.

Orwell, George. *Animal Farm.* New York: Harcourt, Brace and Janovich/ Signet Classics, 1946.

Rifkin, Jeremy. *The Biotech Century: Harnessing the Gene and Remaking the World.* New York: Jeremy P. Tarcher/ Putnam, 1998.

Sax, Boria. *The Frog King: On Legends, Fables, Fairy Tales, and Anecdotes of Animals.* New York: Pace University Press, 1990.

———. "The Mermaid and Her Sisters: From Archaic Goddess to Consumer Society." *ISLE* 72 (summer 2000): 43–54.

———. *The Parliament of Animals: Legends and Anecdotes, 1775–1900.* New York: Pace University Press, 1990.

Scott, Sir Walter. *Letters on Demonology and Witchcraft*. J. and J. Harper, 1832.

Spiegelman, Art. *Maus: A Survivor's Tale* (2 vols.). New York: Pantheon, 1991.

THE MYTHICAL ZOO

Albatross

See Seagull, Albatross, and Other Seabirds

Ant

In the ant's house, the dew is a flood.
—Persian proverb

In Greek mythology, after a plague had wiped out his people, King Aeacus begged Zeus, the supreme god, to give him as many citizens as there were ants in a certain sacred tree. Zeus changed the ants in the tree into warriors. These were the Myrmidons, who later fought under Achilles. Ants are a lot like warriors: They march in columns; they show unbounded courage. No matter how large their foe, they still attack. No matter how many of their number are killed, they will not surrender or retreat. An ant that is decapitated will continue to bite at its adversary. For their size, ants are the strongest creatures in the world, able to carry objects many times larger than themselves.

According to another myth, Zeus changed himself into an ant to make love to the maiden Eurymedusa in Thessaly. She gave birth to a child named Myrmidon, ancestor of the martial race. The efficient Myrmidons not only prevailed in war but also prospered in peace. Like ants, they would diligently work the soil.

Ants have regular access to the mysterious depths of the earth, where metals and jewels are found. Herodotus told of ants in India that were larger than foxes. As they burrowed in the ground, these ants threw up huge heaps of sand that contained gold. The Indians watched from a distance, then quickly packed the sand into bags and carried them away on camels. The treasure hunters had to rely on surprise in these raids, since the ants were extremely swift in pursuit.

"Why bother about the winter?" asked the grasshopper in a famous fable attributed to Aesop. The ant said little but went on storing

1

*Illustration by
Ludwig Becker
of soldier ants on
sentry duty.*

grain. Snow began to fall, and the grasshopper begged for food. "You sang all summer, so now dance all winter," replied the ant. This fable makes ants appear almost as ruthless in their diligence as they are in their wars. "Idler, go to the ant; ponder her ways and grow wise," says the Bible in a passage traditionally attributed to Solomon (Prov. 6:6). Around the world, the proverbial ant has long been synonymous with industry. Tribal healers in Morocco fed ants to lethargic patients.

Creatures that live beneath the earth, the world of the dead, are frightening and mysterious. At festivals of the dead, Jains and certain Hindus feed the ants. West African tribes have traditionally believed that ants carry messages from the gods. In ancient Greece and Rome, ants sometimes appeared in prophetic dreams. When King Midas was a child, ants carried grains of corn to his lips as he slept, a sign that he would one day achieve enormous wealth.

According to Plutarch, when the Greek commander Cimon sacrificed a goat to the god Dionysus during a war with the Persians, ants swarmed around the animal's blood. They carried blood to Cimon and wiped it on his big toe, predicting his imminent death. Ants are still used in divination. To step on ants brings rain. A nest of ants near your door means you will grow rich.

For all their reputation for ruthlessness, ants in folklore often protect the weak and vulnerable. In the story "Cupid and Psyche," told in the novel *The Golden Ass* by first-century Roman author Lucius Apuleius, the young maiden Psyche had fallen in love with Cupid. The goddess Venus, Cupid's mother, did not approve. She captured Psyche, locked her up with a huge stack of many kinds of grain, and demanded that all be sorted by nightfall. The ants pitied Psyche and carried the different grains, one by one, to separate piles.

According to Cornish legend, ants are fairies, which over the centuries have grown ever smaller and are now about to disappear. Other legends make them the souls of unbaptized children, who are admitted neither to Heaven nor to Hell. All such tales reveal a kinship that people feel with ants. Part of the reason for the feeling may be recognition of similarities between their bodies and ours, large heads and hips but slender waists. It may also be that their small size and consequent vulnerability elicit our sympathy.

Ants appear in many European tales as grateful animals. In one fable by Jean de La Fontaine, a dove used a blade of grass to a rescue a drowning ant. Later, a hunter tried to shoot the dove. The ant bit the man on the heel and made his arrow go astray.

In Aztec mythology the seed of maize was once kept in a mountain by red ants. The god Quetzalcoatl transformed himself into a black ant and stole the seed to bring food to humankind. As in so many European stories, grain formed a bond between ants and humanity. The Hopi Indians traditionally believed that the first human beings were ants.

Illustration by Ludwig Becker of ants holding an assembly in a pear tree.

In *Walden*, Henry Thoreau reported going to a woodpile and finding a battle raging between two varieties of ants, with the ground already "strewn with the dead and dying." In one camp were "red republicans"; in the other, "black imperialists." "On every side," Thoreau continued, "they are engaged in deadly combat . . . and human soldiers never fought so resolutely." A valiant Achilles among the red ants came to avenge a fallen comrade. He killed a black Hector, while the enemy cavalry swarmed over his limbs. The gentle hermit of Walden Pond wrote of this carnage with great excitement (pp. 206–207). Perhaps those who believe there are no more heroes today should spend more time around anthills. Ants live in a world a bit like that of old romances, filled with monsters (that is, termites, spiders, woodpeckers, or human beings). Kingdoms with mysterious powers surround the anthill. The ants must constantly battle in order to survive.

Perhaps when kings and lords ruled most of the world, it was easier to identify with ants. The anthill could be seen to be a perfect authoritarian state, one in which everyone accepted his or her role. As

governments became more democratic, however, it became harder to believe that such a society was possible or even desirable. Artists and writers have tried to individualize ants, and that certainly has not been easy.

When people look closely at ants, there is no telling what they may find. Michel de Montaigne reported in "Apology for Raymond Sebond" that the philosopher Cleanthes once observed a negotiation between two opposing anthills. After some bargaining, the body of a dead ant was ransomed for a worm.

Rev. J. G. Wood, in his extremely popular collection of animal anecdotes entitled *Man and Beast* (first published in 1875), gave this report of a lady who had killed several ants:

> After a while, one more (ant) came, discovered his dead companions and left. He returned with a host of others. Four ants were assigned to each corpse, two to carry it and two to walk behind. Changing tasks at times so as not to become weary, the ants eventually arrived at a sandy hill where they dug graves and buried the dead. About six ants, however, refused to help with the digging. These were set upon by the rest, executed and unceremoniously thrown into a mass grave. (p. 42)

Anthills are like metropolises or vast armies, and people can almost never distinguish among individuals. Perhaps, though, even ants can have their nonconformists. The Disney film *Antz* (1998) tells of one ant named Z, who was unable to work or dance in the same way as the others. Gradually, he moved the workers over to his style of thinking. He saved the colony from a flood and married the princess. Did they live happily ever after? The ants started having millions of children, but their anthill did not seem greatly changed. Perhaps the movie is about the loosening of social restraints in the West during the late sixties. "Revolutions may be fun," the message seems to be, "but don't expect too much! Just like ants, we are ruled by our genes."

Nothing we can say about ants is ever quite right. They are not really communist or authoritarian. They don't really even have workers, soldiers, slaves, or queens. As scientists discover more about these creatures, the experience of ants becomes harder to imagine. French author Bernard Werber took up the challenge in his novel *Empire of Ants* (first English edition, 1998). The ants, he explained, communicate mostly by scent, using pheromones, so they are like one enormous mind spread across the globe. A young female ant, separated from her community, set out to found a new anthill. She explored the world of a yard, filled with beetles, termites, and birds, until finally she became queen of one vast colony that was powerful enough to challenge human beings.

Well, ants really do not threaten us, but their society will almost certainly outlast humankind. Ants thrive everywhere, from the Brazilian rain forests to the tiny cracks between the pavements in New York. Though they may appear frail, ants are able to survive even nuclear tests. During the Renaissance, an ant was sometimes depicted devouring an elephant to show the changeable nature of all things.

Selected References

Apuleius, Lucius. *The Golden Asse of Lucius Apuleius.* Trans. William Adlington. London: Abbey Library, ca. 1920.

Davies, Malcolm, and Jeyaraney Kathirithamby. *Greek Insects.* New York: Oxford University Press, 1986.

La Fontaine, Jean de. "The Pigeon and the Ant." In *Selected Fables.* Trans. James Michie. New York: Viking, 1979, p. 49.

Montaigne, Michel de. "Apology for Raymond Sebond." In *The Complete Essays of Montaigne* (2 vols.). Trans. Donald M. Frame. Stanford: Stanford University Press, 1959, vol. 1, pp. 428–561.

Plutarch. *Greek Lives: A Selection of Nine Greek Lives.* Trans. Robin A. Waterfield. New York: Oxford University Press, 1999.

Thoreau, Henry David. *Walden, and Other Writings of Henry David Thoreau.* New York: Modern Library, 1965.

Topsell, Edward, and Thomas Muffet. *The History of Four-Footed Beasts and Serpents and Insects* (3 vols.). New York: Da Capo, 1967 (facsimile of 1658 edition).

Werber, Bernard. *Empire of the Ants.* Trans. Margaret Rocques. New York: Bantam, 1999.

Wood, Rev. J. G. *Man and Beast: Here and Hereafter.* New York: Harper and Brothers, 1875.

Ape and Monkey

How much like us is the revolting ape.
—Attributed to Ennius by Cicero, *De Natura Deorum*

Nowadays, scientists distinguish among species using methods based on evolutionary descent. Earlier methods were less precise but more colorful. The word "monkey" did not enter the English language until the sixteenth century. Prior to then, the word "ape" was the only common term for primates other than human beings. The difference between apes and human beings was never clear either. If somebody called you an ape, it might not be just a metaphor. In *History of Four-Footed Beasts and Serpents, and Insects,* published in 1647, Edward Topsell included the satyr and the sphinx among apes—the term encompassed any creature that was almost "human" but not quite. This sort of definition, and not a conventional biological one, must be used when looking back over the lore of apes and monkeys through the centuries.

Among the most popular religious figures of China is Old Monkey, who was born when lightning struck a stone. Old Monkey broke into heaven, got drunk on celestial wine, erased his name from the book of the dead, and fought back the armies of Heaven. Finally, he caused so much trouble that the gods and goddesses appealed to the Buddha for help. The Buddha sought out Old Monkey, and their dialogue went something like this:

"What do you wish?" the Buddha asked Old Monkey.

"To rule in Heaven," Old Monkey replied.

"And why should this be granted to you?" asked the Buddha.

"Because," said Old Monkey, "I can leap across the sky."

"Why," laughed the Buddha, "I will bet that you cannot even leap out of my hand," and he picked Old Monkey up. "If you can do that, you may rule in Heaven, but if you can't, then you must give up your claim."

Old Monkey made a tremendous jump and soon arrived at a pillar of Heaven. To show that he had been there, he urinated and wrote his name. Then, with another leap, Old Monkey returned to claim his prize.

Illustration of various monkeys from a nineteenth-century book of natural history.

"What have you done?" asked the Buddha.

"I have gone to the end of the universe," said Old Monkey.

"You have not even left my hand," laughed the Buddha, and he raised one finger. Old Monkey recognized the pillar of Heaven and realized that what the Buddha said was true.

The Buddha imprisoned Old Monkey under a mountain for five hundred years. Finally, Old Monkey was rescued by Kwan-Yin, bodhisattva of mercy. To redeem himself, Old Monkey had to guard a Buddhist monk on a dangerous journey from China to India. Old Monkey served faithfully, through fantastic adventures in which he did battle with countless demons and sorcerers, and finally became a Buddha in the end. These adventures were chronicled in the epic novel *Journey to the West*, attributed to Wu Ch'eng-en, in the early sixteenth century. Old Monkey was often depicted alongside solemn portraits of Buddhist sages, but even as a Buddha he retained a mischievous streak.

The monkey-god Hanuman is similarly beloved in the Hindu pantheon, largely because he is capable of both childish mischief and noble sacrifice. When Hanuman was a child, he looked up, saw the sun, and thought it must be a delicious fruit. He jumped to pick it and rose so high that Indira, god of the sky, became angry. Indira hurled a thunderbolt at the intruder, striking Hanuman in the jaw. At this the father of Hanuman—Vayu, the god of winds—became furious and started a storm that threatened to destroy the entire world. Brahma, the supreme god, placated Vayu by granting Hanuman invulnerability. Indira added a promise that Hanuman could choose his own moment of death. Ever since, however, monkeys have had swollen jaws. This story, taken from the *Ramayana*, an ancient Hindu epic, shows the amusement with which apes have generally been regarded throughout the world. Because Hanuman is a monkey, his divinity does not seem intimidating. In the Hindu *Panchatantra* and the early Buddhist Jatakas, the ape was one of the more sensible animals, often serving as chief adviser to the lion king. People in the Far East regard the playfulness of monkeys and apes as divine serenity, not simple frivolity as do people in the West.

To find a major simian figure in Western religion, we must go back to Thoth, the baboon-headed god of the ancient Egyptians. Thoth was the scribe of Osiris, ruler of the dead, and inventor of the arts and sciences. Perhaps in those archaic times reading and writing, still novel and full of mystery, appeared more simian than human. Today, of course, we use language, especially writing, to proudly distinguish ourselves from all other creatures.

By contrast, the peoples of Mesopotamia and Greece often regarded apes as degenerate human beings. According to one Jewish legend, some of the people who built the Tower of Babel were turned into apes. According to another, apes were the descendants of Enosh. On the other hand, some legends also claimed that Adam had a tail like that of a monkey. The debate over whether apes should be considered human probably goes back to the beginnings of civilization. In the religion of Zoroaster, the monkey or ape is the tenth and lowest variety of human beings created by Ohrmuzd.

In many mythologies, apes or monkeys were created as alternative human beings. In Philippine mythology, Bathala, the creator of the world, was lonely and decided to make the first human being out of clay. When he was almost finished, the lump of clay slipped from his hand and trailed to the ground. That created a tail, and the figure became a monkey. Bathala created people on his second try. According to the mythology of the Maya, the Creator once tried to fashion people from wood. They behaved so wickedly that all the animals and deities turned against them. Finally, the few that remained retreated into the forest and became howler monkeys. Then the Creator made human beings out of maize.

Renaissance illustration showing an apelike creature allegedly captured in 1530 in Saxony.

Closely related to apes, at least in folklore, were wild men and women. Perhaps the first of the wild men was Enkidu in the heroic epic of Gilgamesh from Mesopotamia in the early second millennium B.C. Created not by human parents but out of clay by the gods, Enkidu jostled with the beasts at the watering hole. With more than human strength, he overturned the traps of hunters. All who saw him were filled with fear and awe. A sacred prostitute was sent to him, and she taught him the ways of men. He started to drink wine instead of water, and he began to dress as a human being. But then the beasts rejected him, and human sorrow slowed his step.

Body hair, especially on men, has traditionally been a sign of wildness. In the Bible, Esau, eldest son of Isaac and brother of Jacob, was covered with hair. He was also a bit of a wild man, one who liked open country and hunting but was ready to sell his birthright for a bowl of soup. When Isaac was old and blind, he prepared to bless Esau. Aided by his mother, Jacob covered himself up with the fleece of lambs and then went to his father, pretending to be Esau. Isaac insisted on touching his son, but fooled by the fur, Isaac allowed Jacob to steal his brother's benediction (Gen. 27). This story has often been interpreted as a triumph of civilization over savagery.

Apes are forest dwellers. Ape sightings are rare in the wild and usually occur under tense conditions. In the early sixth century B.C., the Carthaginian navigator Hanno led an enormous expedition down the West Coast of Africa. According to his account of the voyage, they sighted a huge mountain called the "chariot of the gods." There, Hanno and his crew confronted wild men and women covered with hair, creatures that threw stones at them and climbed adroitly up the slopes. Ever since, people have speculated whether the wild beings were people in skins, chimpanzees, baboons or, most likely, gorillas. At any rate, the vague rumors of wild men and women began to circulate. Accounts of ape sightings from mariners back from distant lands blended with reports from distant lands of men who had the heads of dogs, men with the feet of goats, men with their faces on their chests, and many other creatures just as strange. Stories of such wild men with clubs were told around the fire and sometimes acted out in medieval pageants.

In the Islamic world as well, the resemblance of apes to human beings was disconcerting, and apes were often invoked to mock or parody humans. The anonymous medieval *Arabian Nights Entertainments* contained a story in which a cruel Jinn, finding his mistress in the company of a man, killed the woman and turned her companion into an ape. The man wandered in simian form until he came to the court of a king, who was amazed at his skill in calligraphy and chess. The king proudly ordered that the ape be dressed in fine silk and fed rare delicacies. A eunuch summoned the princess so that she, too, might see the wondrous animal. On entering the room, the princess immediately veiled her face, for she, as a Muslim, considered it improper for a strange man to see her features. She explained to her father that, unbeknownst to him, she had studied under a wise woman, was herself a great enchantress, and knew that the visitor was not an ape but a man. The king commanded his daughter to disenchant the ape so that he might make this man his vizier. The Jinn appeared, his eyes burning like torches, and the princess began to recite some magic words. As the two traded spells, the Jinn became a lion, a scorpion, then an eagle; the princess became a serpent, a vulture, then a cock. They fought underneath the ground, in water, and in fire, until at last the Jinn was burned to ashes. The princess received a mortal wound as well, but she was able to disenchant the ape before she died.

The Barbary apes (which zoologists do not consider apes at all) are the only primates other than human beings that are somewhat indigenous to Europe. At some point in time, they came over from Africa, though nobody knows if they swam or were carried by boats. At any rate, they were found scattered near the Mediterranean coast until modern times, and a small population still hangs on at the Rock of Gibraltar. The sight of these apes vanishing into the trees certainly contributed to many legends about fairies and wild men. In the Middle Ages, Barbary apes started to become popular as pets of nobles and wandering entertainers. The word "monkey" was probably first used to refer to the Barbary apes. While the etymology is uncertain, "monkey" may have originally been an affectionate diminutive meaning "little monk." Renaissance painters such as Albrecht Dürer often included monkeys in religious and courtly paintings to add a playful touch to otherwise solemn occasions.

At about the same time, a sudden expansion of maritime trade and exploration took Europeans to all the exotic corners of the world. Europeans began to discover the great apes and remote cultures, and sorting the one from the other was not an easy matter. Scientists as well as sailors might often conflate orangutans with gorillas and African tribesmen, all of whom were known mostly through fleeting glimpses and rumor. Tribes in West Africa regarded apes as human. Some believed that chimpanzees could speak but chose not to so that they would not be forced to work. *Orangutan* was initially a Malay word for "wild man." When the Dutch anatomist Nicolaas Tulp dissected the body of an orangutan in 1641, he thought that it was the satyr of classical mythology. A colleague of his, Jacob de Bondt, believed these creatures were "born of the lust of Indonesian women who consort in disgusting lechery with apes" (Dekkers, p. 41).

Explorers in the sixteenth and seventeenth centuries brought back tales of apes living in huts, foraging in trees, and fighting using cudgels. Some people maintained that apes ravished human females or made war on human towns. The enormously popular *History of Animated Nature* published by Oliver Goldsmith during the late eighteenth century tells how apes in Africa would sometimes steal men and women to be their pets. Visitors to Victorian zoos complained that the apes tried to seduce human women. Sometimes apes were even made to put on clothes. It took several centuries to untangle the fantastic accounts.

Literature as well blended folklore about wild men and women with recent accounts of primitives and other primates. In *Gulliver's Travels* by Jonathan Swift (first published in 1726), the hero was marooned on an island and adopted by highly civilized horses. In the woods on the fringes of their settlement were hairy men and women known as "yahoos." These primates constantly wallowed in their own filth. They had long claws and swung through trees. They roared, howled, and made hideous faces. The narrator was filled with revulsion at them, yet he could not help but acknowledge that these creatures were his own kind. Such reaction clearly showed the feelings of Europeans at the discovery of their kinship with apes. Gulliver's disgust with the yahoos anticipated the racism that took such terrible forms in the next few centuries. He reported, with fear but no suggestion of disapproval, that the horses proposed a complete extermination of yahoos.

Apes later figured prominently in racist propaganda. We can see this in the story "Ursprung der Affen" (The origin of apes), told by the late-medieval folk poet and shoemaker Hans Sachs. Jesus, accompanied by Peter, stopped in his wanderings at the house of a blacksmith. Along came an elderly cripple, and Peter asked Jesus to make the invalid young and strong. Jesus promptly consented and asked the smith to heat his furnace. When the fire was blazing, Jesus placed the cripple inside it, where the invalid glowed with light. After saying a blessing, Jesus took the man out and dipped him in water; everyone was amazed to see the cripple transformed into a strong young fellow. After Jesus left, the elderly mother-in-law of the smith sought to be rejuvenated. The smith, who had watched everything, agreed to perform the transformation. After placing the old woman in the furnace, just as Jesus had done with the cripple, the smith realized the magic was not working properly. He pulled out his screaming mother-in-law and dipped her in water. Her screams brought the smith's pregnant wife and his also pregnant daughter-in-law to the scene, where they saw the old woman in the tub howling, with her face wrinkled and distorted. They were so terrified that they give birth to apes instead of human beings.

Apes have long had a reputation for being undignified and immoral. Long before the dawn of Darwinism, the essayist Montaigne, denouncing human pride, had observed in "Apology for Raymond Sebond" that of all animals the apes, "those that most resemble us," were "the ugliest and meanest of the whole herd" (p. 478).

Quasimodo, the hero of Victor Hugo's *Hunchback of Notre Dame*, was certainly based partly on reports of anthropoid apes that were filtering back to Europe when the novel was written in the middle of the nineteenth century. The character was deformed and could barely speak, yet he had superhuman strength and agility. He climbed like an ape among the gargoyles and demons in the remote corners of the cathedral. His tragedy was to be almost human, yet not quite. He could feel the same passions as other men, yet could not share their lives.

Just as the process of distinguishing the apes and men was nearly complete, Charles Darwin announced his theory of evolution with *The Origin of Species* in 1859. Not everybody could understand the book, and some people thought that Darwin was crazy. In a famous debate in 1860, Bishop Wilberforce asked Thomas Huxley whether the ape was on his mother's or his father's side of the family. Huxley replied that rather than be descended from a gifted man who mocks scientific discussion, "I unhesitatingly affirm my preference for the ape" (Barber, p. 27). His brilliant rhetoric may have won the day, but wisecracks about apes for grandparents were constantly made in the vitriolic debate about evolution.

In the early twentieth century, racist caricatures usually showed people, whether African, Jewish, Irish, or Japanese, slouched over in apelike fashion. Adolf Hitler wrote in *My Struggle* (first published in 1926) that Germans must dedicate the institution of marriage to the goal of "bring[ing] forth images of the Lord, not abominations that are part man and part ape" (Sax, p. 54).

Today, rumors continue to circulate about ape-men such as the Yeti. In supermarkets all around the world, tabloids announce such exploits as "I was Bigfoot's Love Slave." Fantastic anthropoid apes entertain us in films, from *King Kong* to *Planet of the Apes*. Our movies are also full of wild men, from Tarzan of the apes to Rambo. Middle-class men in contemporary America now flock to "wild man weekends" in the woods, where they listen to lectures and discuss their problems around a fire.

In the early eighties, experiments in teaching great apes to communicate with human beings, either by computers or by hand signs, generated a great deal of excitement. Jane Goodall and many others observed that apes use tools such as stones to crack nuts and sticks to extract termites from wood. It is odd, though, that people found such observations surprising, since simian use of language and tools had been regularly noted in natural history books until about the end of the nineteenth century. In 1994 Paola Cavalieri and Peter Singer published *The Great Ape Project: Equality beyond Humanity*, a book of essays championing the cause of extending human equality to apes. Few if any of the contributors realized that they were merely reviving a very old debate.

Selected References
Barber, Lynn. *The Heyday of Natural History: 1820–1870*. Garden City, NY: Doubleday, 1980.
Boia, Lucian. *Entre l'ange et la bête: Le mythe de l'homme différent de l'Antiquité à nos jours*. Paris: Plon, 1995.
Cavalieri, Paola, and Peter Singer, eds. *The Great Ape Project: Equality beyond Humanity*. New York: St. Martin's Press, 1995.

Coomarasway, Ananda K., and Sister Nivedita. *Myths of the Hindus and Buddhists*. New York: Dover, 1967.

Corbey, Raymond, and Bert Theunissen, eds. *Ape, Man, and Apeman: Changing Views since 1900*. Leiden: Leiden University Press, 1995.

Dekkers, Midas. *Dearest Pet: On Bestiality*. Trans. Paul Vincent. New York: Verso, 2000.

Goldsmith, Oliver. *History of Animated Nature* (4 vols.). Edinburgh: Smith, Elder/T. Tegg, 1838.

Haraway, Donna. *Primate Visions: Gender, Race, and Nature in the World of Modern Science*. New York: Routledge, 1990.

Montaigne, Michel de. "Apology for Raymond Sebond." In *The Complete Essays of Montaigne* (2 vols.). Trans. Donald M. Frame. Stanford: Stanford University Press, 1959, vol. 1, pp. 428–561.

Sachs, Hans. "Ursprung der Affen." In *Hans Sachsens Ausgewählte Werke* (2 vols.). Leipzig: Insel Verlag, 1945, vol. 1, pp. 166–169.

Sax, Boria. *Animals in the Third Reich: Pets, Scapegoats, and the Holocaust*. New York: Continuum, 2000.

Swift, Jonathan. *Gulliver's Travels*. New York: Penguin, 1987.

Tompkins, Ptolemy. *The Monkey in Art*. Wappinger's Falls, NY: M. T. Train/Scala Books, 1994.

Wu Ch'eng-en. *Journey to the West* (4 vols.). Trans. Anthony C. Yu. Chicago: University of Chicago Press, 1982.

Ass, Mule, and Camel

Orientis partibus
Adventavit Asinus,
Pulcher et fortissimus.
Sarcinis aptissimus.
[From the East
the ass approached,
lovely and very strong.
It carried the sacks.]
—From the carol sung at the medieval Feast of the Ass at Beauvais, France

The ass, or donkey, and camel are, for the most part, animals of peace that help with daily tasks, while the horse excels in arts of war. The ass and camel both have greater endurance than the horse, though they are not as large or fast. The camel thrives especially in hot, dry climates, and the ass is very surefooted in mountainous areas. The ancient Mesopotamians noticed that crossing a mare, a female horse, with a jackass, or male donkey, would produce a mule, which had many advantages of both species. Nevertheless, the mule has sometimes been stigmatized as a product of an "unnatural" union.

The *Avesta*, a scripture of the Zoroastrians, told of an ass with three legs, six eyes, nine mouths, and a single horn. This animal was as large as a mountain and stood in the middle of a wild sea, whose waters it forever purified. This early unicorn symbolized the primeval innocence of a time when the world was new, but it also shows the awe with which the ass was once regarded.

The ass was first domesticated in ancient Egypt around 3000 B.C., well over a millennium before the horse. In the Bible, Job marveled at the difference between the donkeys of god and those kept by human beings:

> Who gave the wild donkey his freedom,
>   and untied the rope from his proud neck?
> I have given him the desert as a home,
>   the salt plains as his own habitat.
> He scorns the turmoil of the town:
>   there are no shouts from a driver for him to listen for.
> In the mountains are the pastures that he ranges
>   in quest of any green blade or leaf. (29:5–8)

The donkey has a reputation as a sort of holy fool, strangely poised between wisdom and stupidity. In this nineteenth-century illustration by J. J. Grandville, a charlatan exhibits a supposedly learned donkey at a fair.

The ass survives precariously in the wild today, but most people think of this animal as fully domesticated. The ass began to acquire new associations through domestication, without casting off old ones, until it became one of the most complex animal symbols of all.

The camel has had much the same fate in Arab lands and parts of Eurasia as the ass has in most areas around the Mediterranean. As the horse took over the more glamorous role of a mount of warriors, the camel, like the ass, was increasingly relegated to being a beast of burden. Although the Bible does not specify this, the Magi, or wise men who brought gifts to the infant Jesus, are traditionally portrayed riding on camels. Though sometimes praised for humility, the camel had the additional reputation of being lascivious. Jeremiah used the camel as a symbol of Israelites who had commerce with heathens:

> A frantic she-camel running in all directions
> bolts for the desert,
> snuffing the breeze in desire;
> who can control her when she is in heat? (2:23–24)

Much later, the Wife of Bath in Chaucer's *Canterbury Tales* urged women to fight their husbands like camels.

A twelfth-century French depiction of a troubadour as a donkey. It is very similar to illustrations from the ancient Near East.

Because of the unstinting service it performed, the Hebrews had a special affection for the ass, much as the Arabs did for the camel. According to the classifications in Leviticus, the ass was an "unclean" animal, yet the people of Israel never regarded it with revulsion. After the asses carried the Israelites and their possessions from slavery in Egypt, Yahweh ordered that every ass be consecrated with the sacrifice of a lamb (Exod. 13:13).

The king of Moab once summoned the magician Baalam to place a curse on the Israelites. Baalam set out on his she-donkey, when an angel, sword in hand, appeared in his path. The donkey turned aside from the road, and Baalam beat her to draw her back. This happened a second time, and then a third. Baalam picked up a stick and began to strike the donkey furiously. The donkey reproached Baalam, saying, "Have I not carried you since you were a young man? Have I ever failed you? Why do you beat me now?" Then Baalam looked up and saw the angel. "It is lucky for you," the angel told him, "that your donkey saw me, though you did not, and turned aside. Had you continued, I would have killed you, but I would have let the donkey live." This story, from the Old Testament (Num. 22:22–35), is one of the earliest and most explicit condemnations of cruelty to animals in the ancient world. For us, perhaps there is another lesson: If people knew a bit more about the proud history of the ass in human culture, being called an "ass" might be taken as a compliment rather than an insult.

The ass was used for work in vineyards and was sacred to Dionysus, the Greek god of wine. The Greeks, however, generally associated the ass with the Phrygians, their traditional enemies. In one legend, Midas, king of Phyrgia and a follower of Dionysus', failed to appreciate the music of Apollo, god of the sun. "You have the ears of an ass," Apollo told Midas. When Midas looked into a stream, he saw that his ears had grown long and hairy. The ears of a donkey became a familiar symbol of stupidity. The foolscap used by jesters in medieval Europe had two points with bells, symbolizing the ears of a donkey. But, however we think they look, donkeys actually hear very well.

In the fables of Aesop, the ass was always a loser. In one tale an ass put on the skin of a lion and roamed about frightening man and beast. A fox heard him braying and said, "Oh, it's only you. I might have been scared myself, if I had not heard your voice." Socrates, in Plato's dialogue "Phaedo," stated that a person who is too concerned with bodily pains or pleasures might after death be reincarnated as a donkey.

The novel *The Golden Ass* by Lucius Apuleius, written in Rome during the first century A.D., looked beyond the image of the donkey as a fool. The hero, Lucius, had an affair with the maid of a great sorceress. When the couple saw the mistress of the house turn herself into an owl and fly away at night, Lucius wanted to do the same. His mistress gave him a potion that was supposed to turn him into a bird. It was the wrong charm, and Lucius became a donkey. His mistress told him that he could be turned back into his true form only by eating roses. When he tried to nibble some roses at an altar, the stable boy chased him away. This began a long series of adventures in which Lucius as a donkey was beaten, forced to carry heavy sacks, and even sexually abused. As a beast, he learned humility and wisdom. When his ordeal was over, he received roses from a priest of the goddess Isis, into whose mysteries he was initiated. One interpretation of the story is that the form of an ass represents the physical body, imprisoning yet challenging the human spirit.

An ass, together with an ox, visited the infant Jesus in the manger. An ass transported the Holy Family to safety in Egypt. Finally, an ass carried Jesus on his entry into Jerusalem. Riding an ass was a sign of majesty for the contemporaries of Jesus. The ass in the Near East was still the mount of kings. Legend has it that the ass still bears a dark cross over its shoulders as a symbol of Christ's passion. When the ass lost prestige, Christians often understood the choice of a mount by Jesus as a sign of his humility. Well into the Middle Ages and the Renaissance, however, clergy preferred to ride on an ass rather than a horse in emulation of Christ.

For many animals in the Western world, popular symbolism has combined radically different traditions of Christianity and paganism, and the ass may be the best example of all. The pagan tradition, which made the ass an object of mockery, has been more dominant. But behind the mockery was usually affection. The ass, unlike the horse, was very rarely accused of being the familiar of a witch or tried in medieval courts.

In ancient Mesopotamian art, we often see the motif of a donkey standing upright on his hind legs, playing the harp and singing. This motif was taken back to Europe by crusaders during the Middle Ages, where it symbolized the divine folly of love. William Shakespeare uses this motif in his play *A Midsummer Night's Dream*. The mischievous fairy Puck gives Bottom, a simple tradesman, the head of an ass. Bewitched by a magic potion, Titania dotes on Bottom for an evening; abashed after the charm wears off, she no longer dares to defy her husband.

The lore of the ass is full of wonders, in the East as well as West, yet almost always with a touch of humor. The Taoist immortal Chang Kwo-lao, an elderly gentleman who rode a donkey for vast distances every day, would fold the donkey up like a piece of paper and put it away whenever he finished a journey.

Medieval people understood that what appeared as foolishness could sometimes be holy innocence, even wisdom. A pageant known as the Festival of the Ass became popular in the northwestern parts of medieval Europe. In Beauvais, France, a splendidly dressed maiden, representing Mary and bearing an image of Christ, would sit on an ass. There would be a magnificent procession from the cathedral to the parish church of Saint Stephen. Instead of praises of Christ, however, the choir would sing a hymn to the ass, and at the end, instead of saying *"Deo gratias,"* or "Thanks to God," the congregation would say "hee-haw, hee-haw, hee-haw." The clergy, of course, often complained about the apparently sacrilegious ceremonies. Nevertheless, the festival was tolerated in the name of both religious tradition and fun.

A worldly equivalent is the donkey whose excrement was gold, a character that appeared in the "Donkey Skin" by Charles Perrault and in many other European fairy tales. The donkey again combined something wonderful with something ridiculous. In the fairy tale "The Magic Table, the Gold Donkey, and the Club in the Sack" by the Grimm brothers, the image was, so to speak, cleaned up. A donkey spewed gold from its mouth whenever a person said the word "Bricklebrit!" The image was a strange anticipation of the automatic teller machines used in banks today.

The camel, however, in addition to sharing with the ass a reputation for foolishness, carried the stigma in European culture of being filthy and ugly, a sort of deformed horse. Medieval bestiaries said that camels are so drawn to slime that they pass up clean waters for dirty ones. This reputation even obscured the grace of the giraffe, which, at least since the time of Pliny the Elder through the Middle Ages, had the misfortune of being considered a camel with spots, or a "cameleopard."

The toughness and endurance of the ass were celebrated in the popular story of the American steelman Joe Magarac; the name Magarac is Slovak for "jackass." "All I do is eatit and workit same lak jackass donkey," said Joe (Botkin, p. 247). He was born from a mountain and had superhuman strength. When there was no more metal to mine, Joe stepped into the furnace and melted himself down into steel. This tale is often taken for folklore, but Owen Francis created the character in an article in the November 1931 issue of *Scribner's Magazine*.

The donkey is now most familiar as a symbol of the Democratic Party in America. The idea was partly inspired by the statement of Ignatius Donnelly to the legislature of Minnesota not long after the Civil War that the Democratic Party was like a mule, lacking both pedigree and posterity. Thomas Nast popularized the symbol in political cartoons. The metaphor may have been first intended as an insult, but the Democrats certainly didn't mind. In fact, they adopted the symbol officially in 1874. Perhaps they realized that the symbolism of the donkey has always had many layers. If the long ears of a donkey suggest foolishness, the large teeth are a formidable weapon. The donkey is tough; it has a devastating kick. The donkey may have a reputation for stubbornness, but isn't that often a virtue in politics?

Illustration by Arthur Rackham showing the tradesman Bottom with the fairy Titania in Shakespeare's "A Midsummer Night's Dream."

Among the most eloquent tributes to animals ever written is *Platero and I* by Juan Ramón Jiménez (first published in 1957). It is a series of remarks addressed by the author to a gentle donkey named "Platero," described as "loving and tender as a child but strong and sturdy as a rock." The donkey is not only a helper but a wonderful listener as well. Together the companions enjoy the flight of butterflies, the playing of children, the touch of water, and all that the richly sensuous life a remote village in Spain has to offer.

As for the camel, a cigarette company has exploited its reputation for sexual potency. The brand known as Camel has as its trademark symbol the animal standing in front of a pyramid. The smoker in the company's advertisements has almost always been male; both the pyramid and the hump of the camel suggest the belly of a pregnant woman—proof of his virility. The advertisers even exploited the reputation of the camel for ugliness by creating the cartoon character Joe Camel, who had the face of a camel and the body of a man, to suggest a blue-collar toughness. Joe was such a commercial success that antismoking activists protested against him, and the ads were made illegal around the end of the nineties. For the most part, however, the camel of Arab lands, like the ass and mule of the Occident, has become a symbol of a vanishing way of life.

In Latin America and parts of the Mediterranean, the mule is the preferred helper of many solitary workers such as peddlers. Even today, in many villages, mules are used to deliver mail. There is often a quiet intimacy between the mules and their handlers, who share a humble status.

Selected References

Apuleius, Lucius. *The Golden Asses of Lucius Apuleius.* Trans. William Adlington. London: Abbey Library, ca. 1920.

Botkin, B. A., ed. *A Treasury of American Folklore: Stories, Ballads, and Traditions of the American People.* New York: Crown Publishers, 1944.

Clutton-Brock, Juliet. *Horse Power: A History of the Horse and the Donkey in Human Societies.* Cambridge: Harvard University Press, 1992.

Dent, Anthony. *Donkey: The Story of the Ass from East to West.* Washington, DC: George G. Harrap, 1972.

Gotfredsen, Lise. *The Unicorn.* New York: Abbeville Press, 1999.

Grimm, Jacob and Wilhelm. *The Complete Grimm's Fairy Tales.* Trans. Margaret Hunt and James Stern. New York: Pantheon, 1972.

Jiménez, Juan Ramón. *Platero and I.* Trans. Eloise Roach. Austin: University of Texas Press, 1983.

Perrault, Charles. "Peau d'Ane." *Contes.* Paris: Gallimard, 1981, p. 95–116.

Schrader, J. L. *A Medieval Bestiary.* New York: Metropolitan Museum of Art, 1986.

B

Baboon
See Ape and Monkey

Badger
See Beaver, Porcupine, Badger, and Miscellaneous Rodents

Bat

> But when he brushes up against the screen
> We are afraid of what our eyes have seen
> For something is amiss, or out of place
> When mice with wings can wear a human face.
>   —Theodore Roethke, "The Bat"

Bats have always presented a problem for those who like to divide things into neat, unequivocal categories. Not only are they nocturnal but they also seem, in other ways, to reverse what appears to be the normal order. They sleep hanging upside down by their feet. They live in shelters such as caves or hollow trees, but they also take advantage of human structures. Like most small animals that are drawn to human habitations, bats have often been identified in folk belief with the souls of the dead. As a result, in cultures that venerate ancestral spirits, bats are often considered sacred or beloved. When spirits are expected to pass on rather than return, bats appear as demons or, at best, souls unable to find peace.

According to one well-known fable, popularly attributed to Aesop, the birds and beasts were once preparing for war. The birds said to the bat, "Come with us," but he replied, "I am a beast." The beasts said to the bat, "Come with us," but he replied, "I am a bird." At the last moment a peace was made, but ever since, all creatures have shunned the bat. The earliest version of this story, by the Roman Phaedrus, contained no explicit moral, and perhaps he intended to suggest that bats prefer human civilization to nature. The learned folklorist Joseph Jacobs, however, appended the lesson: "He that is neither one thing nor the other has no friends" (Aesop, p. 63).

Today taxonomists place bats in a separate order of mammals, but both laypeople and scientists have puzzled for centuries whether bats are avians, flying mice, monkeys, or something else. Revulsion against them, however, is far from universal, and their quizzical faces have often inspired affection. There were no glass windows in the ancient world, and so people had little choice but to share their homes with bats. According to Ovid, the daughters of Minyas had refused to join the revels in honor of Bacchus and stayed at home weaving and telling stories. As punishment, they were turned into bats, but they continued to avoid the woods and flock to houses. In a similar spirit, the medieval bestiaries praised bats for the way they would hang together "like a cluster of grapes," showing affection that was not often found in human beings (White, p. 141). In medieval times it was common for the entire household, from the lord and lady to the serfs, to sleep in the great hall of the manor, and little privacy was available. In such close quarters, they must, indeed, have felt rather like bats in a cave.

In Africa, Swahili-speaking people have believed that after death the spirit of the departed hovers near his or her body as a bat. People in Uganda and Zimbabwe have believed that bats taking wing in the evening are departed spirits coming to visit the living. The flying fox, a large bat found in Ghana, however, is believed to be a demon in league with witches and sorcerers.

Perhaps the most unequivocally favorable view of bats can be found in China, where the word for "bat" also means "joy." In ancient times the Chinese noticed the service that bats provided in eating insects, thus impeding the spread of malaria. Bats seemed to exemplify such Confucian virtues as filial piety, since they would live together in a single cave for many centuries. They were believed to live for centuries, and Shou-Hsing, the god of long life, is depicted with two bats.

Bats did not really come to be thought of as spooky in Europe until the end of the Middle Ages, as folk belief became increasingly equated with witchcraft. Bats came to be regarded as familiars of witches and as a frequent disguise for the Devil. Dragons and demons would often be depicted with the wings of a bat. The association of bats with vampires—that is, the living dead—goes back only as far as the latter half of the eighteenth century, when the zoologist Georges-Louis Leclerc de Buffon examined newly discovered bats from South America. Because the variety sucked small quantities of blood from cattle, though rarely from human beings, he called them "vampires."

At about the same time, gothic horror became fashionable throughout Europe, and popular writers discovered it was piquant to identify bats with vampires.

It was really only in the twentieth century that the new medium of movies established the popular association between the two. In a wave of vampire movies starting in the 1920s, actors such as Bela Lugosi gave Dracula and other vampires the appearance of bats. They would, for example, wear a long black cape that resembled the wings of a bat, large ears, and claws. While some vampires were purely evil, others were grandly tragic, and quite a few were not so different from ordinary human beings. In the 1950s, the popular comic-book character Batman assumed much of the paraphernalia of vampires, but he used these to fight crime rather than to capture souls.

But the mystery of bats has not been diminished by either fantasy or science. In the late twentieth century, the philosopher Thomas Nagel probed the nature of consciousness in a famous essay entitled "What Is It Like to Be a Bat?" He tried to imagine what it might be like to navigate by sonar and decided that the human mind was unequal to the task. His conclusion was that we must recognize facts that we can neither state nor comprehend.

Selected References

Aesop. *The Fables of Aesop.* Edited and retold with notes by Joseph Jacobs. New York: Macmillan, 1910.

Knappert, Jan. *African Mythology: An Encyclopedia of Myth and Legend.* London: Diamond Books, 1995.

Marigny, Jean. *Vampires: Restless Creatures of the Night.* Trans. Lory Frankel. New York: Harry N. Abrams, 1994.

Nagel, Thomas. "What Is It Like to Be a Bat?" In *Moral Questions.* New York: Cambridge University Press, 1985, pp. 169–180.

Nott, Charles Stanley. *The Flowery Kingdom.* New York: Chinese Study Group of America, 1947.

Ovid. *Metamorphoses.* Trans. Rolfe Humphries. Bloomington: Indiana University Press, 1955.

White, T. H., trans. *The Book of Beasts: Being a Translation from a Latin Bestiary of the Twelfth Century.* New York: Dover, 1984.

Bear

> *So watchful Bruin forms, with plastic care,*
> *Each growing lump, and brings it to a bear.*
> —Alexander Pope, *The Dunciad*

Of all animals, the bear is probably the one that most clearly resembles human beings in appearance. Even apes can stand upright only slouched over and with considerable difficulty. The bear, however, can walk and even run on two legs almost as well as a human. The fur of a bear resembles clothing. Like a person, a bear looks straight ahead, but the expressions of bears are not easy for us to read. Often the wide eyes of a bear suggest perplexity, making it appear that the bear is a human being whose form has mysteriously been altered. Bears, however, are generally far larger and stronger than people, so they could easily be taken for giants.

Perhaps the most wonderful characteristic of bears, however, is their ability to hibernate and then reemerge at the end of winter, which suggests death and resurrection. In part because bears give birth during hibernation, they have been associated with mother-goddesses. The descent into caverns suggests an intimacy with the earth and with vegetation, and bears are reputed to have special knowledge of herbs.

At Drachenloch, in a cave high in the Swiss Alps, skulls of the cave bear have been found that face the entrance in what appears to be a very deliberate arrangement. Some anthropologists believe this is a shrine consecrated to the bear by Neanderthals, which would make it the earliest known place of worship. Others dispute the claim; true or not, the very idea is testimony to the enormous power that the figure of the bear has over the human imagination.

A cult of the bear is widespread, almost universal, among peoples of the Far North, where the bear is both the most powerful predator and the most important food animal. Perhaps the principal example of this cult today is that followed by the Ainu, the earliest inhabitants of Japan. They traditionally adopt a young bear, raise it as a pet, and then ceremoniously sacrifice the animal. Before stories of the lion were imported, the bear was regarded throughout northern Europe as the king of beasts. Eskimo legends tell of humans learning to hunt from the polar bear. For the Inuit of Labrador, the polar bear is a form of the Great Spirit, Tuurngasuk.

Countless myths and legends record a sort of intimacy between human beings and bears. The Koreans, for example, traditionally believe that they are descended from a bear. The tiger and the female bear had watched humans from a distance, and they became curious. As they talked together on a mountainside one day, both decided that they would like to become human. An oracle instructed them that they must first eat twenty-one cloves of garlic, then remain in a cave for one month. They both did as instructed, but after a while the tiger became restless and left the cave. The mother bear remained, and at the end of a month she emerged as a beautiful woman. The son of Heaven, Han

Woon, fell in love with her and had a child with her, Tan Koon, who is the ancestor of the Koreans.

The bear was sacred to the Greek Artemis, the Roman Diana, goddess of the moon and protector of the animals. According to the Roman poet Ovid, the god Jupiter once disguised himself as Diana and raped her companion the nymph Callisto. On realizing that Callisto was pregnant, Diana banished the young girl from her presence. Eventually Callisto gave birth to a boy named Arcas. Juno, the wife of Jupiter, turned Callisto into a bear and forced her to roam the forest alone and in perpetual fear. Arcas grew to be a young man. He went hunting in the forest, saw his mother, and raised his bow to shoot her. At that moment, Jupiter looked down,

took pity on his former mistress and brought both mother and son up to Heaven, where they became the constellations of the great and little bear. This is only one version of the story among many, but the Arcadians traditionally trace their origin to Callisto and her son.

The Hebrews, who were herders, regarded carnivorous animals as unclean, and the bear was no exception. In the Bible, the young David protected his flock against bears (1 Sam. 17:34). The bear became a scourge of God when small boys followed the prophet Elisha and made fun of his bald head. Elisha cursed them, and two she-bears came out of the woods and killed the children (2 Kings 2:23–24). According to tradition, however, Elisha was later punished with illness for his deed.

The Tlingit and many other Indian tribes on the northwest coast of the North American continent have told stories of a young woman who was lost in the woods and was befriended by a bear. At first she was afraid, but the bear was kindly and taught her the ways of the forest. Eventually she became his wife. She grew thick hair and hunted like a bear. When the couple had children, she at first tried to teach them the ways of both bears and human beings. Her human family, however, would not accept the marriage, and her brothers killed her husband, whereupon she broke completely with the ways of humans.

The enormous size of the bear, together with its similarity to human beings, often makes it an object of both awe and derision, and dancing bears were until recently a common feature of traveling shows. (Courtesy of the Department of Library Services, American Museum of Natural History, #2A4017)

Many tales pay tribute to the maternal role of the mother bear. Repeating a bit of lore found in the works of Pliny the Elder and other writers of antiquity, medieval bestiaries told of cubs that were completely formless at birth. Their mother would mold them with her tongue, literally licking the cubs into shape.

The mother bear must constantly protect her offspring from the father, who would eat them out of jealousy and hunger. This fierce protectiveness is part of what has moved contemporary American author Terry Tempest Williams to posit a special bond between women and bears. "We are creatures of paradox," she wrote in an essay entitled "Undressing the Bear." She continued, "Women and bears, two animals that are enormously unpredictable, hence our mystery" (p. 108). The name Artemis literally means "bear," as does Arthur, derived from Artus, the name of the legendary king of Britain who led the knights of the Round Table. Such nomenclature suggests a totemic bond between man and bear that goes back to very archaic times.

Many European fairy tales suggest such a bond. For example, according to the Norwegian story entitled "East of the Sun and West of the Moon," recorded by George Dasent, a bear went to the house of a poor family and asked for the daughter in marriage, promising great riches in return. The father persuaded his daughter to reluctantly agree, and the bear carried her home on his back. The bear visited the young woman every night but departed at the break of day. She lived well but was forbidden to know where her husband went every morning. Finally, one night she was overcome with curiosity and lighted a candle, only to see him vanish. Then she had to make a long and perilous journey to the land east of the sun and west of the moon, where she was finally reunited with her husband. Her love broke the enchantment of a sorceress, and he turned out to be a human prince. In another version of the tale, three sisters are talking about the men they will marry, when one says in jest, "I will have no husband but the brown bear of Norway." So it comes to pass, but the couple is permanently united only after many trials and tribulations. These stories belong to the cycle of "Beauty and the Beast" fairy tales in which a bride must learn to see past the bestial appearance of her partner to find a gentle young man.

One tale that seems to lament the loss of intimacy between bears and human beings is the Icelandic saga "King Hrolf and His Champions," from the thirteenth or early fourteenth century. It tells how King Hrolf was drinking with his warriors when the army of Queen Skuld attacked them. Only Bothvar Bjarki, the greatest of the king's knights, could not be found, and all thought he must have been killed or captured. As the battle raged, an enormous bear appeared at the side of

King Hrolf. Weapons simply rebounded from the skin of the bear, and he killed more enemies with his paw than could any five heroes. One of King Hrolf's champions, Hjalti the Magnanimous, ran back to camp, where he found Bothvar in a tent. Outraged, Hjalti threatened to burn the tent and Bothvar. Calmly and a bit sadly, Bothvar rebuked Hjalti, saying that he had proved his courage many times. He was ready to join the battle, Bothvar explained, but could offer his king more help by remaining behind. Indeed, as soon as Bothvar joined the fray, the bear disappeared, for Bothvar and the bear were one. King Hrolf and his champions all fought valiantly, yet they were overwhelmed by the enormous host of Queen Skuld and killed.

Still another such tale is *Valentine and Orson,* which was popular in the Middle Ages and is preserved for us in French and English texts from around the end of the fourteenth century. The story began with the infant Orson lost in the woods. A mother bear took him home to her cave and raised him as one of her cubs. He grew up to be huge, immensely strong, covered with hair, and able to speak only in grunts. For a time, Orson was the terror of the woods, feared by both animals and human beings. When his beloved mother died, Orson let himself be taken by his brother Valentine to the court of King Pepin of France, where he learned the ways of men and became a knight.

There a dreaded warrior known as the Green Knight had captured a princess and challenged to a battle anyone who wished to rescue her. Many of King Pepin's knights took up the challenge, but the Green Knight bested them all and hung them from a tree. Finally came the turn of Orson. When he first jousted with the Green Knight, Orson inflicted several wounds, but he noticed that they healed at once. Realizing the Green Knight could not be defeated in the conventional way, Orson leaped from his horse, threw away his sword, and tore off his armor. Then Orson pulled the Green Knight from horseback and forced his adversary to yield, rescuing the princess and winning her for his bride.

In medieval times, the sport of bear baiting was very popular at country fairs. The dancing bear, clumsily mimicking a human being, was also a favorite entertainment. For all their cruelty, these symbolic affirmations of human dominance perhaps paid the bear a sort of compliment as a representative of natural powers that might inspire fear. Many aristocratic houses adopted the bear as a heraldic symbol, but perhaps resentment against a predatory nobility was taken out on the poor animals. In the medieval tales throughout Europe since the end of the eleventh century, "Bruin" the bear is an aristocrat whose natural strength is no match for the peasant cunning of Renard the Fox.

Legends, however, still show a respect for the abilities and knowledge of bears. Edward Topsell, the Elizabethan zoologist, reported in 1656 that a man was walking along carrying a large cauldron one autumn day when he saw a bear nibble a root, then descend into a cave. The man was curious and started to chew on the root of the same plant. Immediately he began to feel very sleepy, and he was barely able to throw the cauldron over his body. He remembered no more until he lifted up the cauldron to find the last snow melting on a beautiful spring day.

Like all large meat-eaters, bears had become rare by the twentieth century. The terror that bears once inspired came to be remembered though a haze of nostalgia, and the teddy bear became a favorite toy of children. The name comes from a story that had President "Teddy" Roosevelt, an avid big-game hunter, declining to shoot a bear cub, thinking it unsporting to take advantage of the helpless creature.

In William Faulkner's short story "The Bear," a giant brown bear known as Old Ben becomes the symbol of a vanishing wilderness in the American South. As long as he is there, the land remains wild and strangers do not dare to intrude. The hero of the tale is a boy who is learning to be an accomplished woodsman, an occupation that becomes obsolete when a hunting party finally kills Old Ben.

No longer greatly feared, the bear has become a symbol of vulnerability. Everybody in the United States who was born before the seventies or so has seen posters with Smokey the Bear, who was created during World War II to warn people that Japanese shelling might begin a conflagration in the woods of America. When the war ended, the United States Forest Service retained Smokey as a symbol in a campaign to prevent the careless ignition of forest fires. Far from bestial, he has a rather parental image. He wears human clothes and a forester's hat. He is mature, friendly, and a little melancholy. Yet if Smokey seems absurdly civilized, his role remains that of bears since archaic times—protector of the wild.

Selected References

Carpenter, Francis. *Tales of a Korean Grandmother.* Rutland, VT: Charles E. Tuttle, 1973.

Dasent, George. "East of the Sun and West of the Moon." In *Scandinavian Folk and Fairy Tales.* Ed. Claire Booss. New York: Avenel Books, 1984, pp. 63–70.

Faulkner, William. "The Bear." In *Go Down Moses.* New York: Vintage Books, 1970, pp. 181–316.

Jones, Gwyn, trans. "King Hrolf and His Champions." In *Erik the Red and Other Icelandic Sagas.* New York: Oxford University Press, 1991, pp. 221–318.

Shepherd, Paul, and Barry Sanders. *The Sacred Paw: The Bear in Nature, Myth, and Literature*. New York: Viking Penguin, 1992.

Topsell, Edward, and Thomas Muffet. *The History of Four-Footed Beasts and Serpents and Insects* (3 vols.). New York: Da Capo, 1967 (facsimile of 1658 edition).

Watson, Henry, trans. *Valentine and Orson*. Ed. Arthur Dickson. New York: Kraus Reprint, 1971.

Williams, Terry Tempest. "Undressing the Bear." In *On Nature's Terms*. Ed. Thomas J. Lyon and Peter Stine. Austin: Texas A & M University Press, 1992, pp. 104–107.

Beaver, Porcupine, Badger, and Miscellaneous Rodents

Come play with me;
Why should you run
Through the shaking tree
As though I'd a gun
To strike you dead?
When all I want to do
Is to scratch your head
And let you go.
—W. B. Yeats, "To a Squirrel at Kyle-na-no"

From the viewpoint of the lay observer, rats and mice have always seemed a sort of paradigm for other animals. This extends even to creatures that are not rodents—so pigeons are called "rats with wings"; deer, "rats with hooves"; and bats, "mice with wings." Other rodents share the relatively small size and basic form of rats and mice but are usually distinguished by a few dramatic features. There are many varieties throughout the world, many of them picturesque and exotic, including flying squirrels, naked mole rats, kangaroo rats, marmosets, and capybaras.

Among the rodents of greatest folkloric importance is the beaver, which is distinguished by its large flat tail, its huge teeth that can gnaw down trees, and above all, its amazing ability to build. In the ancient world, the most widespread legend about beavers was that they possessed in their testicles a powerful medicine known as castoreum (it is actually in another organ). When a hunter chased a beaver, the beaver would bite off its testicles, giving the pursuer what he probably wanted and thus escaping alive. This was reported by Pliny, Aelian, Horapollo, Cicero, Juvenal, and many others. Priests of Cybele and also a few early Christians practiced self-castration. In Freudian terms, this act might have represented the instinctual renunciations that the founder of psychoanalysis believed were necessary for civilization. Beavers have often been regarded as the most civilized of creatures. At any rate, the legend was often repeated in medieval bestiaries and other manuscripts, where it was interpreted as an allegory of the soul that, pursued by the Devil, must give up all lewdness.

The beaver was a popular totem and often a bearer of culture for Native American tribes. According to the Algonquin, Lenape, Huron, and many other Indians, the beaver first created land, often helped by the muskrat or otter, by dredging up earth from the bottom of the sea. The Blackfoot Indians tell of a man named Apikunni, who had been temporarily banished from his tribe and took refuge during the winter in the beaver house. When he left in the spring, the patriarch of the beaver family gave him a pointed piece of aspen. Using the stick as a weapon, he became the first man ever to kill in war, and so he was welcomed back by his people and made their chief. The Osage tribe traced its origin to a chief named Wasbashas, who was taught to build by beavers after he had married the daughter of their king.

Early explorers were amazed by the size of beaver lodges in the New World. Influenced by the tales of Native Americans, they brought back to Europe fantastic stories of a highly sophisticated beaver society. Beavers were said to build with mortar, use their tails as trowels, and have a system of parliamentary law. By the seventeenth century, the beaver was regularly mentioned, along with the elephant, ape, dog, and dolphin, as perhaps the most intelligent animal after man. Georges-Louis Leclerc de Buffon, a preeminent naturalist of his day, argued that the beaver did not possess extraordinary native intelligence but merely showed what all animals might be capable of were their social cohesion not disrupted by human beings. Oliver Goldsmith, in his enormously popular *History of Animated Nature* (first published in 1774), wrote of America, "The beavers in those distant solitudes are known to build like architects and rule like citizens." He added that the homes of the beavers "exceed the houses of the human inhabitants of the same country both in neatness and in convenience" (vol. 1, p. 176). At about the same time that many Europeans were idealizing the American beaver, colonial trappers were finding it a lucrative source of fur. Greed prevailed over sentiment, as the British, French, and Dutch engaged in the Beaver War, an intense competition for furs that often escalated into armed conflict and drove the beavers in North America close to extinction.

Today, *beaver* is often a slang word for the male sex organ, used most frequently in raunchy magazines for men. Larry Flynt, the owner of *Hustler*, has sometimes had himself depicted as a beaver in cartoons in ads for his magazine. One obvious reason for this usage is the size of the beaver's tail. If, however, the usage ultimately goes

back to the legends of self-castration, it suggests ambivalences that the pornographers prefer not to acknowledge.

Often associated with the beaver in both Europe and America is the porcupine, a rodent known primarily for the spikes covering its back. The most widely spread legend about the porcupine, found in the work of Pliny and many other authors of the ancient world, is that it can shoot its spines when attacked. Aelian added that the porcupine can aim its quills at an attacker with considerable accuracy and that the quills "leap forth as though sped from a bowspring" (vol. 1, book 1, chap. 31). The fiction is still widespread today.

In Native American mythology, the porcupine frequently accompanies the beaver, usually as a companion but occasionally as an adversary. The Haida of the Northwest coast told a story of the war between the clans of Beaver and Porcupine. After Porcupine had stolen Beaver's food, the clan of Beaver placed Porcupine on an island to starve, but the clan of Porcupine rescued their leader when the water froze and they could walk across the ice. The clan of Porcupine then captured Beaver and placed him high in a tree. Beaver could not climb, but he chewed his way down the tree, and the two clans finally made peace.

The beaver and porcupine are known for gentleness, but the weasel has impressed people above all with its fierce temperament. Though usually comparatively small, weasels do not hesitate to do battle with rats or snakes. Pliny the Elder stated that the weasel was the only animal that could defeat the basilisk, a serpent able to kill other creatures with simply a gaze. The diminutive rodent doing battle with such a monster later became a symbol of Christ triumphing over the Devil. In the modern era, as traditional martial virtues have come to be less valued, the reputation of weasels has declined. In Kenneth Graham's *The Wind in the Willows* (first published in 1906), they appear as a vicious yet cowardly mob.

The ermine, a relatively large weasel, was sacred to the Zoroastrians. Because of its white color, it has often been associated with the fierce chastity of a soldier of God, and Mary Magdalene was depicted wearing an ermine coat to show that she had reformed. A popular European legend stated that an ermine, pursued by hunters, would allow itself to be killed rather than soil its beautiful coat with mud.

Still another important rodent in folklore is the badger, which is noted for its powerful front legs and its long claws adapted for digging. Its practice of burrowing under the earth and its nocturnal habits make the badger a creature of mystery. In China and, most especially, Japan, badgers are shape shifters, and many stories are told of spirits haunting old buildings, desolate fields, or ponds that turn out to be badgers. Typical is the story of an ascetic hermit on Mount Atago near Kyoto. A hunter would bring him food every day, and one afternoon the hermit confided to his benefactor that the bodhisattva Fugen visited him every evening upon a white elephant. At the invitation of the hermit, the hunter stayed to see Fugen. At first the hunter was dazzled by the vision, but as he gazed more closely he began to feel suspicious. Finally he shot an arrow at the vision. The bodhisattva immediately disappeared, and there was a rustling in the bushes. "If it had really been Fugen," the hunter told the hermit, "the arrow couldn't have done any damage. So it must have been some monster." The next morning the two followed a trail of blood and found an enormous badger with an arrow through its breast (Tyler, pp. 174–175).

The badger is often thought of as a small bear, and it is one of many animals that have taken the place of the bear in forecasting the coming of spring. The end of the winter was originally indicated by the return of the bears from hibernation. As these large animals became scarce, they were replaced in Germany and much of Britain by the badger. According to a German proverb, "the badger peeps out of his hole on Candlemass Day, and, if he sees the sun shining he draws back into his hole" (Santino, p. 58). In the United States, the woodchuck or groundhog has replaced the badger in forecasting spring. On February 2, the groundhog will lift its head out of its hole. If it sees its shadow, the groundhog will return to its hole and winter will linger six more weeks, but if the groundhog comes out, spring is at hand.

The most beloved rodent in the Northern Hemisphere, however, is the squirrel. It is primarily the squirrel's long bushy tail that differentiates squirrels from rats, yet what a difference that makes in the way the two are regarded. Rats may often be feared and despised, yet squirrels are such a part of our yards and parks that these places would appear desolate without them. Nevertheless, squirrels have been the subject of many ambivalent legends. For the Ainu of Japan, they represented the discarded sandals of the god Aioina, which would never rot, perhaps because squirrels move in spurts that are like footsteps. Malaysians believed squirrels were produced, like butterflies, from the cocoons of caterpillars, and they thought the dried penis of a squirrel was a powerful aphrodisiac. In Norse mythology, the squirrel Ratatosk was the bringer of rain and snow. It moved up and down the tree of life Yggdrasil, constantly trying to stir up strife between the eagle at the top and the serpent at the base. In Irish mythology, the goddess Medb has a bird perched on one shoulder and a squirrel on the other, her messengers for the earth and sky. The habit of hoarding nuts made squirrels symbols of avarice in some medieval bestiaries, but Victorian books of natural history often praised squirrels for their thrift. Today, squirrels thrill urban dwellers with their spectacular leaps between trees or runs along telephone lines over busy highways. Every now and then a squirrel will turn and stare at a person, with a gaze that suggests curiosity but neither fear nor anger. Because they seem completely untroubled by human presence, they reassure us that perhaps we have not alienated ourselves too much from the natural world after all.

Selected References

Aelian. *On Animals* (3 vols.). Trans. A. F. Scholfield. Cambridge: Harvard University Press, 1972.

Bruchac, Joseph. *Native Plant Stories.* Golden, CO.: Fulcrum, 1995.

Gill, Sam D., and Irene F. Sullivan. *Native American Mythology.* New York: Oxford University Press, 1992.

Goldsmith, Oliver. *History of Animated Nature* (4 vols.). Edinburgh: Smith and Elder/T. Tegg and Son, 1838.

Lewinsohn, Richard. *Animals, Men, and Myths: An Informative and Entertaining History of Man and the Animals around Him.* New York: Harper and Brothers, 1954.

Santino, Jack. *All around the Year: Holidays and Celebrations in American Life.* Chicago: University of Illinois Press, 1995.

Sax, Boria. *The Frog King: On Legends, Fables, Fairy Tales, and Anecdotes of Animals.* New York: Pace University Press, 1990.

Tyler, Royall, ed. and trans. *Japanese Tales.* New York: Pantheon, 1987.

Bee and Wasp

Ask the wild bee what the Druids knew.
   —Scottish saying

The word *bee* ultimately goes back to the Indo-European *"bhi,"* meaning "to quiver." The same root is in the Greek *"bios,"* meaning "life." A quiver is the motion of spirit, a pulse, or a breath. Life is a sort of "buzz," a humming in the void. Bees appear primordial. In ancient Egypt, bees sometimes represented the soul. People said that bees were born from the tears of the sun god Ra, or, later, those of Christ.

Bees do not fly mechanically from one place to another. Instead, they often hover pensively in the air. They build complex homes and communities, almost like human cities. Above all else, their ability to produce honey and wax has always seemed wondrous. In Plato's dialogue "Phaedo," Socrates suggested that those who live as good citizens might be reincarnated as bees or other social insects. He meant this transformation to be a reward, of course. It is small wonder that author Maurice Maeterlinck, in the early twentieth century, considered bees the most intelligent of animals next to humankind.

In *Georgics,* Virgil bestowed great praise on bees, hoping to shame his decadent countrymen in Rome:

Alone of living things they hold their young
In common, nor have individual homes:
They pass their lives beneath the might of law:
They know the patriot's zeal, and reverence

For household gods: mindful of frosts to come,
They toil through summer, garnering their grains
Into the common store. While some keep watch. . . .
(part 4, lines 194–200)

According to Virgil, bees neither lost their minds through love nor weakened their bodies through sexual pleasure. They were spared the pains and hazards of pregnancy, since their young spring sponta- neously from plants. Most of all, Virgil admired the patriotism of bees. Spiders, hornets, worms, and other menaces constantly threatened their hives, yet the bees never ceased their vigilance. The individuals sacrificed their lives, but the community survived.

Aristotle had considered the generation of bees "a great puzzle," but he suggested various possibilities. One was that they drew their young from various flowers, while others included copulation and spontaneous generation (book 3, section 10). Virgil told us that the Egyptians near Canopus by the Nile had a rite in which priests would lead a two-year-old bull into a small room. The priests would club the animal to death, then continue to pound the flesh, taking care not to pierce the skin. Next they covered the body with thyme, bay, and other spices. A short time later, bees emerged from the body.

The practice began after the nymph Eurydice, beloved of Or- pheus, departed from her husband into the underworld. The bees died, and they could be brought back only when the spirits of the lovers were placated by the sacrifice of an ox. Persephone, queen of the dead in Greco-Roman mythology, returned yearly from the under-

A worker bee as drawn by Ludwig Becker.

world as vegetation; Eurydice returned as a swarm of bees. Initiates into the mysteries of Dionysus, god of wine and religious ecstasy, had another interpretation of the ceremony: Dionysus had been torn apart by titans as an ox and reborn as a bee.

Like agriculture, tending of bees is very seasonal. Bees die and hives lie dormant in winter. In the ancient and medieval worlds, farmers and their children would watch carefully in spring for signs that the bees were beginning to swarm; then people would gather and follow the bees. They would set up attractive new hives and beat on kettles, believing that the noise would help the bees to settle down. In autumn the farmers would harvest the honey.

Bees are so beloved that people have generally forgiven them their painful sting. In one of Aesop's fables, however, the bees begged Zeus for stings to protect their honey. Zeus was displeased at their covetousness. He granted the request but added that the bees had to die whenever they used their stings. That bees pass away on stinging is true, since they cannot remove the sting without tearing their abdomens. Thus the individual dies for the hive; even a stung person might be moved to forgiveness by the sacrifice.

Sometimes armies have set loose bees against their enemies. Michel de Montaigne reported in "Apology for Raymond Sebond" that when the Portuguese were besieging the town of Tamly, the defenders brought out a great number of hives and placed them around the town wall. Next, residents of Tamly set fires to drive the bees into the invading host. The enemy was completely routed, yet not a single bee was lost. Montaigne does not record how the bees were counted.

The keeping of hives probably began around the seventh century B.C., but bees can't be called "domesticated." Even in hives made by human beings, bees always retain a life of their own. They are full of mystery. Aelian, writing in the first century A.D., reported that bees knew when frost and rain were coming. When bees remained close to their hives, beekeepers warned the farmers to expect harsh weather. If the bees know this, what else might they know as well?

Swarms of bees were closely watched as portents in ancient Rome. Priests used the size and direction of a swarm to foretell fortunes during war. Karma, the Hindu god of love, has a bowstring made of bees, perhaps because discovering love is a bit like a swarm of bees setting off to find a new home. Herodotus, the Greek historian, tells how Onesilus once led some Cyprians in a revolt against the Persian Empire of King Darius. After Onesilus was killed in battle, the people of the Cypriot city of Amathus, who had sided with the Persians, cut off his head and placed it over one of their city gates. After a

while, the skull became hollow. A swarm of bees filled the head with honeycomb. The Amathusians consulted an oracle, who told them to take down the head, bury it, and offer sacrifices every year to Onesilus.

Country people in Europe and North America have traditionally notified the bees when the owner of their property died. There is a description of this ceremony in *Lark Rise to Candleford*, a fictionalized account by Flora Thompson of her childhood in a poor rural family in England during the latter part of the nineteenth century. An elderly woman named Queenie would knock on each hive, as though at a door, and say, "Bees, bless, your master's dead, and now you must work for your missis" (p. 87). At times, rural people would tell the bees a lot more about affairs of the household, and it is not terribly hard to understand why. Working alone in the fields, one might easily feel an urge to talk. If no other people were around, one might speak to whatever seemed most human—that is, to the bees. The word *bee* is sometimes used to refer to activities where people work and talk, for example, a quilting bee or a husking bee. A rumor is sometimes referred to as a "buzz." European peasants have sometimes believed that ancestors return to their property as bees.

People have always considered the honey of bees a divine food. Zeus was raised on the island of Crete drinking the milk of the fairy goat Amalthea and eating the honey of the bee Melissa. In the Bible, Mark tells us that John the Baptist "lived on locusts and wild honey" (1:7). Pliny the Elder wrote that bees placed honey in the mouth of Plato when he was a child, foretelling his later eloquence. The same was later said of Saint Ambrose, Saint Anthony, and other holy men. Cesaire de Hesterbach reported in the early thirteenth century that a peasant once placed the Eucharist in a hive, hoping it would inspire the bees to produce more honey. Later he found that the bees had made a little chapel of wax. It contained an altar on which lay a tiny chalice with the Host.

For some reason, people pair related animals as opposites: the rat and the mouse, the dog and the wolf, the lion and the tiger. The bee is constantly paired with the wasp, which lives in nests instead of hives. One legend from Poland has it that when God created the bees, the Devil made the wasps in a failed attempt at imitation. In a Romanian legend, a peddler persuaded a gypsy to exchange a bee for a wasp by saying that the wasp was larger and would make more honey. All the gypsy got for his greed was a sting.

While the bee is a symbol of peace, the wasp is associated with conflict and war. The Greek comic poet Aristophanes, in his play *Wasps*, compared these insects to jurors, since both came in annoying swarms. Saint Paul seemed to conceive of death itself as an insect, probably a wasp, since he asked, "Death, where is thy sting?" (1 Cor. 15:55). At the end of the Middle Ages, the wasp was frequently the form in which the soul of a witch flew about at night.

Some cultures, however, have admired the martial qualities of wasps. Greek warriors went off to battle with wasps emblazoned on their shields. Among Native Americans and Africans, enduring the stings of wasps can be a test in initiation ceremonies. The wasp was a form often taken by Native American shamans. A wasp killing a grasshopper became a medieval symbol of Christ triumphing over the Devil.

The mason wasp is a deity of the Ila people in Zambia. They believe that the earth was once cold, and so the animals sent an embassy up to heaven to bring back fire. The vulture, eagle, and crow all died on the journey. Only the wasp arrived to plead, successfully, with God. Because it brought fire to the hearths, the wasp now makes its nest in chimneys.

Today in the United States, the acronym "wasp" stands for "White Anglo-Saxon Protestant." The term is usually used in a derogatory way. It suggests a combination of aristocratic restraint and viciousness. A wasp gives little warning yet has a terrible sting. The term "wasp waist" is used to describe people, especially women, who have what is also called an "hourglass figure." This suggests beauty that is obtained in an artificial, calculating sort of way. But if the bee were not thought of as holy, the wasp probably would not be so maligned.

It is hard for people to think of bees as individuals, and even beekeepers can hardly ever distinguish among them. Only the queen—for earlier ages, the king—stands out from the rest. Social insects such as ants and bees may be the inspiration for states in which the individual is subordinate to the state, from ancient Sparta to the Soviet Union. Napoleon took the bee as his emblem. People have constantly aspired to emulate the bees.

Illustration by J. J. Grandville showing a fashionable young lady with a "wasp waist," who is charming but also dangerous.

Edward Topsell, in the mid-seventeenth century, described the society of bees as an ideal monarchy. The king (what we now call the queen) was set apart by his size and royal bearing. His subjects all loved and obeyed him. The court of bees also contained viceroys, ambassadors, orators, soldiers, pipers, trumpeters, watchmen, scouts, sentinels, and far more.

Thomas Muffet, who collaborated with Topsell, has told us that bees "are not misshapen, crook-legged any way, pot-bellied, over close-kneed, bulb-cheeked, great mouthed, lean-chopped, rude foreheads or barren, as many great ladies and noble women are, who have lost the faculty of generation." He went on to say that in the "democratical state" of the bees, everyone is employed in some honest labor. The bees were generated by putrefaction of animals such as oxen, with the kings and the nobility created from the brain and the commoners from the other parts. Muffet added that bees could not endure the presence of lechers, menstruating women, or those who use perfumes (Topsell and Muffet, vol. 3, pp. 892–897).

For others of the Renaissance, these bees seemed a little too perfect, too virtuous, and too austere. Bernard Mandeville, a Dutch physician, satirized them in *The Fable of the Bees* (first published in 1724). The bees appealed to Jupiter to organize their state according to the ideals of perfect virtue. They got rid of the corrupt officials and lazy courtiers. The trouble was that the virtuous replacements didn't know how to get things done. Since the bees no longer produced luxuries such as honey, their economy collapsed. Because the bees lived only for peace, they forgot how to fight. Finally, a few melancholy survivors withdrew into a hollow oak to await their end.

The priestesses of the goddesses Demeter and Rhea were known as Melissae, or bees, a hint that in remote antiquity people may have realized that the bees are a matriarchy. If so, that knowledge was forgotten until the start of the modern era. It was not until the mid-seventeenth century that the Dutch scientist Jan Swammerdam examined bees under a microscope and learned that the so-called king was really a queen. Bees could no longer be used as a model for a perfect kingship.

For the French author Maurice Maeterlinck, around the start of the twentieth century, the religion of the bees was that of progress. "The god of the bees is the future," he wrote in *Life of the Bee*. "There is a strange duality in the character of the bee. In the heart of the hive, all help and love each other. . . . Wound one of them, and a thousand will sacrifice themselves to avenge the injury. But outside the hive, they no longer recognize each other" (p. 43). The bees had become radical socialists, living only for the cause.

During World War II, the distinguished scientist Karl von Frisch was studying bees at the University of Munich. He had been classified as one-quarter Jewish by the Nazi regime, which normally would have deprived him of his job. A disease began to kill off the bees in Germany, however, threatening the orchards, so the government allowed him to continue his work. Pouring his frustrations into work, the introverted von Frisch began to decipher the communication system of bees. They indicate the direction and distance of food by dances within the hive. This remarkable story, though completely true, reads almost like a fairy tale of grateful animals. The scientist seemed to have a covenant, a special intimacy, with bees. As he worked to rescue bees, they saved him. He was then initiated into their society and their speech. Of course, there is a difference. Unlike the heroes of fairy tales, von Frisch published the secrets of bees to the world.

Still, though a bit of the language of bees may be deciphered, only bees themselves may speak it. A person could certainly try doing the dance of bees, but that would be art. It would not impart information. We teach other animals such as chimpanzees to use human language. Then, much of the time, we think of them as imperfect human beings. But people are also, as Virgil knew long ago, imperfect bees.

Selected References

Aristophanes. "Wasps." Trans. Moses Hadas. In *The Complete Plays of Aristophanes.* New York: Bantam Books, 1998, p. 143–184.

Aristotle. *The Generation of Animals* (3 vols.). Trans. A. L. Peck. Cambridge: Harvard University Press, 1953.

Davies, Malcolm, and Jeyaraney Kathirithamby. *Greek Insects.* New York: Oxford University Press, 1986.

Maeterlinck, Maurice. *Life of the Bee.* Trans. Alfred Sutro. London: George Allen, 1908.

Mandeville, Bernard. *The Fable of the Bees: Or Private Vices, Publick Benefits* (2 vols.). Oxford: Clarendon Press, 1924.

Montaigne, Michel de. "Apology for Raymond Sebond." In *The Complete Essays of Montaigne* (2 vols.). Trans. Donald M. Frame. Stanford: Stanford University Press, 1959, vol. 1, pp. 428–561.

Parrinder, Geoffrey. *African Mythology.* London: Paul Hamlyn, 1973.

Plato. "Phaedo." *The Last Days of Socrates.* Trans Hugh Tredennick and Harold Tarrant. New York: Penguin, 1993, p. 93–185.

Thompson, Flora. *Lark Rise to Candleford: A Trilogy.* New York: Penguin, 1973.

Topsell, Edward, and Thomas Muffet. *The History of Four-Footed Beasts and Serpents and Insects* (3 vols.). New York: Da Capo, 1967 (facsimile of 1658 edition).

Virgil. *The Singing Farmer: A Translation of Virgil's "Georgics."* Trans. L. A. S. Jermyn. Oxford: Basil Blackwell, 1947.

Beetle

The poor beetle that we tread upon
In corporal sufferance finds a pang as great
As when a giant dies.
—William Shakespeare, *Measure for Measure* (act 3, scene 1)

Beetles are often found near garbage, around excrement, and in dank areas. People usually associate beetles with filth, squalor, and decay, yet myth often regards these qualities are often a preliminary stage to the creation of life. In ancient times in the Mediterranean region, people believed that life, particularly that of insects, sprang spontaneously from decomposing matter, and a few varieties of beetles came to be regarded as holy. Foremost of these is the scarab beetle, also known as the dung beetle, which has been represented in countless amulets, some of which were found wrapped in cloth together with

A beetle cavalier, drawn by Ludwig Becker, from The Population of an Old Pear Tree *by E. Van Bruyssel (1870).*

mummified corpses. The scarab lives off dung and is frequently seen near farms. It pushes a globe of dung to an underground burrow before consuming it, and to the ancient Egyptians the ball suggested motion of the sun crossing the sky. The scarab was sacred to Ra, god of the sun. The god Khepera, associated with creation and immortality, was depicted with the head of a scarab beetle. The female scarab beetle lays her eggs in a ball that she creates inside her hole. The Egyptians confused the two processes of feeding and reproduction in scarabs, thinking the eggs hatching from the ball were generated spontaneously from the earth.

The Egyptians held a number of other beetles as sacred as well. One long, slender click beetle (*Agypus notodonta*) was sacred to Neith, a very ancient goddess associated with both fertility and war, and it was often depicted on amulets and in hieroglyphs. In the later periods of Egyptian civilization, including the Ptolemaic and Roman eras, beetles were mummified and placed in miniature sarcophagi in expectation that they would enter the next world. According to Louis Charbonneau-Lassay, the veneration of certain beetles eventually spread from Egypt throughout much of the Mediterranean. It also spread south to Africa, to the Hottentots and Kaffirs, who revered the golden-tinted rose beetle up through at least the eighteenth century.

One brightly colored insect, usually orange with black spots, is known as the ladybug in the United States and the ladybird in Britain. "Lady" refers to the Virgin Mary. In France the insect is sometimes called "*poulette à Dieu*," or "chicken of God." These names and the regard with which the insect is viewed hint at a divine role in the religions of antiquity, but this has never been fully explained. One theory is that the beetle was once sacred to Freya, the Scandinavian goddess of love. The association of the ladybug with the sun, however, indicates that its cult may be connected with that of the Egyptian scarab.

To have a ladybug alight on your clothes is considered a sign of good fortune, and you must never kill or injure the creature. You are to send it away with a rhyme, though you may also hurry it along by blowing gently. A common British variant of the rhyme goes:

Lady Bird, Lady Bird,
Fly away home,
Your house is on fire,
Your children will burn. (Baring-Gould, p. 209)

The verse may refer to the ladybug's association with the sun, which could be partly due to the bright orange or red on its back. Another theory is that the lines refer to the burning of hop vines after harvest to clear the fields. Sometimes, if the request is made in additional verses, people have believed the insect will fly to one's sweetheart.

In traditional rural societies, the cycle of putrefaction and renewed life was evident in yearly routines such as fertilizing the land, but it is experienced less intimately in urban life of the twentieth century. The beetle, a form of "vermin," sometimes appears as a symbol of unredeemed filth. In the story "Metamorphosis" by the German-Jewish writer Franz Kafka (first published in 1915), a traveling salesman named Gregor Samsa, subject to degrading demands from both family and work, woke up one day to find he had been changed into a giant insect. Some readers take it for a cockroach, which is now perhaps most intimately associated with squalor and decay. The creature in Kafka's story is indeterminate, but the description of it as lying on its hard back with legs kicking helplessly in the air suggests a beetle. Gregor struggled to communicate what remained of his humanity, until his family eventually tired of caring for him, so he died of neglect and was thrown out in the trash.

Selected References

Arnold, Dorothea. *An Egyptian Bestiary*. New York: Metropolitan Museum of Art, 1995.

Baring-Gould, William S., and Ceil. *The Annotated Mother Goose*. New York: Bramhall House, 1962.

Charbonneau-Lassay, Louis. *The Bestiary of Christ*. Trans. and ed. D. M. Dooling. New York: Parabola Books, 1991.

Fabre, Henri. *Fabre's Book of Insects*. Trans. Mrs. Rodolph Stawell. New York: Tudor, 1935.

Gubernatis, Angelo De. *Zoological Mythology or The Legends of Animals* (2 vols.). Chicago: Singing Tree Press, 1968.

Jones, Alison. *Larousse Dictionary of World Folklore*. New York: Larousse, 1996.

Kafka, Franz. "Metamorphosis." In *The Complete Stories*. Trans. Willa and Edwin Muir et al. New York: Schocken, 1971, pp. 89–139.

Blue Jay

See Crow, Raven, and Other Corvids

Boar

See Pig

Buffalo

See Bull and Cow

Bull and Cow

> *Man in his prosperity forfeits intelligence.*
> *He is the one with the cattle doomed to slaughter.*
> —Psalms 49:20

Bulls and cows are prominent in the Paleolithic paintings on the walls of caves in France, Spain, and other parts of Europe. In the main chamber of the cave at Lascaux, five enormous bulls decorate the ceiling. In the homes of Çatal Hüyük, near Jericho in the Near East, large heads of bulls modeled in clay extend from the walls. These shrines to bulls date back to the middle of the ninth millennium B.C. Similar shrines to bulls have been found in much of the Mediterranean area. Only very slowly did people lose their fear of these giants. Cattle were not domesticated in Europe until around 3,000 B.C., long after other animals such as the dog, sheep, and goat.

Sacred texts in the religion of Zoroaster made man and bull intimate associates. Ohrmuzd made a lone white bull, "shining like the moon," as the fifth act of creation and made the first man, Gayomart, as the sixth. The seed of man and bull were then created from "light and the freshness of sky," so that both would have abundant progeny (Zaehner, pp. 40–41). Zoroastrians believed that when the world drew to an end, Soshyans, a descendant of Zoroaster's, would sacrifice a great bull named Hadhayans, and the fat of the bull would be used to make the elixir of eternal life.

As the largest of domestic animals, the bull was the supreme sacrificial offering throughout almost all of the ancient Mediterranean. Its skin, bones, gristle, and a small bit of its meat were left on the altar for a god, while the humans feasted on the rest of the animal. Some people, however, thought it impious to give the gods such a tiny share. On important occasions, the Hebrews would perform a holocaust, a sacrifice in which the entire animal was offered up to God. The Bible gives a very detailed description of the bull sacrifice that ac-

companied the investiture of priests. Some blood was placed around horns by the altar to purify it, and the rest was poured out onto the ground. Every part of the bull was disposed of according to a precise ritual (Lev. 8:14–17).

In Greece the sacrifice of a bull was generally reserved for tributes to Zeus; in Rome, for tributes to Jupiter. The slaying of the bull became the central rite in the religion of Mithras, which rivaled Christianity in popularity during the latter part of the Roman Empire. Mithras, accompanied by a dog and other animals, would plunge his sword into a great bull at the end of the world so that all things might live again. Artists of the Roman Empire would depict grain sprouting from the wounds of the bull as it was slain by Mithras.

In one myth of the Greeks, Poseidon, god of the sea, gave King Minos of Crete an enormous bull, intending that Minos should offer it back as a sacrifice. But Minos kept the bull instead. This act, an allusion to the first domestication of animals, led to a sequence of events in which great buildings were erected, unnatural acts performed, and people sacrificed. The angry god caused the wife of Minos, Pasiphaë, to fall in love with the bull. She ordered Daedalos, the great inventor, to construct a hollow cow of wood, and she crept inside. From there, she made love to the bull and conceived the Minotaur, a monster with the head of a bull and the body of a man. Deeply ashamed, Minos ordered Daedalos to construct a labyrinth, an underground series of passageways, in which to house the Minotaur. Later, when his son was killed hunting a boar in Athens, Minos demanded that the Athenians send a tribute to him in Crete of seven youths and seven maidens every year as penance. The fourteen were placed in the labyrinth, where they would wander until they were eaten by the monster or else died of hunger. Theseus, a prince of Athens, volunteered to go as one of the youths. Ariadne, the daughter of Minos, fell in love with him. She gave him a ball of yarn to unroll as he wandered through the labyrinth and a sword to do battle with the Minotaur. Theseus killed the creature and escaped from Crete with Ariadne. A short while later, he deserted his benefactress on an island. He went on to kill other monsters and brigands, to defeat the Amazons, and to give Athens its first laws.

The tale mocks the religion, especially the fertility rites, of the Cretans, who were often adversaries of the Greeks. Minos, a fool and tyrant in Greek mythology, appears to have been an actual ruler in Crete. He claimed the bull as an ancestor, and he did indeed have an elaborate palace with underground chambers at Knossos. The Minotaur was a god, whom the Greeks considered a grotesque, unnatural creature. With his horns and his dwelling beneath the ground, he anticipated the Christian Devil.

Cretan wall paintings depicted acrobats turning somersaults on the back of a bull. In the Mesopotamian tale of Gilgamesh, our earliest heroic epic, the Bull of Heaven represented a terrible drought, which came early in the second millennium and may have destroyed the mighty Akkadian empire. The Bull was sent down to earth as a punishment because Gilgamesh and his companion Enkidu had cut down the cedar forests of Lebanon and killed its guardian, Humbaba. The animal immediately killed hundreds of people. Enkidu grabbed the horns of the bull and leapt aside, a bit like the Cretan acrobats. Gilgamesh killed the bull with his sword. But worship of the bull persisted in Mesopotamia. The animal was identified with Anu, the god of the sky, and with Adad, the god of storms. There are a number of depictions of bull-men, which may have sometimes represented Enkidu himself.

In Egypt, the sacred bull Apis was considered an incarnation of the creator god Ptah. Conceived when fire came down from heaven and impregnated a cow, Apis was a unique animal that, legend had it, priests could find by searching among calves for one with very specific markings. He would be black but with an inverted triangle of white on his brow. A mark shaped like the silhouette of a vulture would stretch across his shoulders, and there would be a crescent moon on his sides and a sign like a beetle on his tongue. Once the bull was found, there would be great rejoicing. He would march in a large procession. Women would pray to him for children, and priests would perform sacred rites. Finally, he would be brought to the temple of Ptah, where he would live. When he died, the bull would be consecrated to Osiris, god of the dead, and buried in great splendor. Then priests would search for his successor.

The Greeks and Romans, who had anthropomorphic deities, sometimes thought the animal-gods of Egypt were strange or primitive. Nevertheless, they generally respected the sacred bull Apis. Herodotus recounted how Cambyses, king of the Persians, committed a sacrilege against Apis after conquering Egypt. The new ruler, filled with arrogance, threw his dagger at the bull, striking the animal in the thigh. Then Cambyses had the priests of Apis beaten and forbade them, under penalty of death, to celebrate any festivals. Apis died unattended in the temple and was secretly buried. Shortly afterward, the gods struck Cambyses with madness. He killed his brother, his sister, and many trusted servants in fits of temper. Finally, after he had driven his subjects to revolt, Cambyses accidentally wounded himself in the thigh with his own sword. When he realized that the place of the wound corresponded exactly to where he had struck the sacred bull, Cambyses knew that he was doomed. The wounded limb became infected with gangrene, and he died shortly afterward.

Illustration by Albrecht Dürer to Sebastian Brandt's Ship of Fools *(1494), showing worship of the golden calf.*

The golden calf, which the Israelites worshipped during their flight from Egypt, is a form of the sacred bull Apis. The Hebrews were constantly struggling with the old animal cults, and Moses put this one down with great ruthlessness, killing about 2,000 people. Today, bullfights reenact the struggle against the ancient cult of the bull. It is remarkable that, with all our technology, we still need such ritual affirmations of human dominance.

The many deities of the ancient world who were depicted in the form of a bull also included the Greek Dionysus, Phoenician Moloch, and Syrian Attis. Siva, part of the Hindu trinity, rides on a white bull. He is the god of creativity, a quality vividly embodied in the fecundity of cattle. For this reason the cow and bull are sacred in much of India. The cow and bull are also important in the culture of the Far East, but there they have been viewed with a bit less awe and a bit more intimacy. The ox is a sign of the Chinese zodiac. The sage Lao-tzu has often been depicted riding on a water buffalo, and so are small boys playing the flute. Cattle in Asia are not only admired but often loved as well.

With many animals such as the cat and the dog, worship eventually led to domestication. In a similar way religious awe can evolve into economic power. Cattle in the ancient world, where most exchanges were conducted by barter rather than by money, were a measure of wealth. To show the wealth of Job, the Bible numbers the animals in his herds yet says nothing about money at all. The value of coins, initially, was measured according to the animals they might buy, and the earliest coins are stamped with pictures of cattle. In Homeric times, a talent of gold was the equivalent of an ox. Our word "pecuniary" comes from the Latin "*pecus*," meaning "domestic herd animal."

It is strange that English has no common word that can stand for either bull or cow in the singular. The closest, perhaps, is "bovine," which sounds a bit pedantic. When we speak of a rabbit or spider, the subject may be either female or male. For the cow and bull, however, sexuality is such an intimate part of their identity that, apparently, even the word cannot dispense with gender. The same is true in other languages, for example Latin. Both the bull and the cow are extremely important in the religious history of humanity, but their symbolism is so different that they sometimes hardly seem to be of the same species. As we have seen, the bull is generally associated with generative power and energy. The cow is, by contrast, maternal.

The cow has often been worshipped as a provider of milk. Unlike bulls, cows were seldom sacrificed. In Norse mythology, the creation of the world began when the cow Audhumbla was created from melting frost. She nourished the giant Ymir with rivers of milk. When she grew thirsty, Audhumbla licked grains of salt on ice of the frozen waste. She formed the first man, Buri, ancestor of the gods, with her tongue. The Egyptian goddess Hathor, mistress of the underworld, was often depicted in the form of a cow. As goddess of love, music, and fertility, she was among the most beloved of deities. Once, however, the deities appointed her to punish humankind. She took the form of a lioness and created such devastation that the divinities feared she would destroy every person on the earth. Finally, they gave her wine to calm her. In Greek mythology, Hera, the wife of Zeus, is referred to as "cow-eyed" by Homer. In remote times, she may have been a bovine deity. Her husband, the supreme god, was constantly having affairs with mortals. Once Hera caught him with the maiden Io. Hoping to cover up his transgression, Zeus turned Io into a cow.

Hera saw through the trick. She sent a fly to prod the maiden and drive her over the world.

Hollow images of cows in which people might be buried were made in Egypt and elsewhere in the ancient world. Herodotus told how the daughter of the pharaoh Mycerinus, in her last moments, asked her father that she might still see the sun once a year. Devastated by her death, Mycerinus ordered that a large cow be made of wood. It was hollowed out and covered up with gold. A golden orb representing the sun was placed between the horns. The young woman was buried in the cow. Lamps were kept always burning beside the cow, and once a year it was raised and exposed to the light of day.

What is greatly valued easily becomes an object of contention. Cattle raids were frequent and often led to wars. According to the Greeks, the infant Hermes, who later became messenger of the gods, stole the cattle of the sun god Apollo. Hermes killed two of the animals and locked the rest in a cave. After eating, he strung the guts of the cattle across a tortoiseshell to make the first stringed instrument, a lyre. Apollo, who could tell the future, easily found the thief. The mother of Hermes protested that her son was but an infant and certainly not capable of theft, but Apollo demanded that his property be returned. Finally, though, Apollo exchanged the cattle for the lyre and became the patron of music. The story is about the exchange of the spiritual value of art for pecuniary value, property in the form of cattle.

Perhaps the most important epic of the Celtic people is the *Táin Bó Cuailnge*, or "The Cattle Raid of Cooley." As it began, Queen Medb and her husband, Ailell, were arguing about which of them brought greater wealth to their marriage. They tallied up their goods, item by item, including clothes, jewels, and sheep. Medb was able to match every possession of Ailell's except for a white horned bull named Finnbennach. There was only one bull so fine in all of Ireland. It was named Donn Cuailnge and kept in the province of Ulster. Queen Medb resolved to have that bull. When it was refused to her, she sent an army to take it. The hero Cú Cuchulainn valiantly defended Ulster, but after many battles Medb finally carried off her prize. The story ended as the two bulls fought and Donn Cuailnge was victorious. He wandered about carrying the entrails of Finnbennach on his horns and then finally died. The story is not so different from the plots of many American Westerns, once so popular as cheap paperbacks and early television shows.

The symbolism of animals is often remarkably universal, and similar meanings can frequently be found in cultures that seem to have had little or no contact over centuries or millennia. The American buffalo, much like its relatives, the cow and bull in Eurasian cultures, is viewed as a nurturer among the Native Americans in the West. In *Animals of the Soul*, Joseph E. Brown writes that "because of the overall value of the bison in Oglala (Sioux) religious beliefs, the animals and all parts of it represent some aspect of the sacred . . . " (p. 14). Hunting buffalo was understood as a quest, accompanied by rituals of purification. Every part of the buffalo was used, whether for food, clothing, or the construction of artifacts. The near extinction of the buffalo in the United States during the twentieth century was a systematic attack on the traditional culture of the Indians inhabiting the Great Plains.

Even after millennia of domestication, cattle have not entirely lost their numinous quality. Those who are associated with cattle seem to gain some of their power and virility, at least in popular imagination. This is so for the heroes of ancient epics as well as the gauchos of Argentina and the cowboys of the American West. Eating of beef is still associated with strength and virility. Muscular men are called "beefcake."

Ancestral patterns can be very persistent, even when the culture no longer appears to sanction them. Despite the Christian ban on animal sacrifice, medieval bestiaries often saw a symbol of Christ in the ox or bull that was slain for food. In 1522, desperate to stop the black plague, Pope Leo X allowed bulls to be sacrificed in the Old Roman

Coliseum—to no avail. On farms in England, sacrifices of bulls have been practiced from time to time, even in the twentieth century for such purposes as stopping disease or witchcraft. Bulls have sometimes been killed in very brutal ways, such as being buried upside down or burned alive, when people thought that was what the magic required.

When Emperor Charles V of Spain had a son, later to become Philip II, he celebrated by publicly killing a bull in the marketplace. The most notable example of the survival of animal sacrifice may be the bullfights of the Iberian Peninsula and Latin America. Barbaric as the sport may seem, bullfighting began gaining popularity at the start of the modern era around the sixteenth century. The elaborate ceremony and pageantry that accompany bullfighting date only from around the end of the eighteenth century. The bull is enraged by being kept in darkness and then abruptly exposed to the bright lights of the arena. Lancers on horseback systematically goad the bull, and then, when the animal has been worn out, the matador delivers the fatal thrust with his sword. The contest symbolizes the triumph of the matador's finesse and skill over brute power. Despite the obvious cruelty, matadors insist that they respect and even love the bulls. Fervent aficionados of the bullfight find themselves unable to explain the appeal to others. On a barely conscious level, it is based on the idea that death can release a cosmic energy that may then nourish all of life.

Today, most people live in urban areas and rarely see a bull or cow, yet hamburger is perhaps the favorite food of all. Restaurants and packaging plants constantly invoke the romance of cowboys and the old West. The meat is mixed together to a point where nobody knows which part, much less which animal, is being eaten. The fast-food hamburger is now a symbol of the homogenization of global culture, where all origins and peculiarities are obscured. Chains like McDonald's are constantly vilified, yet they retain enormous popularity.

Cows and bulls, perhaps more than any other animals, have seemed through most of history to embody cosmic energy, which might be worshipped, harnessed, absorbed, or contained. People have felt they drew strength from contact with them, whether by eating or by tending these animals. But today, that cosmic energy has come to seem anonymous, much like the hamburger from a giant franchise.

Selected References
Attenborough, David. *The First Eden: The Mediterranean World.* Boston: Little, Brown, 1987.
Brown, Joseph Epes. *Animals of the Soul: Sacred Animals of the Oglala Sioux.* Rockport, MA: Element, 1992.

Dalley, Stephanie, ed. and trans. *Myths from Mesopotamia: Creation, the Flood, Gilgamesh, and Others.* New York: Oxford University Press, 1992.

Herodotus. *Herodotus* (4 vols.). Trans. A. D. Godley. New York: G. P. Putnam's Sons, 1926.

Lewinsohn, Richard. *Animals, Men, and Myths: An Informative and Entertaining History of Man and the Animals around Him.* New York: Harper and Brothers, 1954.

O'Flaherty, Wendy Doniger. *Women, Androgynes, and Other Mythical Beasts.* Chicago: University of Chicago Press, 1980.

Zaehner, R. C. *The Teachings of the Magi: A Compendium of Zoroastrian Beliefs.* New York: Oxford University Press, 1976.

Butterfly and Moth

I do not know whether I was then a man dreaming I was a butterfly, or whether I am now a butterfly dreaming I am a man.
—Chuang-tzu

The idea of a butterfly or moth as the soul is a remarkable example of the universality of animal symbolism, since it is found in traditional cultures of every continent. The custom of scattering flowers at funerals is very ancient, and the flowers attract butterflies, which appear to have emerged from a corpse. A butterfly or moth will hover for a time in one place or fly in a fleeting, hesitant manner, suggesting a soul that is reluctant to move on to the next world.

The transformation of a caterpillar into a butterfly seems to provide the ultimate model for our ideas of death, burial, and resurrection. This imagery is still implicit in Christianity when people speak of being "born again." The chrysalis of a butterfly may have even inspired the splendor of many coffins from antiquity. Many cocoons are very finely woven, with some threads that are golden or silver in color.

The Greek word *"psyche"* means soul, but it can also designate a butterfly or moth. The Latin word *"anima"* has the same dual meaning. Several gems from ancient Greece depicted a butterfly hovering over a human skull. Late Roman artifacts often portrayed Prometheus making humankind while Minerva stood nearby holding aloft a butterfly, which represented the soul. A story inserted in the first-century novel *The Golden Ass* by Roman-Egyptian author Lucius Apuleius tells of a young girl named Psyche who was given in marriage to Cupid, the god of love, and contemporary illustrations often showed Psyche with the wings of a butterfly. The wings of a butterfly are frequently used to designate the soul in Western art, and they have also been painted on fairies.

In lands around the eastern shores of the Pacific Ocean, the idea that the soul of a person will return in the form of a butterfly that hovers around the grave of the body is widespread. In Indonesia and Burma, people have traditionally believed that if a butterfly enters your house, it is likely to be the spirit of a deceased relative or a friend. On the island of Java, it is traditionally believed that sometimes during sleep the soul flies out in the form of a butterfly. You should never kill a butterfly, since a sleeping person might then die as well.

Their close association with flowers helps to make butterflies a symbol of both fecundity and transience.

The Chinese sage Chuang-tzu, one of the disciples of Lao-tzu, the founder of Taoism—used to flutter about as a butterfly at night. On waking, he would continue to feel the motion of wings in his shoulders, and he was unsure whether he was truly a butterfly or a man. Lao-tzu explained to him, "Formerly you were a white butterfly which . . . should have been immortalized, but one day you stole some peaches and flowers. . . . The guardian of the garden slew you, and that is how you came to be reincarnated" (Werner, p. 149).

The way certain butterflies perform a courting dance—each partner moving off in various directions yet always coming back to the other—has made these insects symbols of conjugal love, especially in Japan. Lafcadio Hearn has collected a Japanese story of an old man named Takahama who was nearing death. A nephew was sitting at his bedside when a white butterfly flew in. It hovered for a while and perched near Takahama's head. When his nephew tried to brush it away, the butterfly danced around strangely and then flew down the corridor. Surmising that this was no ordinary insect, the nephew followed the butterfly until it reached a gravestone and disappeared. Approaching to examine the grave, he found the name Akiko. On returning to his uncle, he found Takahama dead. When the boy told his mother about the butterfly, she was not in the least surprised. Akiko, she explained, was a young girl that Takahama had planned to marry, but she died of consumption at the age of eighteen. For the rest of his life, Takahama had remained faithful to her memory and visited her grave every day. The nephew then realized that the soul of Akiko had come in the form of a butterfly to accompany the spirit of his uncle to the next world.

The soul of a beloved also takes the form of an insect, probably a butterfly, in the ancient Irish saga "The Wooing of Etian." The god Mider had fallen in love with a mortal named Etian, but the goddess Fuamnach struck the young woman with a rowan wand and transformed her into a puddle. As the water dried, it became a worm, which was then changed into a "scarlet fly." "Its eyes shone like precious stones in the dark, and its color and fragrance would sate hunger and quench thirst in any man; moreover, a sprinkling of the drops it shed from its wings could cure every sickness . . . " (Gantz, p. 45). The insect accompanied Mider as he traveled and watched over him as he slept, until Fuamnach sent a fierce gale to blow it away. Pursued constantly by the goddess, the insect was finally carried by wind into the goblet of a chieftain's wife, who drank it and gave birth to Etain 1,012 years after the infant had been first conceived. Mider had searched for her for a thousand years, but when he finally found her, she was the wife of the king of Ireland. Finally, after Mider had won his wife from the king in a game, the lovers flew away in the form of swans.

Biologists distinguish between butterflies and moths by anatomical features that strike laypeople as arcane, but folk culture usually distinguishes in a very simple manner—moths are nocturnal while butterflies are diurnal. Furthermore, butterflies have many dazzlingly bright patterns of color, while moths tend to be shades of white and brown.

When homes were lighted by candles or tapers at night, people were particularly fascinated by those moths that would fly toward the fire even when that meant they would expire in a sudden blaze. In one of his most famous poems, "Blissful Longing" ("Selige Sehnsucht"), Johann Wolfgang von Goethe used this motif as a symbol of the soul's desire for transcendence. The poem tells of a moth drawn to a flame and ends with these words:

Dost thou shun the great behest,
   This, *Become by Dying!*
Thou art but a sorry guest
   On this dull earth staying. (p. 95)

While many people find the poem beautiful, some critics have been troubled by the romantic celebration of death.

A less mystical but perhaps more compassionate view of such an event is given by the early-twentieth-century British author Virginia Woolf in her essay "The Moth." She tells of watching a moth dance about by day as its motions became gradually fainter. Many times she gave the moth up for dead, only to see it flutter once again. Finally, when the tiny body relaxed and then grew stiff, she felt awed by both the power of death and the courageous resistance of the spirit against so formidable an antagonist.

As the pace of modern life has become increasingly frantic, people have come to admire the leisurely flight of the butterfly. As W. B. Yeats puts it in his poem "Tom O'Roughley":

'Though logic-choppers rule the town,
And every man and maid and boy
Has marked a distant object down,
An aimless joy is a pure joy,'
Or so did Tom O'Roughley say
That saw the surges running by,
'And wisdom is a butterfly,
And not a gloomy bird of prey. (p. 141)

Sometimes the way a butterfly moves from flower to flower has also been decried as lack of commitment, and Yeats, in the same poem, calls it "zig-zag wantonness" (p. 141). Today many ecologists regard butterflies as a keystone species, and they will count butterflies per acre in an attempt to determine the health of an ecosystem, perhaps in a manner not altogether different from that of diviners in the ancient world.

Selected References

Gantz, Jeffrey, ed. and trans. *Early Irish Myths and Sagas.* New York: Penguin Books, 1982.

Goethe, Johann Wolfgang von. "Blessed Longing." Trans. John Weiss. *Representative German Poems.* Ed. Karl Knotz. New York: Henry Holt, 1985, p. 95.

Hearn, Lafcadio. *Kwaidan: Stories and Studies of Strange Things.* Rutland, VT: Charles E. Tuttle, 1971.

Werner, Edward T. C. *Ancient Tales and Folklore of China*. London: Bracken Books, 1986.

Woolf, Virginia. "The Death of a Moth." In *The Death of a Moth and Other Essays*. New York: Harcourt, Brace, 1942, pp. 3–6.

Yeats, W. B. "Tom O'Roughley." In *The Poems of W. B. Yeats*. New York: Macmillan, 1983, p. 141.

C

Camel
See Ass, Mule, and Camel

Carp
See Salmon and Carp

Cat

> *The cat is the only animal to have succeeded in domesticating man.*
> —Marcel Mauss

A cat has enormous eyes that shine especially dramatically when the rest of its body is shrouded in darkness. Because the pupils of the cat constantly expand and contract to adjust to the level of light, they seem like the waxing and waning moon. The lunar cycle, in turn, is closely bound up with the menstrual cycle of women. Most civilizations, especially Indo-European ones, have thought of the moon as feminine (a partial exception is the Germans, for whom the word for "moon"—*Mond*—has a masculine gender).

The position of women in patriarchal societies is a bit like that of cats in homes. In many ways, cats may be subordinate to the master or mistress of the house. Nevertheless, their manner always suggests confidence and power. They are able to bestow affection and appreciation without debasing themselves. Furthermore, the intense attachment that cats develop to their homes is a bit like the domestic role that women have often played. Jean Cocteau called the cat "the soul of a home made visible" (Delort, p. 426). The troubled partnership of cat and dog in many human homes often resembles that of women and men.

We can also think of the cat within the home as the secret wildness in every person that survives despite the regimentation of our public lives. The confident bearing of cats suggests secret knowledge, which people have both valued and feared.

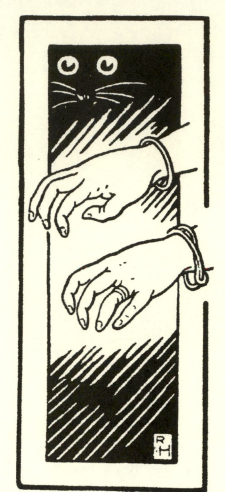

Illustration by Richard Heighway to Aesop's fable of "The Cat Maiden."

"When I play with my cat, who knows but that she regards me more as a plaything than I do her?" wrote Michel de Montaigne in "Apology for Raymond Sebond" (p. 444). Touch or pet a cat and there may be sparks! Cats are constantly rubbing their backs against any available surface, so static electricity builds up in their fur. People have always been mystified by the ability of cats to survive after falling from tall trees or buildings. No wonder cats have always seemed magical.

The curvilinear design of the feline body and the cat's rhythmic way of walking are very feminine. No doubt this is why so many archaic goddesses were closely associated with cats. The Greek Artemis, goddess of the moon, fled to Egypt and changed herself into a cat to escape the serpent Typhon. A panther was sacred to the goddess Astarte, the Mesopotamian equivalent of Aphrodite. She was often portrayed standing upright and riding on her mascot. The Hindu goddess of birth, Shasti, also used a cat as her mount. Freya, the Norse goddess of love, rode in a chariot drawn by cats.

Perhaps most important, the Egyptian goddess Bast was depicted with the head of a cat and the body of a woman. Our word *puss* or *pussy* for cat comes from Pasht, an alternative name for Bastet. The yearly festival of Bastet, held in autumn, was the most splendid celebration in all of Egypt. Hundreds of thousands of people would come on boats, singing and clapping to the music of castanets. They would offer sacrifices at the temple of Bastet, then feast for several days.

The Egyptians punished unsanctioned killing of a cat with death. Diodorus Siculus reported that in the middle of the first century B.C. a member of a Roman delegation to Alexandria accidentally killed a cat. A crowd stormed his house. Not even fear of Rome could keep the local citizens from punishing the perpetrator with death. Several superstitions about cats probably go back to ancient Egypt, and many people still say that killing a cat brings bad luck.

According to Herodotus, the entire family in an Egyptian home would go into mourning when a cat died. All members would shave their eyebrows to show their sorrow. Dead cats were taken to the city of Bubastis, where they were embalmed and ceremoniously buried. Hundreds of thousands of mummified remains of cats have been found in Egyptian tombs. Veneration of the cat eventually reached far beyond the Mediterranean, and Robert Graves has reported in *The White Goddess* that when Saint Patrick arrived in Ireland, there was a shrine in a cave at Connacht where the oracle was a black cat upon a chair of silver.

A fable known as "The Cat Maiden," traditionally attributed to the Greek Aesop, records a triumph of feminine wiles over masculine power. The gods and goddesses were arguing about whether it was possible for a thing to change its nature. "For me, nothing is impossible," said Zeus, the god of thunder. "Watch, and I will prove it." With that, he picked up a mangy alley cat, changed it into a lovely young girl, had her dressed in fine clothes, instructed her in manners, and arranged for her to be married the next day. The gods and goddesses looked on invisibly at the wedding feast. "See how beautiful she is, how appropriately she behaves," said Zeus proudly. "Who could ever guess that only yesterday she was a cat!" "Just a moment," said Aphrodite, the goddess of love. With that, she let loose a mouse. The maiden immediately pounced on the mouse and began tearing it apart with her teeth. This fable has been written down in many versions, some of which date back to the fifth century B.C. in Greece. Perhaps in some still earlier version, the cat was Aphrodite herself.

"Dick Whittington and His Cat," an early rags-to-riches tale from England, shows how cats were valued in the early modern period by those engaged in trade. The hero, Dick Whittington, was an impoverished young man in London who had worked hard and managed to buy a cat, which he lent to a ship's captain. The captain sold the cat for a vast fortune to the king of the Moors, who was plagued by rats. Dick became a wealthy man and was Lord Mayor of London in the late thirteenth and early fourteenth centuries, though the tale was not written down until much later.

Aboard ships, cats were used as mascots and to catch mice. Virtually all mariners were male. Sailors sometimes believed the presence of a woman on board, or even the mention of a woman's name, would bring ill luck. The cat, often the only female on the ship, was a mediator with the feminine powers of the weather and the sea. Mariners predicted weather by watching the cat. When the cat washed its face, they would expect rain. When the cat was frisky, they would expect strong winds. Cats would also know if the ship was about to sink. Every detail of the cat's behavior would be closely scrutinized for portents.

Superstitions about cats are almost as diverse as they are numerous. A black cat, for example, is usually thought of as a sign of bad luck, while a white cat means good luck. Sometimes, however, this has been reversed. Wives of mariners in England would keep black cats as a charm for the safe return of their husbands at sea, a practice that people in other communities could misinterpret as witchcraft.

In Renaissance Europe, cats were often thought to be the familiars of witches, and black cats in particular were frequently named as such in the witch trials. Jean Boille, who was burned as a sorceress at Vesoul in 1620, claimed to have seen demons and cats participating together in sexual orgies at the witches' Sabbath. A pact with the Devil was sealed with a paw print placed on the body of a witch. The Black Witch of Fraddan flew through the air at night on an enormous cat. In the early thirteenth century, the bishop of Paris, Guillaume d'Auvergne, claimed that Satan appeared to his followers in the form of a black cat and they had to kiss him beneath the tail.

Diabolic, and sometimes almost as frightening as the Devil himself, is the King of the Cats in Irish folklore. Sometimes the King is black and wears a silver chain, but he cannot always be recognized. Lady Wilde in *Legends of Ancient Ireland* tells of a man who once, in a fit of temper, cut off the head of a domestic cat and threw it into a fire. The eyes of the cat continued to glare at him from within the flames, and the feline voice swore revenge. A short time later the man was playing with a pet kitten; suddenly the kitten lunged, bit him on the throat, and killed him.

When people are fond of certain animals, they assume the animals will also be beloved by the gods and goddesses, and they offer them up as sacrifices. The ancient Egyptians may have punished the killing of a cat outside of a temple with death, but they offered thousands of cats to Bastet, generally by breaking their necks. Christianity officially rejected animal sacrifice, but ceremonial killing of cats continued for thousands of years. Cats were burned alive on Ash Wednesday in Metz and other Continental cities during the Middle Ages to produce the ash for the mass. In England, the effigy of Guy Fawkes that was ceremonially burned every year sometimes contained a cat that would howl as the flames rose. Cats have been found walled up alive in the foundations of several medieval buildings, including the Tower of London. This was the theme of Edgar Allan Poe's famous horror story "The Black Cat." Terrified that his wife was a witch and her black cat the Devil, the narrator killed his wife and built a wall to conceal her body. The cat howled from behind the wall until the police came.

Toward the end of the Middle Ages there were few cats left in Europe. Their absence led to a great increase in rats and diseases, including bubonic plague. The few cats that had survived the persecutions came to be highly valued. For the first time, Europeans began to realize that cats were not only useful but also loyal and affectionate. Benevolent cats began to appear in fairy tales, though they still usually seemed to have something a little disturbing about them. In "The White Cat" by Madame D'Aulnoy, a magical feline guided the hero through all sorts of trials and tribulations. Finally, the cat cast off its skin, became a woman, and married him. Then she burned the skin; after all, would the man want his wife changing shape and casting spells? Perhaps the magic here is the power of young love, to be put away as a person enters maturity.

In "Puss in Boots" by Charles Perrault, a cat loyally helps a young man. To win a fortune for him, however, the two must connive and deceive everybody else. Master Puss makes up a title, "the Marquis of Carrabas," for the young man. Then the cat tells harvesters that they will be chopped up into little pieces if they don't tell the king their land belongs to this marquis. At the request of the cat, the ogre who really owns the land in question transforms himself into a mouse. The cat immediately pounces on the mouse, eats him, and takes over the ogre's castle for the young man. Finally, the young man has so much wealth that he can marry the king's daughter. If the story were told from another point of view—say, that of the ogre—the reader could easily take this cat for the Devil. At any rate, it is great having such a cat on your side.

In folklore, the animals in a household often make up their own little society, a sort of microcosm. The dog, of course, is among the most domesticated of animals, while the rodents are completely wild. The cat is in between. The dog and cat are constantly quarreling and making up. Sometimes they cooperate to help their master, but the old enmity can break out at any time. The cat and mouse, by contrast, are mortal enemies. The mice in the household hardly ever defeat the cat, though they often manage to get away. The situation is a bit like a troubled family of human beings, where mother and father quarrel and the children suffer. In a tale traditionally attributed to Aesop, the mice meet in council to decide how to protect themselves against the cat. One mouse proposes that they fasten a bell around the cat's neck to warn them when she approached. After the proposal is warmly applauded, an old mouse stands up and asks, "But who is going to bell the cat?"

Buddhists take a negative view of the cat, though they have seldom carried this to the extremes we find in the West. The Jatakas, ancient Buddhist fables, in describing the animals assembled around the deathbed of Buddha to pay him homage, note that the cat was taking a nap and didn't come. According to another traditional tale, Maya sent a rat with medicine for the ailing Buddha, but the cat killed the rat, so Buddha perished. Nevertheless, cats were regularly kept as mousers in households of China, Japan, and other countries of the Far East. Artists were often fascinated by their alertness, their sensitivity to subtle sounds and motions. For such a common animal, cats were notably absent from the Chinese zodiac, in part because they were closely associated with the element of earth.

For all their differences, Christianity and Buddhism have both tended to be suspicious of archaic magic. Perhaps this is part of the reason the cultures that have grown around these religions so often view the cat, the most magical of animals, with mistrust. Islam may be a legalistic religion, yet the Koran delights in extravagant tales of the supernatural; consequently, Muslims have always been lovers of cats. According to legend, Muhammed once found his cat Meuzza sleeping on his robe. So as not to disturb his pet, the prophet cut off a sleeve and put on the rest of the garment. When he returned, Meuzza bowed to him in gratitude. Mohammed blessed the cat and her descendents with the ability to fall and land on their feet. When cats enter a mosque, it means good luck for the community. In one story from Oman, told by Inea Bushnaq, a cat caught a mouse and was about to devour it; the mouse begged to be allowed a prayer before death. When the cat agreed, the mouse suggested that the cat pray as well. The cat raised its arms and the rat escaped. When a cat rubs its face, the story concluded, it is remembering the smell of the rat.

At the beginning of the nineteenth century, the German writer E. T. A. Hoffmann took on the formidable task of trying to imagine the feelings of a cat in *The Life and Opinions of Kater Murr*. A passionate if somewhat reluctant romantic, Hoffmann felt cats were like those who work magic in verse or paint. Like artists, cats have mysterious insights. Like artists, cats often seem vain and impractical. Both cats and artists have an odd combination of innocence and guile. The cat Murr, who tells his story, affectionately mocks his master. He has adventures climbing the rooftops of the town. He reminds the reader in his preface, "Should anybody be bold enough to raise doubts concerning the worth of this extraordinary book, he should consider that he confronts a tom-cat with spirit, understanding, and sharp claws" (vol. 2, p. 11).

Poets always love mystery, and so they also love cats. W. B. Yeats and T. S. Eliot are among the many who have found inspiration in cats, but the most famous poem of all about cats is "My Cat Jeoffrey" by Christopher Smart. The author takes precisely the characteristics that have impressed people as diabolic and uses them to make the cat a symbol of Christ:

> For he keeps the Lord's watch in the night against the
> adversary.
> For he counteracts the powers of darkness by his electrical skin
> & glaring eyes.
> For he counteracts the Devil, who is death, by brisking about
> the life. (p. 28)

For Smart, the many paradoxes that surround the cat are a proof of divinity.

The decades immediately following World War II saw a romanticizing of alienation in the United States and Europe. In the slang of the Beatnik movement, a "cat" became somebody who preferred the colorful life of the streets to the mainstream of American society. In the last few decades of the twentieth century, cats have replaced dogs as the most popular pet in the United States. Some reasons for this preference are pragmatic. Cats are smaller, eat less, need less space to exercise, and are less expensive to care for than dogs. For those who find the emotional exuberance of dogs embarrassing, cats seem to offer emotional support without sacrifice of decorum. The relationship of cats to people can be warm and nurturing yet with a distance of respect, intimate yet full of riddles.

Selected References

Aesop. *The Fables of Aesop.* Ed. Joseph Jacobs. New York: Macmillan, 1910, pp. 180–182.

Briggs, Katharine. *Nine Lives: The Folklore of Cats.* New York: Dorset Press, 1980.

Bushnaq, Inea, ed. and trans. *Arab Folktales.* New York: Pantheon, 1986.

Dale, Rodney. *Cats in Boots: A Celebration of Cat Illustration through the Ages.* New York: Harry N. Abrams, 1997.

D'Aulnoy, Marie-Catherine. "The White Cat." Trans. Minnie Wright. In *The Blue Fairy Book.* Ed. Andrew Lang. New York: Dover, 1965, pp. 157–173.

Delort, Robert. *Les animaux ont une histoire.* Paris: Éditions du Seuil, 1984.

Graves, Robert. *The White Goddess: A Historical Grammar of Poetic Myth.* New York: Farrar, Straus and Giroux, 1993.

Herodotus. *Herodotus.* (4 vols.). Trans. A. D. Godley. New York: G. P. Putnam's Sons, 1926.

Hoffmann, E. T. A. *The Life and Opinions of Kater Murr.* In *Selected Writings of E. T. A. Hoffmann* (2 vols.). Ed. and trans. Leonard J. Kent and Elizabeth C. Knight. Chicago: University of Chicago Press, 1969.

Houlihan, Patrick F. *The Animal World of the Pharaohs.* New York: Thames and Hudson, 1996.

Jacobs, Joseph, ed. "Dick Whittington and His Cat." In *English Fairy Tales.* New York: Dover, 1967, pp. 167–178.

Montaigne, Michel de. "Apology for Raymond Sebond." In *The Complete Essays of Montaigne* (2 vols.). Trans. Donald M. Frame. Stanford: Stanford University Press, 1959, vol. 1, pp. 428–561.

Perrault, Charles. *Perrault's Fairy Tales.* Trans. A. E. Johnson. New York: Dover, 1969.

Poe, Edgar Allan. *Complete Stories and Poems of Edgar Allan Poe.* New York: Doubleday, 1966.

Smart, Christopher. "My Cat Jeoffrey." In *Animal Poems,* ed. John Hollander. New York: Knopf, 1994, pp. 27–31.

Lady Wilde (Speranza). *Ancient Legends, Mystic Charms, and Superstitions of Ireland: With Sketches of the Irish Past.* Galway: O'Gorman, 1971 (1888).

Centaur

See Horse

Chimpanzee

See Ape and Monkey

Cicada

See Grasshopper, Locust, Cricket, Cicada, and Mantis

Clam

See Starfish, Clam, Octopus, and Other Creatures of the Sea Floor

Cock and Hen

> *It faded on the crowing of the cock.*
> *Some say that ever, 'gainst that season comes*
> *Wherein our Savior's birth is celebrated,*
> *The bird of dawning singeth all night long;*
> *And then, they say, no spirit dare stir abroad,*
> *The nights are wholesome, then no planets strike,*
> *No fairy takes, nor witch hath power to charm,*
> *So hallow'ed and so gracious is that time.*
> —William Shakespeare, *Hamlet,* (act 1, scene 1; said after the ghost
> of Hamlet's father had vanished upon the crowing of a cock)

Aelian wrote in the second century A.D. of two Greek temples separated by a river, one consecrated to Hercules and the other to his wife,

Two cocks fighting over a hen in an illustration from the mid-nineteenth century by J. J. Grandville.

Hebe. Cocks were kept in the temple of the god, and hens in that of the goddess. The roosters would cross the waters once a year to mate, returning with any male offspring and leaving the females for the hens to raise. The arrangement is not very plausible, among other reasons because cocks generally cannot stay together without fighting, which is why barnyards have only one. Nevertheless, this account shows how cock and hen, even more than other animals, seem to be defined by their gender, to the point where they hardly appear to belong to the same species. Both cock and hen were indeed kept for sacrifice in temples throughout the ancient world from Egypt to Greece. On the altars, their entrails were used to predict the future.

Until historically recent times, even urban dwellers would generally be awakened by the call of a rooster at dawn. From ancient times through much of the Middle Ages, the crowing of the cock at certain times was so predictable that it was used to signal the changing of the guard. It had a triumphant ring and was said to frighten away the spirits of darkness. The crowing of a cock served as the voice of conscience in the Bible after Peter had denied knowing Jesus, since the sound moved him to tears of regret (Matt. 26:75). The red comb of a cock heightened its association with the sun. Cocks have always been celebrated for their fierceness, as they seemed to lord over the barnyard.

The cock is also a solar animal in East Asia, where it is the tenth sign of the Chinese zodiac. According to one Japanese tale, the sun

The cock outsmarts the fox in this medieval fable, retold by La Fontaine and illustrated by J. J. Grandville.

goddess Ameratsu, angry at the violence of the storm god, moodily withdrew into a cave, leaving the world in darkness. When a cock crowed, she wondered if the dawn had come without her and went to the entrance of her cavern to find out. There, indeed, it was bright day.

Hens, by contrast, are symbols of domesticity and maternal care. Especially when brooding on their eggs, they seem unconcerned about all else, even the cock. In the Bible, Jesus says, "Jerusalem, Jerusalem . . . how often have I longed to gather your children, as a hen gathers her chicks under her wings, and you refused!" (Matt. 23:37).

Long before Christ, the cock symbolized resurrection. The cock was associated with Asclepius, the Greek god of healing, who as a mortal physician once raised a man from the dead. The last words of Socrates, as recorded in Plato's dialogue "Phaedo": "Crito, we ought to offer a cock to Asclepius. See to it and don't forget" (section 118a). Perhaps Socrates wished to thank the god for spiritual healing as he moved on to the next world.

Cockfighting has been a popular sport since ancient times, and its willingness to fight another to the death has made the cock a symbol of the warrior spirit. Before such battles as Marathon and Salamis, commanders would rouse their men to battle by showing them fighting cocks. The general Themistocles ordered an annual cockfight in Athens to commemorate the victory of the Greeks over the Persians. Fighting cocks were also used to predict the outcome of a battle. In the medieval Japanese *Tale of the Heike*, a local warlord used a cockfight to decide which side to take in the war between the Heike and Genji clans. He matched seven cocks that were white, the color of the Genji, against seven that were red, the color of the Heike. When all of the white cocks proved victorious, he knew that he should take the side of the Genji.

In an Irish tale that relates the call of the rooster to the resurrection, a group of unbelievers sat around a fire over which a cock is boiled. "We have buried Christ now," said one, "and he has no more power to rise from the dead than the cock in this pot." Immediately the cock leaped up and crowed three times, saying, "The Virgin's son is saved" (O'Sullivan, p. 53).

The cock also experiences a sort of resurrection in a famous story from the work of Alcuin, a learned monk at the court of Charlemagne. A rooster, boasting of his powers, forgot to remain watchful and suddenly found the jaws of a wolf had closed about his neck. The cock begged to hear the wolf sing just once, so he would not have to die without hearing the wonderful harmonies of a lupine voice. The wolf opened his mouth to grant the request, at which point the cock immediately flew up to a tree and admonished the wolf, saying, "Whoever is taken in by false pride will go without food" (Ziolkowski, p. 241). The jaws of the wolf here represent the grave or, perhaps, the gate of Hell, and the bird is saved not only by his cleverness but also by grace. In later versions the adversary of the cock was usually the fox, and the story has been retold by Marie de France, Geoffrey Chaucer, and countless other fabulists from the Middle Ages to the present.

Since the cock and hen are so quintessentially male and female, people have often viewed any violation of their sexual roles with horror. According to traditional belief in cultures from Germany to Persia, a hen that crows like a cock augurs terrible fortune and has to be killed immediately. Similarly, a number of cocks were judicially condemned to death in the Middle Ages for laying eggs. Writing around the end of the twelfth century, Alexander of Neckam stated that an egg laid by an old cock and incubated by a toad could produce a "cockatrice," a serpent able to kill with a glance.

Today, the proud society of the barnyard has almost disappeared, and most people rarely see fowl before it reaches the supermarket or the dinner plate, though heraldic roosters still decorate packages of cereal and many other products. Smaller farms, often run by humane activists, still raise free-range chickens. Cockfighting is now illegal in the United States and most of Europe, but people, particularly from Latin America or the Caribbean, still engage in it, believing they are preserving the values of a more heroic age.

Selected References

Aelian. *On Animals* (3 vols.). Trans. A. F. Scholfield. Cambridge: Harvard University Press, 1972.

Alexander of Neckam. *De Naturis Rerum.* Ed. Thomas Wright. London: Longman, Green, Longman, Roberts and Green, 1963.

Gubernatis, Angelo De. *Zoological Mythology or the Legends of Animals* (2 vols.). Chicago: Singing Tree Press, 1968.

Hawley, Fred. "The Moral and Conceptual Universe of Cockfighters:

Symbolism and Rationalization." *Society and Animals* 1, no. 2 (1993): 159–168.

McCullough, Helen Craig, trans. *The Tale of the Heike.* Stanford: Stanford University Press, 1988.

O'Sullivan, Patrick. *Irish Superstitions and Legends of Animals and Birds.* Dublin: Mercier Press, 1991.

Plato. *The Last Days of Socrates.* Trans. Hugh Tredennick and Harold Tarrant. New York: Penguin, 1993.

Ziolkowski, Jan M. *Talking Animals: Medieval Latin Beast Poetry, 750–1150.* Philadelphia: University of Pennsylvania Press, 1993.

Cow

See Bull and Cow

Coyote

See Fox, Jackal, and Coyote

Crane

See Heron, Ibis, Crane, and Stork

Cricket

See Grasshopper, Locust, Cricket, Cicada, and Mantis

Crocodile

> *How doth the little crocodile*
> *Improve his shining tail,*
> *And pour the waters of the Nile*
> *On every golden scale!*
> *How cheerfully he seems to grin,*
> *How neatly spreads his claws,*
> *And welcomes little fishes in*
> *With gently smiling jaws!*
> —Lewis Carroll, *Alice's Adventures in Wonderland*

Crocodilians, including crocodiles and alligators, are the only large, partially terrestrial animals that do not hesitate to attack human beings. Since our traditions tend to make the food chain into a metaphysical hierarchy, this makes them appear to challenge human supremacy. What makes crocodiles even more frightening is the suddenness with which they strike. Most of the time, they appear utterly lethargic, yet they can rouse themselves almost instantly and attack, for short periods, with remarkable speed. Sometimes a lunge will thrust a crocodile partially out of the water until, for a second or so, it seems almost to be standing upright.

Illustration entitled "The Lying Demon" from a religious tract, Philadelphia, ca. 1900. The deceiver is accompanied by a crocodile, symbol of hypocrisy.

Unlike lions, for example, crocodiles can still inspire a sort of primeval terror, yet they do not seem entirely alien to us. The expressions in the eyes of most reptiles are almost impossible for us to read, but those of crocodiles sometimes appear to share a glimmer of human awareness. Female crocodiles care briefly for their young, and according to some observers, crocodiles may even engage in communal hunts. The upturned mouth of a crocodile can appear to be a perpetual smile, but the large teeth that always protrude on the sides give it a sinister aspect.

Crocodiles are closely identified with wetlands and, in consequence, with irrigation and fertility. According to legend, Menes, the first king of Egypt, was hunting when he fell into a swamp. His dogs failed to help him, but a friendly crocodile ferried the monarch to safety on its back. At the place where he arrived in safety, Menes founded the city of Crocopolis, where the crocodile-god Sebek was worshipped. Much the same story was later told of Saint Pachome, who founded a monastic order in Egypt during the third century. He was so beloved of animals that crocodiles would ferry him across the Nile River to whatever destination he might indicate.

The Greek historian Herodotus reported that Egyptians in some districts killed and ate crocodiles, but those in others considered the animals sacred. In Crocopolis priests would place a tame crocodile in a temple, and golden ornaments would be placed in its ears and bracelets on its legs. Pilgrims would bring the holy crocodile special offerings to eat, and after death, it would be embalmed and placed in a coffin. Herodotus, who visited the labyrinthine temple containing the remains of crocodiles and kings at Crocopolis, wrote, "Though the pyramids were greater than words can tell, . . . this maze surpasses even the pyramids" (book 2, section 148).

Other mythologies throughout the world reflect admiration for the crocodile and its power. The dragon of Chinese mythology, which appeared to the emperor Fu Hsi out of the Yellow River, resembled a crocodile with its teeth and short legs, though stylized almost beyond recognition. A Muslim legend from Malaysia held that Fatima, daughter of Muhammed, created the first crocodile. In some parts of Java, mothers would traditionally wrap the placenta of their children in leaves and place it in a river as an offering to ancestral spirits that had become crocodiles.

But terror and scorn for the crocodile go at least equally far back in history. In paintings to illustrate *The Egyptian Book of the Dead*, the goddess Ammut would be shown waiting hungrily to devour those who were found wanting, as a soul was weighed in balance. In this capacity, she had the head of a crocodile, as well as the forepart of a lion and the hind legs of a hippopotamus. Several monsters of legend to whom human sacrifices were made may originally have been crocodiles. In Greek mythology, for example, the Ethiopian maiden Andromeda was chained to a rock to be eaten by such a creature before the hero Perseus saved her. Human sacrifices to crocodiles of people chained beside a lake or river have been widely practiced from Africa to Korea.

The crocodile has been closely associated with magic from time immemorial. In one Egyptian text from the early second millennium B.C., a sorcerer made a wax crocodile and threw it into the Nile River. It immediately grew large and devoured his wife's lover. Sorcery is always closely linked with deception, and in Western Europe the crocodile has been a symbol of hypocrisy. Bestiaries would report that crocodiles weep as they eat human beings. Naturalist Edward Topsell wrote in 1658 that the crocodile, "to get a man within his danger, he will sob, sigh, and weep, as though he were in extremity, but suddenly he destroyeth him." Topsell noted that, according to other observers, the crocodile wept after eating a man, much as Judas had cried after betraying Christ (vol. 2, p. 688).

Several cultures, Arabs and some African tribes, for example, have offered accused criminals to crocodiles as a test, and those people who were eaten or bitten were presumed to be guilty. In the Middle Ages, the entrance to Hell was sometimes depicted as a huge jaw filled with teeth, often resembling that of a crocodile. The idea that crocodiles eat only the guilty has persisted into the latter half of the twentieth century among the Turkana people who live around Lake Rudolph in Kenya. When Alistair Graham saw them wading casually into waters filled with crocodiles, he was told by a tribesman, "My conscience is clear; therefore, I am in no danger" (Graham, p. 68).

In the British classic for children *Peter Pan* (first published in 1904), James M. Barrie created the villain Captain Hook. A hypocritical murderer like the crocodile of legend, the captain is called Hook for an iron claw that has replaced one of his hands. His hand was bitten off by a crocodile, which liked the morsel so much that it has followed Hook ever since, though the beast does not seem to threaten anybody else. The crocodile has also swallowed a clock, and the captain is terrified whenever he hears it tick. Eventually Hook is thrown to the crocodile, the clock stops, and the captain goes contentedly to his death, a bit like the victim of a human sacrifice who believed that to be eaten was an exalted destiny.

Selected References

Alderton, David. *Crocodiles and Alligators of the World.* New York: Blanford, 1998.

Arnold, Dorothea. *An Egyptian Bestiary.* New York: Metropolitan Museum of Art, 1995.

Barrie, James M. *Peter Pan.* New York: Barnes and Noble Books, 1995.

Graham, Alistair. *Eyelids of Morning: The Mingled Destinies of Crocodiles and Men.* New York: A and W Visual Library, 1973.

Herodotus. *Herodotus* (4 vols.). Trans. A. D. Godley. New York: G. P. Putnam's Sons, 1926.

Ions, Veronica. *Egyptian Mythology.* New York: Peter Bedrick Books, 1982.

Topsell, Edward, and Thomas Mullet. *The History of Four-Footed Beasts and Serpents and Insects* (3 vols.). New York: Da Capo, 1967 (facsimile of 1658 edition).

Waddell, Helen, trans. *Beasts and Saints.* Grand Rapids, MI: William B. Eerdmans, 1996.

Crow, Raven, and Other Corvids

This is a story about crows: One is for sorrow. Two is for mirth. Three is a wedding. Four is a birth.

—American nursery rhyme

Birds of the Corvidae family, or corvids, particularly crows and ravens, are creatures of paradox. Their black plumage, slouching posture, and love of carrion sometimes make them appear morbid, yet few if any other birds behave in as playful a manner as they do. Even their voices are at once harsh and spirited. Ravens are larger than crows. They are relatively solitary and make their nests far from human beings, while crows generally move about in flocks and are attracted to human settlements by the promise of food. Both, however, are associated with death and share a reputation as birds of prophecy. They are also monogamous, making them symbols of conjugal fidelity. People probably did not distinguish sharply among ravens, crows, rooks, and related birds in the ancient world, and they all appear much the same in heraldry. The blue jay is one corvid that is not black, but among the Chinook and other Native Americans along the northwest coast of the United States and Canada it shares the family reputation as a trickster. Sometimes identified with corvids in myth is the vulture, which the Egyptians associated with Nekhbet and other goddesses.

The ambivalent character of ravens is apparent in the Bible, where, though described as "unclean," they sometimes appear to have a special intimacy with God. After the Flood had raged for forty days, Noah sent out a raven to find land. It flew back and forth until the waters receded but did not return (Gen. 8:6–8). Later, however, ravens fed the prophet Elijah every morning and evening after he had fled from Ahab into the wilderness (1 Kings 17:4). According to the Talmud, when Abel had been slain, Adam and Eve, who had no experience with death, did not know what do. A raven slew one of its own kind, dug a hole, and performed a burial, thus demonstrating to the first man and woman how the dead ought to be treated. In gratitude, God feeds the children of the ravens, which are born white, until they grow black plumage and can be recognized by their parents.

The crow even taught people how to die in a myth of the Murinbata, an aboriginal people of Australia. Crab demonstrated what she believed was the best way to die by going to a hole and casting off her wrinkled shell. Then she waited for a new one, so that she might be reborn. Crow responded that there was a quicker, more efficient way, rolled his eyes, and immediately fell over.

The Greek historian Herodotus wrote that two "black doves"

flew from Thebes in Egypt; one settled in Libya while the other went on
to Greece and settled in the sacred
grove of Dodona, where it rustled the
leaves and brought forth the
prophetic voice of Zeus. Herodotus
believed the birds were originally
dark-skinned priestesses, but scholars have suggested that they may
have been crows or ravens.

Closely bound with their reputed wisdom is their reputation for
longevity, and corvids can indeed
live for decades. In *The Birds,* by the
Greek comic playwright Aristophanes, crows are said to live for five
times the life of a human being. In
the dialogue by Plutarch entitled
"On the Use of Reason by So-Called
'Irrational' Animals," the wise pig
Gryllus states that crows upon losing

a mate will remain faithful for the remainder of their lives, seven
times that of a human being. Precisely because of this reputation for
fidelity, however, the Greeks and Romans considered a single crow at
a wedding to be an omen of possible death to one partner.

The god Apollo took the form of a crow or hawk when he fled to
Egypt to escape the serpent Typhon. The crow remained sacred to
Apollo, but the relationship between the god and corvids was not without ambivalence. As Ovid tells the story in *Fasti,* Phoebus (Apollo) was
preparing a solemn feast for Jupiter and told a raven to bring some water from a stream. The raven flew off with a golden bowl but was dis-
tracted by the sight of a fig tree. Finding the fruits unfit to eat, the raven
sat beneath the tree and waited for them to ripen. He then returned
with a water snake that he claimed had blocked the water, but the god
saw through this lie. As punishment for lateness and for deceit, the god
later decreed that the raven from that time on could not drink of any
spring until figs had ripened on their trees. A constellation of depicting
a raven, a snake, and a bowl was placed in the sky, and the voice of the
raven is still harsh from thirst in the spring. The call of the raven was
often said to be *"cras,"* Latin for "tomorrow," and through the Renaissance the raven often symbolized the procrastinator.

The intelligence of crows and ravens has amazed people from

*Illustration by
Albrecht Dürer
to Sebastian
Brandt's* Ship
of Fools *(1494).
The raven tells the
fool "cras," Latin
for "tomorrow,"
leading him to
procrastinate.*

ancient times. A fable about this, traditionally attributed to the legendary Aesop, is "The Crow and the Pitcher." A thirsty crow came upon a pitcher of water but was unable to reach inside and drink. The bird began to pick up pebbles and drop them one by one into the pitcher until the water had risen to the top. The usual moral given this story is, "Necessity is the mother of invention." This is one anecdote that could well be based on fairly accurate observation.

The Romans viewed birds as mediators between gods and human beings, at times in homey as well as solemn ways. Pliny the Elder told of a raven that had been born on the roof of a temple in Rome that had flown down to the shop of a shoemaker. The owner, wishing to please the gods, welcomed the bird. By watching the customers, the raven soon learned to talk. Every day he would fly to the podium across from the forum and greet Emperor Tiberius by name. Then he would fly around and say hello to various men and women before returning to the shop. One day a neighbor killed the raven, perhaps thinking the bird had left some droppings on his shoes. The people of Rome were incensed and lynched the man. Then they gave the raven a splendid funeral in which Ethiopian slaves carried the bier and many people left flowers along the path.

On the European continent, where there are few vultures, corvids would always hover above a battlefield and later descend to eat the corpses. Two ravens perched on the shoulders of the Norse Odin, who was intimately associated with battles. They were named *Huginn* (thought) and *Muninn* (memory), and they flew all over the world to bring news to the god. The Celtic war goddess known as the Morrígan would take the form of a raven or crow and come as a herald of death. When the hero Cúchulainn had been mortally wounded, he tied himself to a tree and stood with his sword in hand. His enemies watched from a distance but did not dare approach until a crow, the goddess Badb, perched on his shoulder. In one of many versions collected from oral traditions, the traditional British ballad "The Twa Corbies" begins:

There were three ravens on a tree,
They were as black as black might be:
The one of them said to his mate,
"Where shall we our breakfast take?"—
"Downie in yonder green field,
There lies a knight slain under his shield. . . . (Hall, p. 373)

The ravens find they must take their meal elsewhere, for this knight is guarded by his dogs, hawks, and wife. In many wars, however, it gave soldiers a sense of foreboding to see corvids following their armies and hovering over the battlefield.

The giant Bran, traditionally depicted with a raven, was mortally wounded while leading an army of Britons against the Irish. At his command, his followers beheaded him and carried the head to the site of the Tower of London for burial so that it might serve as a charm to protect Britain. This is the origin of the legend that Britain will never be successfully invaded as long as ravens remain in the Tower. Such pagan legends eventually led to the demonization of crows and ravens at the end of the Middle Ages, when they were often seen as either familiars of witches or a form in which witches flew about at night.

Illustration by Richard Heighway to Aesop's fable of "The Crow and the Pitcher."

Rooks share the reputation of the more illustrious ravens for wisdom, but they are more approachable. In *Precious Bane* by Mary Webb (first published in 1924), a novel about peasant life in the English countryside during the early nineteenth century, a family told the rooks when the old master of the house died so that the birds would not bring ill luck by deserting the home. The new master of the house observed the tradition cynically, remarking quietly that he was very fond of "ricky pie," that is, pie made of rook meat (chap. 5). The birds rose and circled thoughtfully but then returned to their branch, letting the people know they intended to stay. Their hesitation, however, left a sense of foreboding, and the farm was soon struck by disaster.

Though sometimes birds of ill omen in China, crows can also be symbols of fidelity in love. A collection of Taoist lore usually entitled *Strange Stories from a Chinese Studio (Liao Chai Chih I)*, written in the latter part of the seventeenth century, tells of a young man from Hunan named Yü Jung who had failed his examinations and was, in consequence, unable to find employment. Desperate and hungry, Yü Jung stopped at the shrine of Wu Wang, the guardian of crows, and prayed. After a while, the attendant of the temple approached and offered him a position in the Order of the Black Robes. Delighted to have found a way to earn his living, Yü Jung accepted. The attendant gave him a black garment. Putting it on, he was transformed into a crow. Soon he married a young crow named Chu Ch'ing, who taught him corvid ways. Unfortunately, he proved too impetuous, and a mariner shot him. The other crows churned up the waters and made the mariner's boat capsize, but Yü Jung suddenly found himself once again in human form, lying near death on the temple floor. At first he thought the whole adventure had been a dream, but he could not forget the joys he had known as a crow. Eventually he recovered, passed his exams, and became prosperous, but Yü Jung continued to visit the temple of Wu Wang and made offerings to the crows. Finally, when he sacrificed a sheep, Chu Ch'ing came to him and returned his black robe, and Yü Jung again took on a corvid form.

In the story "Herd Boy and the Weaving Maiden," popular in many versions throughout East Asia, corvids come to the aid of lovers. The daughter of the king of Heaven, who would weave the silk of clouds, married a humble herdsman, and the two spent so much time together that they neglected their duties. The father finally placed the Weaving Maiden in the western sky and the herd boy in the eastern sky, where they were separated by a river of the Milky Way. One day every year the crows and magpies gather and form a bridge across the sky so that the lovers may be briefly reunited.

The lore of corvids among Native Americans is perhaps even more varied than that in Europe or Asia. The major themes, prophesy and death, are much the same, though the tales of the Indians are often richer in humor. Among the Haida Indians and related tribes along the American Northwest coast, the raven is at once a sage and trickster. They tell a story about how once there was no light in the world, and everything had to be done in complete darkness. All light was held in a box kept in the house of the chief of Heaven. Raven didn't like that, and he conceived a plan to steal the light. First, he transformed himself into a cedar leaf floating in a stream where the daughter of the chief of Heaven went to drink. She gave birth to him, and for many days he played as an infant in the house of the chief. After a while, Raven began to cry and clamor for the box that held the light. The chief, who was charmed by his young grandson, let Raven hold the box. Then Raven put on his wings and carried the container through the sky. Dazzled by all the new things he saw, Raven dropped the box, and the light broke into many fragments, which became the stars, the moon, and the sun.

In the Ghost Dance religion founded by the Paiute Indian shaman Wovoka near the end of the nineteenth century, the crow was the messenger between the world of human beings and that of spirits. Indians from many tribes in the American Southwest, together with some whites, engaged in an ecstatic dance to bring about the regeneration of the earth. The celebrants wore crow feathers, painted crows upon their clothes, and sang to the crow as they danced. Sometimes they sang of Wovoka himself, flying about the world in the form of a crow and proclaiming his message.

Corvids have always figured prominently in poetry, and the most famous example is Edgar Allan Poe's poem "The Raven" (first published in 1845). The narrator asked a raven that had flown into his chamber whether he could be reunited with his deceased beloved:

> "Prophet!" said I, "thing of evil! prophet still, if bird or devil!—
> Whether tempest sent, or whether tempest tossed thee here
>   ashore,
> Desolate yet all undaunted, on this desert land enchanted—
> On this home by Horror haunted—tell me truly, I implore—
> Is there—is there balm in Gilead?—tell me—tell me, I implore!"
> Quoth the Raven "Nevermore." (pp. 11–13)

The bird gazed imposingly, as befitted a messenger from the world of spirits, but revealed nothing.

In literature of the twentieth century, corvids are sometimes archaic deities that now rebel against the order of the universe. In a volume of poetry entitled *Crow* (1971), British poet Ted Hughes constructed a personal mythology. A figure named Crow continually does battle with cosmic powers; he may be defeated or victorious but always survives.

In "Vincent the Raven" (first published in 1941) Portuguese author Miguel Torga tells a story about the raven that accompanied Noah. Vincent becomes increasingly restless. Though not personally mistreated, he becomes angry that the animals and the earth should be punished for the crimes of humankind. At last he leaves the Ark unbidden, perches on the peak of Mount Ararat, and calls out his defiance to God. The flood continues to rise, but Vincent refuses to leave. God, realizing that should he drown Vincent, his creation would no longer be complete, finally relents and reluctantly allows the water to recede.

But ravens and crows are not at all endangered. Corvids are found nearly everywhere in the Northern Hemisphere, from remote cliffs and forests to cities. They neither fear man nor need him, and their resilience constantly inspires our respect.

Selected References

Elston, Catherine Feher. *Ravensong: A Natural and Fabulous History of Ravens and Crows.* Flagstaff, AZ: Northland, 1991.

Giles, Herbert A., trans. *Strange Stories from a Chinese Studio (Liao Chai Chih I).* New York: Boni and Liveright, 1926.

Hall, S. C., ed. "The Twa Corbies." In *The Book of British Ballads.* London: George Routledge and Sons, 1879, pp. 373–374.

Hughes, Ted. *Crow: From the Life and Songs of the Crow.* New York: Harper and Row, 1971.

Poe, Edgar Allan. "The Raven." In *Last Flowers: The Romance Poems of Edgar Allan Poe and Sarah Whitman.* Providence: The Poet's Press, 1987, pp. 11–13.

Toperoff, Shlomo Pesach. *The Animal Kingdom in Jewish Thought.* Northvale, NJ: Jason Aronson, 1995.

Torga, Miguel. "Vincent the Raven." In *Farrusco the Blackbird and Other Stories from the Portuguese.* Trans. Denis Brass. London: George Allen and Unwin, 1950, pp. 83–88.

Webb, Mary. *Precious Bane.* New York: The Modern Library, ca. 1960.

Cuckoo, Nightingale, Lark, Woodpecker, and Other Musical Birds

No more than ever seems it rich to die,
To cease upon a midnight with no pain,
While thou are pouring forth thy soul abroad
In such an ecstasy!
Still wouldst thou sing, and I have ears in vain—
To thy high requiem become a sod.
—John Keats, "Ode to a Nightingale"

Before the modern era, the sounds of nature were everywhere, day and night. Buildings, even medieval castles with walls thick enough to resist sieges, were not constructed to keep them out. Sounds of birds, most especially, were used to mark both the hours of the day and the seasons. The cuckoo is the bird of spring, while the lark sings in the early morning and the nightingale during the night. This gave them significance at once practical and poetic, as is illustrated by this exchange in Williams Shakespeare's *Romeo and Juliet,* taking place after a night of love:

Juliet: Wilt thou be gone? It is not yet near day;
It was the nightingale, and not the lark,
That pierced the fearful hollow of thine ear;
Nightly she sings on yon pomegranate tree:
Believe me, love, it was the nightingale.
Romeo: It was the lark, herald of the morn,
No nightingale. (3.5)

Until the modern period, when clocks became relatively inexpensive and accurate, the songs of birds were constantly used to signal the time of day and night. The association of birdsong with hours is why many of the first affordable clocks used a mechanical cuckoo to announce the hours.

The song of the cuckoo traditionally announces the beginning of the growing season with an outpouring of exuberant energy. Farmers understood it as a signal to begin planting, but spring is above all the season of love. Through most of history, apart from the high Middle Ages and the nineteenth century, amorous passion has been regarded with suspicion, and that may also be said of the cuckoo. Its song has traditionally been a good omen for those who planned to marry but a warning of possible adultery for those already wedded.

Pliny the Elder suggested that hawks transformed themselves into cuckoos, since the hawks seemed to vanish at about the same time as cuckoos became numerous. He observed, however, that hawks would eat cuckoos if they did meet. The idea reflected the bird's reputation for treachery, since, as Pliny put it, "the cuckoo is the only one of all the birds that is killed by its own kind" (book 10, section 21). This superstition has continued into the twentieth century in parts of Europe.

According to one myth, Zeus first made love to Hera after he had moved her to pity by appearing in the form of a disheveled little cuckoo. The bird was one of Hera's attributes and adorned her scepter. Indian poets knew the cuckoo as the "ravisher of the heart" (Gubernatis, vol. 1, p. 226), and the god Indra also assumed the form of a cuckoo for the purpose of seduction.

The idea that the cuckoo is an adulterer has at least some distorted basis in observation, since the European cuckoo will lay its eggs in the nest of another bird. The egg containing the young cuckoo will generally hatch first, and the fledgling will push the other eggs from the nest. Pliny explained this by saying that all other birds so hated the cuckoo that it would not dare make a nest, for that would be vulnerable to attack. The only way the cuckoo could procreate would be by concealing the identity of its offspring.

The use of the word *cuckold* for a man whose wife is unfaithful goes back to *The Owl and the Nightingale*, a poetic dialogue on love and marriage written in England around the end of the twelfth century. And Shakespeare wrote in his play *Love's Labor's Lost*:

When daisies pied, and violets blue,
And lady-smocks all silver hue,

Do paint the meadows with delight,
The cuckoo then on every tree
Mocks married men; for thus sings he,
    "Cuckoo;
Cuckoo, cuckoo" O word of fear,
Unpleasing to the married ear! (5.2)

In an era when marrying for love was still a somewhat revolutionary idea, the cuckoo increasingly came to represent sexual energy, while the nightingale was more romantic.

Although the cuckoo of literature is masculine, the nightingale is usually female in Western culture, and people have found her song less exuberant than sweet and sad. Her tragedy, as told by Appollodorus, began as Procne, a princess of Athens, married King Tereus of Thrace. They had a son named Itys. Tereus raped Philomela, his wife's sister, and then cut out her tongue so she could not reveal his crime. Philomela wove characters telling her story into a robe and gave it to Procne, who then killed Itys, boiled him, and served him up to his father, Tereus, in revenge. When the king realized what had happened, he set out in pursuit of the two sisters. The women prayed to the gods, who then turned Procne into a nightingale, Philomela into a swallow, and Tereus into a hoopoe. Latin authors, however, confused the two sisters and called the nightingale Philomela, a name later used by poets throughout Europe, perhaps because the song of a nightingale seemed to belong less to a killer than to an innocent victim. According to Pliny the Elder, the nightingale's song was so beloved in Rome that caged nightingales there commanded the sort of prices paid for slaves.

In *The Owl and the Nightingale*, the songster becomes an advocate for courtly love and the owl accuses her of promoting licentiousness. In traditions of the Near East, the nightingale is masculine and in love with the rose, a tragic passion incapable of consummation, but the Islamic world shared Western ambivalence about romantic passions. In *The Conference of Birds*, written by Sufi poet Farid Ud-Din Attar in Persia around the end of the twelfth century, the hoopoe summoned the birds to a pilgrimage to their king, the Simorgh. The nightingale responded that the rose flowered only for him and he could not leave her for a single day. The hoopoe then replied that the love of the rose was a superficial illusion, and the rose really mocked the nightingale by fading in a day.

In the tenth-century Islamic fable *The Island of Animals*, however, the nightingale proved to be the most eloquent and sensible of the animals. He surpassed even such fine speakers as the jackal and the bee, as the beasts, claiming mistreatment, brought suit against people before the king of Djinn. When a man from Mecca and Modena argued that human beings were especially favored by God, the nightingale carried the day by replying that humans therefore had special responsibility not to abuse other creatures.

In Russia, by contrast, nightingales were often associated with witchcraft. There was a great demand for caged nightingales to sing in the homes of aristocrats and wealthy merchants. Peasants hired to capture the birds would have to wander about the woods at night following the birds' sounds, and they often feared becoming victims of enchantment. In Russian folklore, Nightingale was a monstrous brigand who was half bird, nested in oak trees, laid in wait for travelers on the road to Kiev, and could whistle up a wind strong enough to kill human beings.

The lark begins to sing early in the morning before the sun has even risen, and so it has been associated with beginnings. In *The Birds* by the Greek comic playwright Aristophanes, the lark boasts that it is older than not only the gods but also the very earth itself, an idea perhaps inspired by the lark's ability to sing in flight. When the lark's father died, there was no ground in which to bury him, so the lark had to bury its daddy in its head.

As is true with so many other things, people tend not to appreciate animals until they begin to disappear. As Europe industrialized and birds became less common, Romantic poets of the nineteenth century celebrated birdsongs with perhaps unprecedented intensity. The singing of birds represented a sort of poetic inspiration that was utterly natural and spontaneous. Among the most famous lyrics of the period were "Ode to a Nightingale" by John Keats and "To a Skylark" by Percy Bysshe Shelley, in which the poets long to enter the world of joy that could inspire the songs of a bird. Hans Christian Andersen celebrated the beauty of nature over the creations of humankind in "The Emperor's Nightingale," a fairy tale about a mechanical bird that fails to sing as sweetly as a bird in the wild.

An elegiac poem, which perhaps marks the end of this tradition, is "The Darkling Thrush" by Thomas Hardy, published in the first years of the twentieth century, which concludes:

At once a voice arose among
  The bleak twigs overhead
In a full-hearted evensong
  Of joy illimited;

An aged thrush, frail, gaunt, and small,
   In blast-beruffled plume
Had chosen thus to fling his soul
   Upon the glowing gloom.

So little cause for carolings
   Of such ecstatic sound
Was written on terrestrial things
   Afar or nigh around,
That I could think there trembled through
   His happy good-night air
Some blessed hope whereof he knew
   And I was unaware. (pp. 1743–1744)

As the twentieth century progressed, writers increasingly thought references to nightingales or larks as an outmoded poetic contrivance.

The woodpecker is not so much a singer as a musician, but its sound announces the start of the rainy season in many cultures. The sound of a woodpecker knocking its beak against a tree resembles martial drumming and resonates loudly through the forest. The woodpecker was sacred to Ares, the Greek god of war. Romulus and Remus, the legendary twins who founded Rome, were suckled by a wolf and fed by a woodpecker. Ovid in his *Metamorphoses* told of the witch Circe, who changed a young man named Picus, son of the Roman god Saturn, into a woodpecker after he had refused her advances. Jacob Grimm and other scholars derived Beowulf, the name of the Anglo-Saxon epic hero, from "bee-wolf," meaning woodpecker, though that etymology is not generally accepted. Seen more as a fighter than a lover, the woodpecker has never been terribly popular, yet it may do better than songbirds in the raucous popular culture of the latter twentieth century. One of the most popular cartoon characters has been the violent and frequently amoral trickster Woody Woodpecker.

Selected References

Apollodorus. *The Library of Greek Mythology.* Trans. Robin Hard. New York: Oxford University Press, 1997.

Aristophanes. *The Birds.* Trans. Alan H. Sommerstein. New York: Dover, 1999.

Attar, Farid Ud-Din. *The Conference of Birds.* Trans. Afkham Darbandi and Dick Davis. New York: Penguin, 1984.

Gubernatis, Angelo De. *Zoological Mythology or the Legends of Animals* (2 vols.). Chicago: Singing Tree Press, 1968.

Hardy, Thomas. "The Darkling Thrush." In *The Norton Anthology of English Literature*. Vol. 2, 5th ed. Ed. M. H. Abrams. New York: W. W. Norton, 1986, pp. 1743–1744.

Johnson-Davies, Denys, trans. *The Island of Animals*. Austin: University of Texas Press, 1994.

Pliny. *Natural History* (10 vols.). Trans. H. Rackham, W. H. S. Jones, et al. Cambridge: Harvard University Press, 1953.

Pollard, John. *Birds in Greek Life and Myth*. New York: Thames and Hudson, 1977.

Ryan, W. F. *The Bathhouse at Midnight: Magic in Russia*. University Park: Pennsylvania State University Press, 1999.

Shakespeare, William. *Love's Labor Lost*. New York: Viking Penguin, 2000.

———. *Romeo and Juliet*. New York: Dover, 1993.

Stone, Brian, trans. *The Owl and the Nightingale/ Cleanness/ St. Erkenwald*. 2nd ed. New York: Penguin, 1988.

D

Deer
See Hart and Hind

Dog

> Ay, in the catalogue ye go for men;
> As hounds, and greyhounds, mongrels, spaniels, curs,
> Shoughs, water-rungs, and demi-wolves, are clept
> All by the name of dogs. . . .
>   —William Shakespeare, *Macbeth* (act 3, scene 1)

In Eurasia around 12,000 B.C.—or much earlier, according to some theorists—the dog became the first animal to be domesticated by human beings. Cats continue to appear wild even when raised in the family living room. Sheep and cattle generally stay together in herds, even under human direction. In the continual war between man and nature, only dogs appear to be on our side. According to a legend of the Tehuelche Indians, after the sun god had created the first man and woman, the deity immediately created a dog to keep them company. Emotionally, dogs seem akin to human beings. Some people believe that dogs are the only animals apart from humans that can feel guilt. Others dismiss that perception as an anthropomorphic illusion or even hypocrisy. People often regard dogs as icons of either the faithful companion or the sycophant. In much the same way that the dog joins the realms of culture and nature, the mythic dog serves as a mediator between life and death.

In ancient Egypt, dogs and cats were the most beloved of pets. According to Herodotus, when the family dog died every person in the household would shave his or her entire body, including the head, in mourning. Many Egyptian pictures have been preserved through the ages of people caressing dogs, as well as using them in the hunt. While cats were associated with the sun god Ra, dogs were associated with the underworld and with death. The appearance of the Dog Star, Sirius, was a sign to people that they should prepare for the rising of the Nile River. Plutarch, however, reported in his essay "Isis and Osiris" that when the blasphemous conqueror from Persia, Cambyses, had slain the sacred bull Apis, only dogs would eat the body, and so the dog lost its status as the most honored animal among Egyptians.

Throughout the ancient world, owners were interred with their dogs. Tombs with canine effigies or canine corpses alongside human bodies have been found throughout Eurasia and in parts of Africa as well as in pre-Columbian America. Just as dogs led hunters tracking game through the wilderness, they were expected to guide people through the next world. In Egypt, dogs were associated with Anubis, god of the dead, who is most often depicted with a human body and the head of a jackal or dog.

Lady Wilde has written of dogs in Ireland: "The peasants believe that the domestic animals know all about us, especially the dog and the cat. They listen to everything that is said; they watch the expression of the face and can even read the thoughts. The Irish say it is not safe to ask a question of a dog, for he may answer, and should he do so the questioner will surely die" (p. 146). The dog certainly shares the life of human society more intimately than any other animal. This, of itself, can make people feel uneasy. Human beings view dogs with a strange combination of affection and contempt, of domination and fear.

Though dogs are occasionally seen as solar animals, they are usually associated with the moon. Perhaps this is because they howl at the moon, as do their relatives, wolves, coyotes, and jackals. By extension, dogs are also associated with night and with death. In Greek mythology, they are companions of the lunar goddesses Artemis and Hecate. The association of dogs with the star Sirius reaches all the way from Mexico to China.

Their sense of smell gave dogs an ability to guide people in the hunt. A dog would know the location of game that was not even remotely visible. After the hunt, a dog guided people through the woods back to their settlement. We should remember that this was long before the use of the compass or of even remotely accurate maps. This ability must have impressed people as miraculous. It is small wonder that a vast range of cultures on every continent has regarded dogs as guides to the world after death.

Many cultures view the howling of dogs as an omen of death. According to Jewish tradition, dogs can see the angel of death. In Virgil's *Aeneid*, dogs howl at the approach of the goddess Hecate. Several

HIS MASTER'S VOICE

traditions also make dogs the guardians of the underworld. The best known of such sentries is Cerberus, who keeps watch at the entrance to Hades in Greco-Roman mythology. According to Hesiod, this dog had fifty heads, though later writers reduced the number to three. In Norse mythology, the abode of the dead is watched over by the dog Garm. When the final battle at the end of the world comes, Garm will swallow the moon. This monstrous dog will finally do battle with the god Tyr, and both will be slain. In Hinduism and Buddhism, two dogs accompany Yama, the lord of the dead. They each have four eyes and serve their master by searching out those who are about to die. In Aztec mythology, the departed soul descended to the underworld and came to a river guarded by a yellow dog. In European folklore, demonic dogs accompanied the Wild Huntsman across the sky in his search for lost souls. To even hear the hounds meant that you would die soon. A black dog was a frequent omen of doom. In the lore of western England, the devil's Dandy Dogs passed over the moors during storms. They breathed fire and tore hapless strangers to pieces.

The name of Cúchulainn, the popular hero of Celtic myth, literally means "hound of Ulster." When he killed the ferocious hound of a smith, Cúchulainn had to take on the role of the creature he had killed. When roused to battle, his appearance changed. His eyes bulged or contracted. His jaw opened from ear to ear, like that of a dog, while a light like the moon rose in his head. When three witches in the form of crows tricked him into eating the flesh of a dog as well as violating other taboos, Cúchulainn was killed.

In the religion of the Aztecs, the canine deity Xotol was intimately associated with the world of the dead. At one point human beings died out and the gods wished to bring them back. Xotol traveled beneath the ground to obtain the bone of the departed races. The god of the dead pursued him in anger. Xotol stumbled and fell, breaking the bone into many pieces, but he recovered and brought the bones back to the surface of the earth. The gods sprinkled the bones with their blood, and the pieces became human beings of many shapes and sizes.

A further reason dogs have been associated with death is that throughout the ancient world feral dogs roamed in packs in search of carrion, including the bodies of human beings. The greatest disgrace for a corpse in most cultures of the Mediterranean was to be eaten by dogs. In Homer's *The Iliad,* the Trojans feared such would be the fate of Hector's body. In *Antigone* by Sophocles, the heroine feared this would be her brother's fate if he was not given a proper burial. In Ovid's *Metamorphoses,* Actaeon experienced an especially demeaning death: he was changed by the goddess Diana into a stag and killed by his own hounds. In the Bible, because Jezebel, wife of King Ahab of Israel, spread the worship of Baal, the prophet Elijah prophesied that dogs would devour her body (1 Kings 21:23). Jehu later ordered her thrown down from a window, and those who went to bury her found only the skull, feet, and hands (2 Kings 9:34–37).

Dogs were held in special reverence in Persia. According to legend, Cyrus, who founded the Persian Empire, was left out to die at birth but was suckled by a dog. In the religion of Zoroaster, which began in Persia, a dog had to accompany a funeral procession to ensure a peaceful journey to the next world. The Zoroastrians believed that dogs were able to see spirits and could protect families from evil powers that human beings were not even aware of. To express their gratitude for the protection, families were expected to feed hungry dogs, using ritualistically prepared food. The members of the family then said prayers as the dogs ate. Dogs guarded the Cinvat Bridge that led to the next world, protecting the righteous but leaving the unrighteous to demons. In the religion of Mithras, the major rival to Christianity in the latter part of the Roman Empire, a dog would be among the animals to accompany Mithras at the sacrifice of a great bull to rejuvenate the world. After the sacrifice, the dog would lap up the blood that had been spilled.

Just as the dog guards the home, dogs in the ancient world were also thought to guard the body from demons or disease. In Mesopotamia, the dog was sacred to Gula, the Babylonian goddess of healing. At times Gula was represented as a bitch suckling her pups.

When in human form, she was accompanied by dogs. Many dog figurines have been found in her temple, and they were used to ward off illness. In Greece, a dog generally accompanied Asclepius, the legendary doctor who once raised a man from the dead. In the Middle Ages, Saint Roch, who is invoked for protection against diseases, was also depicted with a dog. The holy man worked with victims of bubonic plague. One day, however, he himself was stricken, and sores appeared on his body. Saint Roch wandered into the woods to die, when a dog came up and licked the sores. With the help of the dog, who brought him bread, Saint Roch miraculously recovered.

The ancient tradition in which the dog serves as a guardian to the next world is reflected in medieval burials. The lord and lady of the house would often be buried with their dogs. Splendid sculptures and bas-reliefs on graves show the deceased stretched out with a faithful dog at his or her feet. Today, dogs are often buried in pet cemeteries and more seldom with their masters, yet many people still hope to be reunited with a beloved pet in the world beyond.

Dogs were, for the most part, favorably regarded in the Greco-Roman world as well. Many people find the most touching scene in Homer's *The Odyssey* to be when the hero finally returned home and was recognized only by his hound Argos. The dog wagged its tail and then died. The Greeks and Romans sometimes wrote very affectionate epitaphs for their dogs.

The philosopher Diogenes, a contemporary of Alexander the Great's, called himself a "hound." Members of his school were known as "cynics," after the Greek word for "doglike." Like dogs, they lived in the society yet did not fully belong to it. Since that time, dogs have often symbolized alienation. Diogenes not only praised the fidelity and the modest needs of dogs but also admired their lack of shame, since they would not hesitate to urinate or copulate in public.

Ancient authors such as Ctesias and Pliny the Elder wrote of the cynopheli, who had human bodies and the heads of dogs. The legend probably originated in Egypt, where the creatures could have been inspired partly by baboons. Through the Middle Ages, travelers spread accounts of dog-men in distant lands. They were among the many marvels reported of the mythical kingdom of Prester John in India. Saint Christopher is often portrayed with the head of a dog. One popular legend had it that Saint Christopher was from a race of cynopheli. They were fierce and ate human flesh. They had no language beyond a bark. In answer to his prayer, God gave him human speech. To account for his strange appearance, another legend suggested that Saint Christopher was once extraordinarily handsome. He prayed to God for the head of a dog so that women would leave him in peace. The figure ultimately goes back to the jackal-headed Egyptian deity Anubis. Soldiers of Alexander of Macedonia conflated Anubis with their god Hermes, since both were guardians of the dead. They called this composite deity Hermanubis and erected a temple to him in Alexandria. His temple became one of the most popular shrines in the ancient world. In time, his cult was absorbed into Christianity.

A version of this deity also entered Chinese legend. One very popular tale had a dog marrying a princess. Barbarians had invaded from the west, and the desperate emperor promised that anybody who could drive back the enemy could marry his daughter. A dog heard the pledge, crept behind enemy lines, and killed the opposing commander; he chewed off his victim's head, brought it back, and presented it to the emperor. When they discovered what had happened, the barbarians withdrew. The dog, who could speak like a human being, then reminded the emperor of his promise. When the emperor objected that marriage between a person and an animal was impossible, the dog replied that he could be made human by being placed under a bell for 280 days, provided that nobody disturbed him in the interim. This was done, but when only one day remained, the emperor was overcome with curiosity and lifted the bell, only to see a creature with a human body and a canine head. The marriage went ahead as planned; members of the tribe known as the Fong of Fuzhou claim to be descended from the couple.

Being close to humanity has by no means necessarily worked to the advantage of dogs. We often try to judge dogs by human standards, which may not always be appropriate. We include them in human hierarchies, which means they are at or near the bottom of the scale. The epithet "dog" traditionally suggests a combination of contempt and mistrust, such as masters would feel for their slaves. We use the term "ass kisser," taken from the greeting behavior of dogs, to describe hypocritically servile people.

Partly in reaction to other cultures, especially that of Egypt, the Hebrews developed a repugnance for the dog. Not only is the dog an "unclean" animal in the Old Testament, but a revulsion against the dog is expressed repeatedly in very graphic terms: "As a dog returns to its vomit, so a fool reverts to his folly" (Prov. 26:11). The view in the New Testament is not much more generous. Revelations lists "dogs" among those who must remain outside the kingdom of Heaven, together with "fortunetellers," "fornicators," "murderers," "idolaters," and "everyone of false speech and false life" (22:15).

When people vilify an animal, they are usually reacting against others who regard the creature as sacred. The Hebrews were very fastidious about the preparation of food, and they insisted that animals be slaughtered according to prescribed rituals. For other cultures of the Near East, the hunt using dogs was often sacred. The Hebrews took a dim view of the hunt in general, and they regarded meat touched by hunting dogs as unclean. This meant that dogs had little chance to display their most spectacular abilities. Dogs are often compared to the enemies of Israel in the Old Testament:

> Yahweh, God of Sabaoth, God of Israel,
> Up, now, and punish these pagans, show no mercy to these
> villains and traitors!
> Back they come at nightfall,
> Snarling like curs,
> Prowling through the town. (Ps. 59:5–6)

It took some time for dogs to be accepted as pets. In 1613, Margaret Barclay of Scotland was tried for witchcraft. With the assistance of another woman, Isobel Insh, and in the company of a black lapdog, she allegedly had made clay images of mariners and their boat one night. Then, together with the dog, she had gone down to the shore and cast these images into the waves. Immediately the water had turned red and the sea had begun to rage. At about the same time, a ship had gone down near the coast, killing all the crew except two men. The daughter of Isobel Insh, a girl of only eight, was called in to testify. She claimed to have witnessed the witchcraft and added that her mother had been present only at the making of the clay images and not when the spell was cast. The child went on to testify that the dog gave off fire from his jaws and mouth to illuminate the scene. Margaret Barclay was forced to confess under torture. Though she later retracted the confession, she was executed.

Islam as well takes a negative view of dogs, though there are noteworthy exceptions. Moslem tradition places nine animals in heaven, including two dogs. One is the dog of the apocryphal prophet Tobit. The other is Kasmir, the dog of the Seven Sleepers of Ephessus, from a Christian legend that passed over into Islam. Seven young Christians took refuge in a cave to escape persecution by the Roman soldiers during the reign of Decius. They slept for two hundred years. After waking, one of them went into town to purchase provisions. He was amazed to find that almost everyone had converted to Christianity. According to the Koran, Kasmir kept watch outside the cave for the entire time, not eating, nor drinking, nor sleeping himself.

Just as many tales celebrate the fidelity of dogs, others lament the inability of human beings to reciprocate this loyalty. The most famous is the Irish tale of the thirteenth-century Welsh prince Llywelyn and his hound Gelert. The prince had gone hunting and left the dog to guard his infant son. He returned to find the boy missing and Gelert covered with blood. Horrified, Llewelyn immediately killed Gelert with his sword. Then, looking closely, he found the baby sleeping peacefully on the ground beside the body of a serpent that Gelert had killed.

Almost the same story is told of Guinefort, a greyhound on the estate of Villars near Lyons in France. After the dog had saved a baby from a snake and after being killed by the master of the house, the body of Guinefort was thrown into a well. The grave of the dog became a site of pilgrimages, where parents would bring sickly or deformed children to be healed. Monks in a nearby monastery looked on in consternation as peasant women prayed to the dog, hung swaddling clothes in nearby bushes, and practiced what seemed to be pagan rituals.

The absolute fidelity of a dog to its master is a central virtue of the feudal world. With the rise of the middle class in Victorian times, unconditional fidelity became a nostalgic remembrance of the Middle Ages. Since one could no longer demand such loyalty of men, one valued this virtue all the more in hounds. One story that was constantly retold is that of the "Dog of Montargis." The dog belonged to a courtier of Charles V of France named Aubry, who was murdered in the wood of Montargis near Orléans in 1371. The dog was the only witness and followed the murderer, Robert Macaire, everywhere, constantly barking in an accusatory manner. Finally, a duel between the dog and man was arranged. After being badly defeated, Macaire confessed to his crime and was executed.

There are countless stories throughout the world of dogs that killed themselves after their masters had died, often by refusing all food. Pliny the Elder wrote of a dog named Hyrcanus that threw itself on the blazing funeral pyre of its master. Seldom do people pass the test of canine loyalty. One of the few who did is Yudhisthira, in Hindu myth, when he was invited to enter Heaven without his dog. There was thunder, then a great light. He could see the god Indira waiting for him in the divine chariot. Invited to enter, Yudhisthira stepped aside so the dog might go first. Indira objected, saying that the presence of a dog would defile Heaven. Yudhisthira replied that he could conceive of no greater crime than to send the faithful dog away. At that moment the dog was transformed into Dharma, the god of righteousness. The words of Indira had been a final test, and Yudhisthira had shown his worthiness through fidelity to his companion.

During the Nazi period, the dogs of Adolf Hitler became a public obsession. Hitler was fanatically possessive of his dogs and would not allow anybody to touch his puppy named "Wolf." The regime wanted to promote unquestioning obedience, a quality that people found in dogs. Hitler once said that he trusted nobody but his girlfriend, Eva, and his dog, Blondie. Even with the fall of Nazi Germany, people's fascination with Hitler's dogs continued almost unabated. People wondered especially about Blondie during Hitler's final days. Did he really risk his life to walk her every day in spite of bombs? How did Hitler take his final leave of Blondie and her pups? Did he personally administer cyanide to her, or did he delegate the task to the SS? Author Günter Grass satirized the obsession with Hitler's dogs in his novel *Dog Years*. Perhaps much of the fascination comes from the juxtaposition of great guilt and innocence—one of the worst mass murderers in history and a blameless animal.

Dogs have also served as surrogates for human beings in space. The first living creature to be sent into orbit was a Samoyed named Laika, launched in a Soviet satellite in 1957. After six days the oxygen ran out and she died, but her corpse remains in orbit to this day. For many, she has come to symbolize the fragility of all life in this age of scientific exploration. Two years later, another Soviet husky, Otvazhnaya, was sent into space, together with a rabbit, and safely returned.

Dogs seem to not only reflect but also exaggerate the ideals of the society in which they are kept. In aristocratic societies they were valued according to their ancestry. Like kings and queens, the thoroughbred dogs in noble houses had recorded bloodlines that went back several generations and fabricated ones that went back to remote antiquity. As society industrialized, dogs became a nostalgic reminder of the rural past. Especially in the fifties and early sixties, dogs such as Lassie and Rin Tin Tin were enormously popular on American television. But it is not easy for most people to keep a dog humanely in increasingly urbanized communities. Today, the keeping of dogs mirrors to the point of parody the commercial values of contemporary Western culture. Dogs have special gyms, fashions, gourmet foods, therapists, beauty parlors, and almost everything that people have. But dogs, like people, pay for all of this luxury with freedom. In the last decades of the twentieth century, most urban communities have prohibited dogs from running free even in city parks.

As the role of the dog in our lives is slowly reduced, the symbolic importance of dogs may even be increasing. In this age of electronic security systems, dogs are relatively inefficient at guarding the home. Nevertheless, most people have seen the cartoon dog McGruff, in a trench coat and floppy hat, who tells people on television to "take a bite out of crime." Dogs are used to sell a vast variety of products related to security, from alarms to software programs against computer viruses.

Our commercial culture today can sometimes make fantasies so vivid that reality seems . . . well, almost irrelevant. Among the most familiar canines on television is Spuds McKenzie, who is used to advertise light beer. In 1990, Spuds made *People* magazine's list of the world's ten best-dressed men. Not only does Spuds pitch a product that is not at all for dogs, but the canine model for this distinctly masculine persona is actually a bitch.

Not everybody likes dogs, but those who do are very passionate about them. Dogs often appear helpless, yet they are usually pretty able to take care of themselves. This combination of vulnerability and strength makes dogs, for good or ill, so very "human."

Selected References

Christie, Anthony. *Chinese Mythology*. New York: Barnes and Noble Books, 1996.

Comfort, David. *The First Pet History of the World*. New York: Fireside, 1994.

Leach, Maria. *God Had a Dog: Folklore of the Dog*. New Brunswick, NJ: Rutgers University Press, 1961.

Menache, Sophia. "Dogs: God's Worst Enemies?" *Society and Animals* 5, no. 1 (1997): 23–44.

Plutarch. "Isis and Osiris." In *Plutarch's Moralia* (15 vols.). Trans. Frank Cole Babbit et al. Cambridge: Harvard University Press, 1962, vol. 5, pp. 3–384.

Schwarz, Marion. *A History of Dogs in the Early Americas*. New Haven: Yale University Press, 1997.

Scott, Sir Walter. *Letters on Demonology and Witchcraft*. New York: J. and J. Harper, 1832.

Thurston, Mary Elizabeth. *The Lost History of the Canine Race: Our 15,000-Year Love Affair with Dogs*. New York: Avon Books, 1996.

White, David Gordon. *Myths of the Dog Man*. Chicago: University of Chicago Press, 1991.

Wilde, Lady [Speranza]. *Ancient Legends, Mystic Charms, and Superstitions of Ireland: With Sketches of the Irish Past*. Galway: O'Gorman, 1971 (1888).

Donkey

See Ass, Mule, and Camel

Dove and Pigeon

Pigeons in the grass, alas.
—Gertrude Stein

Doves seem holy and clean, but pigeons appear commonplace and dirty. Nevertheless, the two are very closely related in biology and closely associated in folklore. In ancient texts it is often impossible to know which is meant, and perhaps the best way to think of these birds is as the sacred and profane aspects of a single creature.

A grove near the city of Dodona contained one of the most ancient and venerable oracles in Greece. According to legend, a black dove from Egypt alighted there. As it moved among the oak trees, the branches would rustle and speak to the priests in the voice of a woman. In the time of Homer, the shrine at Dodona was the most revered in all the land.

In the ancient world, doves were often associated with prophecy. In *The Voyages of the Argo*, Apollonius of Rhodes told how the Greek heroes in search of the Golden Fleece found their way through a sea barred by the Clashing Rocks, which would continually open and close. They released a dove. It passed between the rocks, so the heroes knew they could navigate unscathed. In Virgil's *Aeneid*, doves guided Aeneas through a forest to a golden bough, which he needed to enter the world of the dead. Even Christianity, which often took a dim view of pagan oracles, was full of stories in which doves assist in divination, perhaps because doves seemed above every suspicion of evil. One apocryphal gospel had a dove from heaven alighting on the staff of Joseph and anointing him as the husband of Mary.

Of course, whatever pleased the gods would be offered up to them in the ancient world. For the Hebrews, doves and pigeons were the only birds that might be offered for sacrifice (Lev. 1:14), and they were the favorite sacrifice of people who could not afford sheep or oxen.

The biblical book of Genesis states that "God's spirit hovered over the water" (1:2). This image certainly suggests a bird, and it has usually been depicted as a dove. During the Flood, Noah sent out a dove. When it returned with an olive branch, he knew that the waters had begun to subside. In Christianity, the dove represents the Holy Spirit. A dove descended on Jesus at his baptism. In pictures of the Annunciation, the dove has traditionally been portrayed descending to Mary from God the Father as she becomes pregnant with the infant Jesus. The scene recalls the amorous adventures of Zeus, for example, when the god assumed the form of a swan to impregnate the maiden

Leda. The dove, usually painted directly between Mary and God the Father, seemed to shield Mary with its purity.

The dove was sacred to many goddesses of the ancient world. Doves drew the chariot of Aphrodite, the Greek goddess of love. Though sometimes thought promiscuous, Aphrodite became a guardian of chastity when the hunter Orion attempted to break into the home of the Pleiades, the seven daughters of Atlas and Pleione. She changed the girls into doves so they might escape by flight, and Zeus later transformed them into stars.

Doves fed the legendary Assyrian queen Semiramis, daughter of the goddess Derceto, when she was abandoned as an infant in the desert. They were also closely associated with the Roman Venus, the Babylonian Ishtar, and the Semitic Astarte. The following amorous symbolism enters the Judeo-Christian tradition through the biblical "Song of Songs," which probably referred to turtledoves:

> The season of glad songs has come,
> the cooing of the turtledove is heard.
> The fig tree is forming its first figs
> and the blossoming vines give out their fragrance.
> Come then, my love,
> my lovely one, come.
> My dove, hiding in the clefts of the rock,
> in the coverts of the cliff,
> show me your face,
> let me hear your voice. . . . (2:12–14)

Jews and Christians have interpreted this song of love as an allegory of the longing of the soul for God. The image of the dove has always served to spiritualize erotic desire. It is also a symbol of conjugal fidelity. According to the medieval German poet Wolfram von Eschenbach in his epic *Parzifal*, a dove that has lost its mate would always perch on a withered branch.

The Holy Spirit is traditionally spoken of with a masculine pronoun. Nevertheless, it is hard to think of it in that way. The Trinity and the very concept of God seem unbalanced without some feminine element. Several heretical groups have identified the dove with the feminine concept of "Sophia," or divine wisdom, as well as with Mary herself. The wings of a dove, spread out and pointing downward, are sometimes stylized in Christian art to form an M for Mary.

When Christianity was introduced into Russia, people were forbidden to eat the flesh of doves. The dove is also important in the

Grail romances. In Eschenbach's *Parzifal*, written in Germany around 1200, a dove visited the Castle of the Grail every year on Good Friday to bring the Host from Heaven. The dove was also the badge of the Knights of the Grail. European folklore made the dove the one shape that the Devil could not assume. The dove was also one of the very few common animals that were never mentioned as familiars of witches.

In the ancient world, several cultures sometimes portrayed the soul as a dove. There is an enormously moving sculpture in New York City's Metropolitan Museum of Art from the grave of a Greek child who died in the mid-seventh century B.C. The young girl holds a pair of doves or pigeons in her hands, and her lips touch the beak of one. The doves are to go on and have the marriage and family that were denied the maiden. The dove was the symbol of Saint Scholastica, founder of a convent and the patroness of rain. Her twin brother, Saint Benedict, visited her on her deathbed. When she died, Saint Benedict saw her soul ascend to Heaven in the form of a white dove.

A Greek grave relief from the island of Paros, ca. 455–450 B.C. This girl is remembered caring for animals, perhaps at the annual festival of Artemis. She kisses one of two doves or pigeons, which will go on to have a family though fate denied that privilege to her.

The dove is also holy in Islam. Christian polemicists sometimes tried to discredit Islam by claiming that Mohammed had a dove feed from his ear. This was allegedly a trick to make his followers believe that the Holy Spirit was giving him advice.

In their collection of German legends, the Grimm brothers tell how a dove saved the town of Höxter. This community had held out valiantly against the mighty army of the Holy Roman Empire during the Thirty Years' War. At last, when other attempts had failed, the imperial generals ordered their troops to bring in the heavy artillery and bombard the town into submission. In the evening, a soldier was about to light the fuse of the first cannon when a dove flew down and pecked his hand, forcing him to drop the kindling. The soldier took this as a sign from God, and he refused to fire. This delayed the bombardment long enough for Swedish troops to arrive and lift the siege.

The dove, particularly in a drawing by Pablo Picasso, was a symbol of the peace movement during the Cold War. Is the dove a little too perfect? It suggests eroticism without lewdness and virtue without self-righteousness. It is rare, indeed, for any symbol to be accepted with so little ambivalence. Perhaps it is possible in this case because the pigeon functions as a sort of double to the dove, deflecting any resentment.

When people do distinguish between doves and pigeons, the rock doves become the black sheep of the family. The urban pigeons descended from the rock doves, which originally came from the northern coasts of the British Isles. People have not always distinguished very sharply between pigeons and doves. Pigeons were often trained to carry messages in the Roman Empire. This probably contributed to the role of a dove in Christianity as a sort of messenger from God. In Christian paintings the dove of the Annunciation was often portrayed as a white rock dove, with a very broad fanlike tail rather than the narrower tail of the turtledove and related varieties.

The passenger pigeons of North America, once so numerous that they darkened the skies, were driven to extinction in the early twentieth century. Now they are remembered as a symbol of human rapacity and the lost bounty of the New World. Poet Wallace Stevens probably had the passenger pigeon at least partially in mind when he wrote "Sunday Morning" in 1915. It ends with the lines:

> And, in the isolation of the sky,
> At evening, casual flocks of pigeons make
> Ambiguous undulations as they sink,
> Downward to darkness, on extended wings. (p. 41)

But pigeons generally blend in so well with our urban environments that most people hardly even notice them. The few who do pay attention find much beauty in their enormous variety of patterns and tones, caused largely by the mixing of urban and feral birds. Pigeons thrive in cities because the facades of buildings resemble the stony landscapes of their original homes. People sometimes call pigeons "rats with wings." It is now illegal to feed them in New York City, though many people, especially immigrants from the Mediterranean, do anyway.

There are small but devoted circles of pigeon fanciers who race the birds and display them at pigeon shows. While lovers of many animals, such as horses and cats, tend to be female and aristocratic, pigeon enthusiasts are generally male and blue-collar. They identify with the toughness of these birds, which can survive easily in the roughest of neighborhoods.

Mourning doves are also found in New York and other cities, although they are not as common. They are a bit smaller, have a delicate call, and often seem like feminine counterparts to the more masculine pigeons. Most of the time, mourning doves are even more unobtrusive. Few people ever even think, at least consciously, of a connection between the dove on the street and the one in church. But isn't it like that with many religious symbols?

Selected References

Benwell, Gwen, and Arthur Waugh. *Sea Enchantress: The Tale of the Mermaid and Her Kin.* London: Hutchinson, 1961.

Charbonneau-Lassay. *The Bestiary of Christ.* Trans. D. M. Dooling. New York: Parabola Books, 1991.

Eschenbach, Wolfram von. *Parzifal.* Trans. A. T. Hatto. New York: Penguin, 1980.

Grimm, Jacob, and Wilhelm. *The German Legends of the Brothers Grimm* (2 vols.). Ed. and trans. Donald Ward. Philadelphia: Institute for the Study of Human Issues, 1981.

Staal, Julius D. W. *The New Patterns in the Sky: Myths and Legends of the Stars.* Blacksburg, VA: McDonald and Woodward, 1988.

Stevens, Wallace. "Sunday Morning. *Stevens/ Poems.* New York: Knopf/ Everyman's Library, 1993, pp. 40–41.

Dragon
See Snake, Lizard, and Related Animals

Duck
See Swan, Goose, and Duck

Eagle

He clasps the crag with crooked hands;
Close to the sun in azure lands,
Ringed with the azure world, he stands.
The wrinkled sea beneath him crawls;
He watches from his mountain walls,
And like a thunderbolt he falls.
—Alfred Lord Tennyson, "The Eagle"

The symbolism of no other animal is quite so simple and unambiguous as that of the eagle. The majestic bird is associated with the sun and, largely by implication, with monarchs. Eagles have remarkable eyesight and appear able to gaze directly into the sun. Contrary to their reputation, they are not exceptionally high flyers as compared with other birds, but they are extremely powerful and are often able to lift large prey such as sheep or monkeys. Perhaps their remoteness also contributed to an exalted reputation, since they prefer rocky cliffs or tall trees for their nests. Though eagles may be majestic, we should remember that royalty has never been universally beloved.

This symbolism of the eagle was already clearly established in the ancient Mesopotamian poem about Etana, possibly the first ruler ever to have his story written down. The epic of Etana begins with an eagle and a serpent swearing an oath of friendship to each other before Shamash, the god of the sun. The eagle lived in the top of a tree and the serpent at its base, and for a time they and their young shared every kill. One day the eagle ate the young of the serpent, who then burrowed in the carcass of a bull. As soon as the eagle approached to eat, the serpent bit it, cut its wings, and threw the bird into a pit to die of hunger and thirst. Shamash sent the hero Etana to rescue and nurse the eagle, which became his guide. Etana mounted on the back of the eagle to fly up to the heavens to ask Ishtar, a goddess of fertility, for the plant of birth so that he might have a son. The last sections of the manuscript are fragmentary, but Etana apparently did attain his goal and founded the first Sumerian dynasty.

The ascent of Etana is depicted on many seals, and the story seems to have had a wide influence. The Greeks later retold the episode of the two quarreling animals as an Aesopian fable called "The Eagle and the Fox." The eagle violated a friendship by eating the young of the fox, which then set fire to the eagle's tree in revenge. The motif of a tree with an eagle at the top and a hostile serpent at the base, however, has often been found in myth and legend, and an example is Yggdrasil, the Norse tree of life. The story of Etana may well have influenced the Greek myth of Ganymede, a young man who was abducted by Zeus, in the form of an eagle, so that he might serve on Olympus as cupbearer of the gods. Eagles are, however, entirely capable of carrying off an infant or small child, and perhaps the story goes back to such a tragic incident.

The eagle was sacred to Zeus, and the god of thunder sent an eagle to eat the liver of the disobedient titan Prometheus each day, as he lay chained to a rock in the Caucasus Mountains. The liver would grow back during the night, and the cycle continued until the eagle was finally slain with an arrow by Hercules. The Roman standard was an eagle, and conquered peoples often adopted the symbol.

The eagle is the initial inspiration for a huge range of mythological figures. The double-headed eagle first appears on Hittite reliefs in Mesopotamia. From there it spread to the Byzantine Empire, and today it is a symbol of Russia. The Assyro-Babylonian epic poem "Anzu" told of a lion-headed eagle so powerful that it could cause whirlwinds simply by flapping its wings. It once stole the Tablets of Destiny from Enlil, the god of the sky, and briefly ruled the world. Mysterious figures, sometimes known as "demon-griffins," were carved on palace walls of the Assyrian king Ashurnasirpal II. They had the bodies of men but the heads and wings of eagles, and they held up a pinecone in one hand, perhaps to enact a fertility rite.

The lion shared a solar association with the eagle, and their features were often blended. Perhaps related to the lion-headed eagle, or Imdugud, is the first griffin, which had the face of an eagle, the body of a lion, and, sometimes at least, wings. The griffin first appeared in the art of Mesopotamia but quickly spread to Greece and beyond. Herodotus believed a griffin lived in the mountains of India, where it made a nest of gold. Dante placed a griffin in Paradise, where it drew the chariot of the church.

Closely related to the griffin was the Hindu Garuda, the king of birds and the mount of the god Vishnu. Garuda had the wings and beak of an eagle, and the rest of his body was human, but his vast form could darken the sky. Also inspired largely by the eagle were several other huge birds of legend such as the Arabian Roc and the Persian Simorgh.

In Christianity, the eagle became the symbol of Saint John the Evangelist and is always depicted on the ground by his side. According to *The Golden Legend*, written by Jacobus de Voragine in the late thirteenth century, this is because John once said, "The eagle . . . flies higher than any other bird and looks straight into the sun, yet by its nature must come down again; and the human spirit, after it rests awhile from contemplation, is refreshed and returns more ardently to heavenly thoughts" (vol. 1, p. 54). But like an eagle, John soars straight to the mystical heights at the start of his gospel: "In the beginning was the Word . . ."

Medieval bestiaries reported that when an eagle grew old it would first find a fountain. Then it would fly directly into the sun until its wings were singed and it fell into the waters. After repeating this three times, the eagle would once again be filled with youthful vigor, much like Christ, who rose from the dead on the third day after his burial.

One of the very few literary works in which eagles are viewed not with awe but with tenderness is "The Parliament of Fowles" by Geoffrey Chaucer, written in the late fourteenth century. On Saint Valentine's Day, the birds gathered at the temple of Venus to choose their mates. Several birds paid court to the lovely female eagle that sat in the hand of the goddess. When they had all set forth their claims, Nature ruled that the female eagle herself should make the choice, thus upholding love over politics. Lords and princesses, after all, are still human beings, just as even eagles are birds.

In many ways the Native American view of the eagle was surprisingly similar to that of Europeans. The Plains Indians, most especially, admired the strength of the eagle and associated the bird with the sun. Eagle feathers represented solar rays, and they were used on headdresses and shields to indicate skill in war or hunting. The Indians also stylized the eagle into a mythical creature—the thunderbird. The beating of its wings causes thunder, while its beak is like lightning.

The eagle is a bit like singers and actors who, after achieving great popular success, find themselves dominated by their public image. People have trouble comprehending that the eagle, so mighty in legend, can be very vulnerable in fact. This creature has been so prominent in symbolism over millennia that people even have trouble thinking of it as a genuine animal, and the cultural significance of the eagle seems to provide it with little protection. In countries such as the United States and Germany, eagles remain endangered despite being national emblems.

Selected References

Black, Jeremy, and Anthony Green. *Gods, Demons, and Symbols of Ancient Mesopotamia: An Illustrated Dictionary.* Austin: University of Texas Press, 1992.

Brown, Joseph Epes. *Animals of the Soul: Sacred Animals of the Oglala Sioux.* Rockport, MA: Element, 1992.

Chaucer, Geoffrey. "The Parliament of Fowles." In *The Works of Geoffrey Chaucer.* 2nd ed. Ed. F. N. Robinson. Boston: Houghton Mifflin, 1961, pp. 309–318.

Dalley, Stephanie, ed. *Myths from Mesopotamia: Creation, the Flood, Gilgamesh, and Others.* New York: Oxford University Press, 1993.

Nigg, Joe. *The Book of Gryphons.* Cambridge, MA: Applewood Books, 1982.

Voragine, Jacobus de. *The Golden Legend: Readings on the Saints* (2 vols.). Trans. William Granger Ryan. Princeton, NJ: Princeton University Press, 1995.

White, T. H., trans. *The Book of Beasts: Being a Translation from a Latin Bestiary of the Twelfth Century.* New York: Dover, 1984.

Williams, Ronald J. "The Literary History of a Mesopotamian Fable." *The Phoenix* 10, no. 2 (1956): 70–77.

Earthworm

See Worm

Elephant

Elephants are always drawn smaller than life, but a flea always larger.
—Dean Swift

The elephant is set apart from other creatures by its immense size, its enormous tusks, and above all, its prehensile trunk. Rough as the skin of an elephant may appear, the trunk has such fine coordination that it can be used to pick flowers or lift small coins. But this strange, paradoxical nature has made people identify intensely with the elephant, since the animal seems to share with humans an alienation from the natural world. Cicero wrote in the first century B.C. that "although there is no animal more sagacious than the elephant, there is also none more monstrous in appearance" (book 1, section 97). No other animal has been so intensely and consistently anthropomorphized. The eyes of an elephant are disproportionately small and on opposing sides of the head, but the folds about the eyes give them enormous expressiveness. Their gaze can be so intense that one popular book on animals in the late twentieth century was entitled *When Elephants Weep,* despite the fact that crying is a human trait that elephants do not actually share.

Pliny the Elder spoke for many when he said the elephant was the animal "closest to man as regards intelligence" and added that "the elephant has qualities rarely apparent even in man, namely honesty, good sense, justice, and also respect for the stars, sun, and moon" (book 8, chap. 1). One traditional description of humanity is *"homo religiosus,"* but elephants, according to tradition, share even the religious impulse. Pliny wrote that elephants would come down from the mountains of Mauritania to bathe in the river Alimo and pay homage to the moon. This theme was frequently repeated in Christian Europe, where the religious impulse of elephants was regularly praised and their paganism ignored. In the latter eighteenth century, Marcel LeRoy, forester to the king of France, wrote that "many authors say this animal is lacking in nothing but the worship of God, while others accord it that virtue as well" (vol. 3, p. 99). Even today, the debate as to whether elephants are religious has not been entirely resolved. For centuries, elephants have been said to bury their dead, and researchers in the latter twentieth century confirm that they at least cover their dead with vegetation.

Most of our elephant lore comes from India, where the elephant may have been domesticated as early as the middle of the third millennium B.C. According to the Indians, after the sun had been hatched from a cosmic egg, the god Brahma took the two shells in his hands and began to chant. Out of the shells emerged the elephant Airavata, which later became the mount of the god Shiva, followed by fifteen other cloud elephants. They and their progeny could fly about and change their shape at will. One day, however, the young elephants on earth became too boisterous and disturbed the sage Palakapya, who cursed them and relegated them to the ground.

Up through at least the nineteenth century, elephants continued to be accorded superhuman abilities, including total recall and life spans of centuries. But even as these ideas have been debunked, remarkable new qualities of elephants have been discovered. People had long puzzled over the social cohesion of elephants, and in the 1980s researchers discovered they communicate with ultrasound— that is, by means of frequencies inaccessible to the human ear.

Among the most beloved deities of the Hindu pantheon is Ganesha, the mischievous god of wisdom, who has a human body and an elephant head. He is usually depicted riding on a rat and has a potbelly and a broken tusk. There are many stories that explain his origin and odd appearance. According to one, when the god Siva was away, his consort Parvati was lonely and desired a son. She covered her body with scented lotion, rubbed off the dirt, formed it into a young man, and directed him to guard her home. After a while Siva returned and demanded admittance. The young man refused to let him pass. A fight ensued and Siva beheaded his adversary. When she saw what had happened, Parvati was so furious that she threatened to destroy the entire world if Siva did not restore her son to life. To do this Siva needed another head, so he sent his servants in search of one. They came upon an enormous elephant, decapitated the animal, and returned to their master, who placed the head of the elephant on the body of the young man.

Among the incarnations of Buddha was an albino elephant, and such animals are traditionally held in great honor in Southeast Asia. The conception of Gautama, who was to become Buddha, resembles that of Christ, but the mediator of that virgin birth was not a dove but an elephant. Queen Sirimahamaya dreamed that she had been transported to a palace on a mountain peak. An elephant, bearing a lotus, approached her and bowed. She heard the call of a bird and awoke, pregnant with the redeemer.

The elephant entered European awareness at the battle of Hydaspes, when Alexander the Great invaded India and faced King Porus, whose army included 200 mounted elephants. Alexander was finally victorious, but the power of the elephants so awed his troops that his generals refused to venture any farther east. At the end of the third century B.C., Pyrrhus, the king of Epirus in Greece, used elephants to defeat the Romans in several battles until his outnumbered army was finally overwhelmed. In 219 B.C. the Carthaginian general Hannibal crossed the Alps with an army that included elephants and inflicted many defeats on the Romans, though his troops, too, finally succumbed to the superior numbers and discipline of the Romans. It is interesting that the Romans, despite experiencing the damage elephants inflicted in battle, rarely included these animals in their legions. One reason may be that the Romans were aware of the military limitations of elephants, which, even when trained, were unpredictable in battle.

The reason may also be simply that the Romans were too fond of elephants to use them in such a manner. They were slain in Roman circuses, but the spectacles were not very popular. Pliny recorded that on seeing one elephant killed with a javelin in the arena at a festival organized by Pompey, the other elephants tried to break through iron railings. "But when Pompey's elephants had given up hope of escape,

THE

ELEPHANT,

ACCORDING to the account of the celebrated BUFFON, is the moſt reſpectable Animal in the world. In ſize he ſurpaſſes all other terreſtrial creatures; and by his intelligence, makes as near an approach to man, as matter can approach ſpirit. A ſufficient proof that there is not too much ſaid of the knowledge of this animal is, that the Proprietor having been abſent for ten weeks, the moment he arrived at the door of his apartment, and ſpoke to the keeper, the animal's knowledge was beyond any doubt confirmed by the cries he uttered forth, till his Friend came within reach of his trunk, with which he careſſed him, to the aſtoniſhment of all thoſe who ſaw him. This moſt curious and ſurpriſing animal is juſt arrived in this town, from Philadel- phia, where he will ſtay but a few days.———He is only four years old, and weighs about 3000 weight, but will not have come to his full growth till he ſhall be between 30 and 40 years old. He meaſures from the end of his trunk to the tip of his tail 15 feet 8 inches, round the body 10 feet 6 inches, round his head 7 feet 2 inches, round his leg above the knee 3 feet 3 inches, round his ankle 2 feet 2 inches. He eats 130 weight a day, and drinks all kinds of ſpirituous liquors; ſome days he has drank 30 bottles of porter, drawing the corks with his trunk. He is ſo tame that he travels looſe, and has never attempted to hurt any one. He appeared on the ſtage, at the New Theatre in Philadelphia, to the great ſatisfaction of a reſpectable audience.

A reſpectable and convenient place is fitted up adjoining the Store of Mr. Bartlet, Market- Street, for the reception of thoſe ladies and gentlemen who may be pleaſed to view the greateſt natural curioſity ever preſented to the curious, which is to be ſeen from ſunriſe till ſundown, every day in the week.

☞ The Elephant having deſtroyed many papers of conſequence, it is recommended to viſitors not to come near him with ſuch papers.

Admittance *ONE QUARTER OF A DOLLAR*———Children *ONE EIGHTH OF A DOL- LAR.*

NEWBURYPORT, Sept. 19, 1797.

In the late-eighteenth and early-nineteenth centuries elephants were grandly displayed as wonders of the world and drew large crowds. Little attention was paid to their diet or treatment, however, and this one is said on some days to have drunk "30 bottles of porter, drawing the corks with his trunk." (Courtesy of the New York Historical Society, negative # 23508) they played on the sympathy of the crowd, entreating them with indescribable gestures. They moaned as if wailing, and caused the spectators such distress that, forgetting Pompey and his lavish display devised so to honor them, they rose in a body, in tears, and heaped dire curses on Pompey . . . " (book 8, chap. 21). The resulting loss of popular support, Pliny believed, was partly responsible for Pompey's defeat by Julius Caesar not long afterward.

Harun ar-Rashid gave an elephant as a gift to Charlemagne and his court. A few European princes of the late Middle Ages imported elephants as exotic trophies, to display their splendor and power. In general, Europeans of the Middle Ages knew elephants only through ancient books and confused reports by mariners, but the animals were far from forgotten. As their physical presence vanished, their symbolic importance increased, and no painting of Noah and the Flood was complete without an elephant.

According to one medieval bestiary, elephants lived for hundreds of years. Other bestiaries held that when an elephant couple wanted to have a child, they would go eastward toward Paradise until they came to the Mandragora, the Tree of Knowledge. First, the elephant wife would eat from the tree. Then she would give some of the fruit to her husband, at which point the two would copulate and immediately conceive. The elephants were like the first Adam and Eve, except that the fruit from the Tree of Knowledge was not forbidden to them and they could freely enter or leave the Garden of Eden. The author also says of elephants, "They never quarrel with their wives, for adultery is unknown to them. There is a mild gentleness about them, for, if they happen to come across a forwandered man in the deserts, they offer to lead him back to familiar paths" (White, p. 28).

In most of the Arab world, the elephant was only slightly less exotic than in the West, and it was held in much the same high regard. The seventh voyage of Sinbad the sailor, from the medieval *Arabian Nights Entertainments,* contains an episode that anticipates modern ecological and humanitarian concerns. After Sinbad is captured by pirates and sold into slavery, at the direction of his new master he hides in a tree and shoots arrows at a herd of elephants to obtain their tusks for ivory. This continues for a few days, but then the elephants surround him and uproot the tree. Sinbad expects the elephants to kill him, but instead they take him to their graveyard so that he may peacefully obtain their ivory.

Meanwhile, in Africa, elephants were very much a physical reality, and the practical problems of living alongside the animals restricted their appropriation in fantasy or symbolism. They were a copious source of meat but also a formidable challenge to hunters. An Ashanti proverb goes, "If you follow an elephant, you don't have to knock the dew from the grass" (Courlander, p. 131). Strength and power rarely go together with cunning in folklore, and African tales often present the elephant as mighty but naive. According to a Mbochi tale, the animals once selected the elephant as their king. As the elephant was going to his coronation, the hare lay in his path and pretended to be terribly ill. The elephant did not wish the hare to miss the great event and lifted the little fellow upon his back. When they reached the council of animals, the hare protested that the elephant had carried him on his back—as the rider, he was superior to the beast of burden. The animals crowned not the elephant but the hare as king.

Africans traditionally hunted elephants primarily for meat, so both the danger and the bounty obtained from a single kill kept slaughter within limits. With colonization and the advent of modern weapons, the demand for ivory has placed the once vast populations of elephants in danger. Desperate to stop poaching, some African governments in the latter twentieth century have imposed the death penalty for killing elephants. Elephants are accorded an ironically human status, both as objects of slaughter and protection.

Selected References

Cicero. *The Nature of the Gods.* Trans. Horace C. P. McGregor. New York: Penguin, 1972.

Courlander, Harold. *A Treasury of African Folklore: The Oral Literature, Traditions, Myths, Legends, Epics, Tales, Recollections, Wisdom, Sayings, and Humor of Africa.* New York: Marlowe, 1996.

Courtright, Paul B. *Ganeśa: Lord of Obstacles, Lord of Beginnings.* New York: Oxford University Press, 1985.

Delort, Robert. *The Life and Lore of the Elephant.* Trans. I. Mark Paris. New York: Harry N. Abrams, 1992.

LeRoy, Marcel. "Lettres sur les animaux." *Variétés litteréraires recueil des pieces tant originales que trauites, concernant la philosophie, la littérature et les arts.* Paris: Lacombe, 1768, vol. 3, pp. 1–173.

Pliny the Elder. *Natural History: A Selection.* Ed. and trans. John F. Healey. New York: Penguin, 1991.

Sax, Boria. *The Frog King: On Legends, Fables, Fairy Tales, and Anecdotes of Animals.* New York: Pace University Press, 1990.

Sillar, F. C., and R. M. Meyler, eds. *Elephants, Ancient and Modern.* New York: Viking Press, 1968.

White, T. H., trans. *The Book of Beasts: Being a Translation from a Latin Bestiary of the Twelfth Century.* New York: Dover, 1984.

English Robin

See Wren and English Robin

Ermine

See Beaver, Porcupine, Badger, and Miscellaneous Rodents

F

Falcon and Hawk

I caught this morning morning's minion, kingdom of daylight's dauphin,
*   dapple-dawn-drawn falcon, in his riding*
Of the rolling level underneath him steady air, and striding
High there, how he rung upon the rein of a wimpling wing
In his ecstasy!

—Gerard Manley Hopkins, "The Windhover"

The falcon turning and circling overhead is a stirring sight even today, and we can only imagine how inspiring it must have seemed before human beings had learned to fly. The peregrine falcon, which is indigenous to Egypt, not only is capable of elaborate aerial maneuvers, but also has been clocked at the fastest speed of any bird. A poem on a fragment of pottery from the vicinity of ancient Cairo celebrated the sun god Ra in his incarnation as a falcon:

You awaken in beauty, o falcon of morning,
You lion of the night,
You worthy bringer of light,
That opens the eyes . . ." (trans. Boria Sax, after the German
   version of Günter Röder.)

Since Egyptian times, the falcon has remained a symbol of transcendence and of love.

The Egyptians also depicted their god Horus, who came to be partially conflated with Ra, as a falcon. After Osiris had been murdered by his wicked brother, Set, Isis, wife of Osiris, conceived Horus as she mourned by hovering over the body of her husband in the form of a kite. Horus later defeated Set in combat to gain dominion over Egypt, but he lost one eye in the battle, which was replaced by the god Thoth. As the Egyptians realized, raptors have remarkable eyesight, and the lost "eye of Horus" was frequently represented as a protective talisman in Egyptian culture. The motif eventually entered Christianity as the "all-seeing eye of God."

Although biologists now place hawks and falcons in separate families, ancient and medieval people did not distinguish clearly between the two. Egyptian representations of the god Horus combined features of several species, though the most important model is probably the peregrine falcon. In what is probably the oldest animal fable to have come down to us from the Greeks, Hesiod used a hawk to represent the inexorable power of fate. A hawk had caught a nightingale in his claws and carried her high into the clouds, at which point she began to weep. The hawk rebuked her, saying, "Goodness, why are you screaming? . . . He is a fool who seeks to compete against the stronger: he both loses the struggle and suffers injury on top of insult" (*Works and Days*, p. 43). The context, however, made this fable ambiguous, since Hesiod in the following passage urged his brother to refrain from violence, saying that justice would triumph over force in the end. Perhaps Hesiod was assuming his readers knew of a now lost ending in which the call of the nightingale brought help and the hawk was punished.

Falconry goes back to very ancient times and has been practiced throughout Eurasia, but its greatest popularity was probably in the European Middle Ages. The Holy Roman Emperor Frederick II, who was known for his prodigious learning, wrote a treatise on falconry. Hunting with falcons became a favorite recreation of medieval lords and ladies, who would ride out on horseback in the spring, dressed in elaborate finery and with the hooded birds perched on their wrists. When the eyes of the falcon were uncovered and the bonds released, the people would vicariously participate in the pursuit of game.

Wooing was frequently compared to the hunt in medieval times, and metaphors from falconry were often used to describe amorous relationships. The medieval troubadours and minnesingers often celebrated the falcon as a symbol of unhindered love. "The Falcon" by minnesinger Dietmar von Aist begins:

> By the heath stood a lady
>   All lonely and fair;
> As she watched for her lover,
>   A falcon flew near.
> "Happy falcon!" she cried,
>   Who can fly where he list
> And can choose in the forest
>   The tree he loves best!" (p. 1)

She goes on to compare her knight to a falcon and to long for his return.

Not only proper falcons but also a variety of other birds of prey, including hawks, were used in hunting. Sir Gawain, the greatest of King Arthur's knights in early tales, though less significant in the later ones, is called Gwalchmai, meaning "hawk of May," in early Welsh tales. He appears to be a version of the Irish hero Cúchulainn, whose father was the sun, so perhaps the name comes from the raptor's archaic solar associations. Merlin, the legendary magician of Arthur's court, also takes his name from a raptor that was sometimes used in falconry.

The Irish poet W. B. Yeats used the image of a circling falcon to represent the social and cosmic order in his poem "The Second Coming," which begins:

Turning and turning in the widening gyre
The falcon cannot hear the falconer;
Things fall apart; the centre cannot hold;
Mere anarchy is loosed upon the world,
The blood-dimmed tide is loosed, and everywhere
The ceremony of innocence is drowned. (p. 178)

Later references in the poem to Egyptian culture indicate that Yeats may have connected his falcon with the deity Horus. The image of a circling falcon, however, also suggested a bomber, particularly since the poem was published in a brief period of peace between the two world wars.

Selected References
Charbonneau-Lassay, Louis. *The Bestiary of Christ.* Ed. and trans. D. M. Dooling. New York: Parabola Books, 1991.

Hesiod. *Theogony/ Works and Days.* Trans. M. L. West. New York: Oxford University Press, 1988.

Matthews, John. *Gawain and the Goddess: Restoring an Archetype.* London: Aquarian/Thorsons, 1990.

Röder, Günter, trans. "Gebet des fälschlich Verurteilten an die Sonne" [ancient Egyptian poem]. *Der Tierkreis: Das Tier in der Dichtung aller Völker und Zeiten.* Ed. Karl Soffel and Klabund. Berlin: Erich Reiss Verlag, 1919, p. 1

von Aist, Dietmar. "The Falcon." Trans. E. Taylor. In *Representative German Poems: Ballad and Lyrical.* Ed. Karl Knortz. New York: Henry Holt, 1885, p. 1.

Yeats, W. B. "The Second Coming." In *The Poems of W. B. Yeats.* New York: Macmillan, 1983.

Flea

See Fly, Louse, and Flea

Fly, Louse, and Flea

> *Little Fly*
> *Thy summer's play*
> *My thoughtless hand*
> *Has brush'd away*
> *Am I not*
> *A fly like thee?*
> *Or art not thou*
> *A man like me?*
> —William Blake, "The Fly"

The authors of the ancient world generally did not distinguish sharply among the different types of small insects that might be a minor, if persistent, irritation, and the term *fly* is used here loosely as a general designation for them. In the biblical book of Exodus, the fourth plague sent by Yahweh when the pharaoh refused to release the Israelites was a plague of gadflies that filled the palaces (8:1–20), a particularly insulting punishment since these insects are generally attracted to cattle. The Egyptians, however, seem to have admired the appearance of houseflies, which they frequently used in decorative pins. Pendants of gold in the form of flies were awarded to soldiers for valor.

In the play *Prometheus Bound* by the Greek tragedian Aeschylus, Hera changed the maiden Io into a heifer as punishment for having an affair with Zeus. Then the goddess sent a gadfly to drive the unfortunate creature across Europe and Asia. A similar image is used, though in a positive way, in Plato's "Apology," where Socrates compared himself to a gadfly sent by God to prod the Athenians out of their complacency. In a similar spirit, the Greek poet Melegros called upon a mosquito to buzz in the ear of his beloved to remind her of his love. In many cultures, especially in East Asia, insects have represented the soul. In *Journey to the West*, a mythological epic written by Wu Ch'eng-en in late medieval China, Old Monkey sometimes took the form of a fly to escape from demons or to elude detection.

Among the Montagnards of Vietnam, fireflies have traditionally been considered the spirits of departed heroes. In Japan and China, fireflies are the companions of impoverished scholars engaged in nocturnal study. Because they provide moments of illumination, short poems written on fans or pieces of silk have been known as fireflies.

The name of the demon Beelzebub, originally a Phoenician deity, literally means Baal of the Flies or Lord of the Flies. In the Old Testament, Beelzebub tempted King Ahaziah of Israel away from Yahweh (2 Kings 1:2–6), and later he was called the "prince of devils" (Matt. 12:24; Mark 3:22; Luke 12:15). In the Christian Middle Ages, demons were frequently depicted as flies, and so people often thought of swallows and other insectivorous birds as holy. There are several stories of devils taking the form of insects to enter the bodies of people by mouth. According to a local chronicle, for example, in 1559 a maiden in the Harz Mountains near Joachimsthal inadvertently swallowed an evil spirit, disguised as a fly, in her beer. The demon immediately possessed her and began to speak through her, though it was finally exorcised by the parish priest.

Before improvements in hygiene in the modern period, lice could be found in the hair and on the body of nearly everybody, from king to peasant. Though a perpetual annoyance, they could also serve as a means of social bonding. To pick lice off a person was a service that might be performed by parents for children or servants for masters. It was even a ritual of courtship and love, performed by couples. The presence of an inordinate number of lice might indicate either coarseness or, for ascetics, a lack of worldly concern. Thus, Julian the Apostate, the austere Roman emperor who attempted to revive paganism, once compared the lice running freely in his beard to wild beasts in a forest.

Fleas also tended to be thought of in a familiar and, at times, even affectionate way, though they were by far the most dangerous insects of the lot. Though it was not realized until the end of the nineteenth century, fleas had been carriers of many diseases, including bubonic plague. In the Renaissance, references to fleas became a humorous convention in poetic diction. Among the most famous examples is "The Flea" by John Donne, a poem in which the author requests sexual favors from a woman by showing how their blood has mingled in the body of a flea:

> Oh stay, three lives in one flea spare,
> Where we almost, nay more than married are.
> This flea is you and I, and this
> Our marriage bed, and marriage temple is;
> Though parents grudge, and you, we are met,
> And cloistered in these living walls of jet.

When the young woman kills the flea, the speaker concludes:

> Just so much honor, when thou yield'st to me
> Will waste, as this flea's death took life from thee.

The words, however, certainly seem ironic from today's perspective, since we know that fleas carried bubonic plague, which wiped out entire villages in the early seventeenth century when this poem was written.

But insects, like rats, are now often put in the service of medicine. Apart from human beings and perhaps rodents, the drosophila fruit fly has become the most studied animal in the world. Scientists have found that the genetic code of the fruit fly is easy to manipulate and has many affinities with that of human beings. In hope of correlating them with parts of the genome, all features of the creature's life, from anatomy to courtship dances, have been intricately observed. One journalist recently remarked that researchers who study fruit flies "are easily provoked into confessing that they think of people as large flies with wigs" (Wade, p. F1)

Selected References

Davies, Malcolm, and Jeyaraney Kathirithamby. *Greek Insects.* New York: Oxford University Press, 1986.

Donne, John. "The Flea." In *Animal Poems.* Ed. John Hollander. New York: Knopf, 1994, pp. 127–128.

Evans, E. P. *The Criminal Prosecution and Capital Punishment of Animals: The Lost History of Europe's Animal Trials.* Boston: Faber and Faber, 1988.

Melegros. "The Mosquito." In *Poems from the Greek Anthology.* Ed. and trans. Dudley Fitts. New York: New Directions, 1956, p. 26.

Wade, Nicholas. "The Fly People Make History on the Frontiers of Genetics." *New York Times* (April 11, 2000): F1–4.

Zinsser, Hans. *Rats, Lice, and History.* New York: Macmillan, 1963.

Fox, Jackal, and Coyote

You can think, study, brood, and gloss
More on Renard than on anything else.
—Anonymous, "The Romance of Renard"

The fox and jackal are predators of moderate size, which has probably made them easier for most people to identify with than the awesome lion or the ferocious wolf. The fox and jackal are almost interchangeable in the literature of the Near East; in fact, it is usually difficult for translators to know which of the two is meant in passages. Both of these canids are renowned for their cleverness. The sagacity of animals in folklore is often a rationalization of magic, and archaic manuscripts confirm that these animals once appeared as powerful sorcerers. The coyote is a canid of about the same size as the fox and jackal, but it is indigenous to the New World. In a striking instance of the universality of animal symbolism, the coyote has much the same role in Native American lore as that of its cousins in Eurasia.

In one of the very earliest literary manuscripts that have come down to us, written in Mesopotamia about the middle of the third millennium, a fox brings back the son of Enlil, god of the air, from the netherworld. The Sumero-Babylonian god of magic, Enki, was closely associated with a fox. In another cuneiform manuscript, Enki had disobeyed Ninhursag, the great earth mother, and she punished him with the curse of death. The other gods gazed on helplessly as Enki sank into oblivion, when the fox appeared and brought the deity back. The tale probably originated with a shamanic trance, in which Enki entered the realm of the dead as his body was possessed by a fox.

By the second millennium the role of the fox as a trickster was already established in Mesopotamian animal proverbs, which are the ancestors of the fables attributed to the legendary Greek Aesop. A Babylonian tablet known as *The Fable of the Fox*

Print by Ando Hiroshigi from "Hundred Famous Views of Edo." This shows the foxes that are said to gather annually at Oji near Tokyo. A large number of foxes at the congregation, according to legend, means a plentiful harvest the next year. The flames emanating from the foxes are known to the Japanese as "kitsune-bi" or "foxfire." They can sometimes signal mischief, but in this case it is a sign of fecundating power. (The Metropolitan Museum of Art, #MM60544B)

from around the middle of the second millennium told of a fox, a wolf, and a dog who brought suit against one another before a lion. They accused one another of sorcery, theft, and, most especially, of provoking the gods into sending a terrible drought that threatened to destroy the world. Much of the manuscript is missing, but the fox seemed to carry the day with its cleverness. In the final tablet we learn that rain had come and the fox was entering the temple in triumph.

The Egyptian equivalent of this magical fox was the god Anubis, shown with the head of an animal that may be either a dog or a jackal. The jackal's burrowing instinct may have suggested intimacy with the earth, while its habit of scavenging may have contributed to an association with the dead. Anubis was a psychopomp, who guided the dead to their place of judgment. He would weigh the heart of the deceased against Maat, the spirit of cosmic order, which was often represented by an ostrich feather. If the heart sank on the scales, the deceased would be devoured by demons, but if the heart rose, he or she might join the god Ra and sail across the sky in the boat of the sun.

The fox was a trickster in the fables attributed to Aesop in Greco-Roman civilization. It constantly matched wits with other animals, though it was generally obsequious to the lion. The most famous of these tales was known as "The Fox and the Grapes," and the story could hardly be simpler. A fox looked up at grapes on a trellis. It tried repeatedly to reach them by jumping, but without success. Finally, the fox said, "They are probably sour anyway" and walked away. This anecdote has been told in various eras with different morals. In medieval versions the fox is called wise, while in modern ones he is mocked as foolish. For a trickster, even a frustrated one, wisdom and foolishness are often very close indeed.

The Bible, however, took a less anthropomorphic view of animals, which were often credited with pathos but rarely with wit. Foxes were associated with trickery, but this was as hapless implements rather than perpetrators. Samson caught 300 foxes (or, possibly, jackals), tied them in pairs by their tails, fastened a torch to each pair, and set them loose in the cornfields of the Philistines (Judg. 15:4). The fox received increasing attention and respect in Jewish literature of the Diaspora, where political sensitivities forced leaders to express themselves indirectly by means of fables and parables.

Rabbi Akiba ben Joseph once defied Roman authorities by teaching the Torah. When a follower asked him if he was afraid of the government, he replied with the following story. A fox once asked some fish why they kept moving from one place to another, and they replied they were fleeing the nets of the fishermen. The fox invited the fish to come out on dry land and live with him in peace. A wise fish replied that the danger they faced in their own element must be much less than what they would face in a foreign one. In a similar way, the Jews would face greater danger if they abandoned their traditions. The Talmud also contains many stories that celebrate the wit and wisdom of the fox. Without their own army or police, the Jews of the Diaspora had to live by wit and diplomacy, and they often identified with the crafty fox with respect to both its virtues and its failings.

The dual nature of the jackal and the fox is especially clear in the Hindu-Persian *Panchatantra*, also known as *The Fables of Bidpai*, which was probably written down in about the second or third century B.C. The frame of this collection of stories concerned two jackals, the devious Damanaka and the honest Karataka, at the court of the lion king. Damanaka became jealous when the lion adopted the ox Sanjivaka as his favorite. Against the counsel of his companion, the insidious jackal stirred up strife between the lion and ox by telling each lies about the other. Finally, Damanaka provoked the former friends to engage in a bat-

Illustration by Richard Heighway to Aesop's fable of "The Fox and the Mask."

tle, in which the lion was wounded and the ox was slain. The debates and intrigues provide occasions for all of the various characters to tell stories in support of their advice.

With trickster figures, excessive cleverness is often a form of folly. In one of the tales of Bidpai, a jackal had strayed into the city, where it was chased by dogs. In desperation, it jumped into an enormous vat of blue dye to hide. When it could no longer hear any barking, the jackal slowly climbed out and then returned to the jungle. When the other creatures saw the strange blue beast passing, they were terrified and thought it must have supernatural powers. The blue jackal was declared king. It made the lion prime minister, and the elephant and monkey became royal attendants. The jackal assigned some role in its kingdom to every creature except for the other jackals, which were banished out of fear that they might expose the king as a mere jackal. One day, however, the blue jackal heard other jackals howling in the distance. Unable to restrain itself, it began to howl with them. Realizing what had happened, the other beasts were outraged and tore the blue jackal to pieces.

The *Panchatantra* was translated into Arabic by Mohammed al Haq, and then it became known as *Kalila wa Dimna*. The Arab version, in turn, was translated into Latin and eventually into all major European languages during the late Middle Ages and Renaissance. It became the basis for the cycle of Renard the Fox stories, which were first written down in French toward the end of the twelfth century and then quickly spread throughout Europe. The fox here is the clever peasant who outwits the other animals, especially its more powerful, aristocratic adversaries such as the wolf and bear. The fox's opponents end up ruthlessly beaten, cuckolded, maimed, eaten, and otherwise destroyed. Any sympathy we may have for the fox as the "underdog" is at least severely tested by its unscrupulousness. Depending in part on the class affiliation of the authors of various manuscripts, Renard comes across as a thorough villain, a flawed hero, or simply a figure of raucous fun. In one popular story the lion is ailing, and the fox convinces the king of beasts that the cure is to wrap himself in the skin of the wolf. The wolf, Renard's great adversary, accordingly is flayed, but the lion dies soon after, leaving Renard alone in triumph. Such sophisticated authors as Geoffrey Chaucer, Jean de la Fontaine, and Johann Wolfgang von Goethe retold folktales of Renard.

Readers will find a complex and thoughtful perspective in the *Fox Fables* of the French rabbi Berechiah ben Natronai ha-Nakdan, sometimes known as the Jewish Aesop. These fables, written in Hebrew around the end of the twelfth century, are a bit reminiscent of the Old Testament, filled with violence and iniquity yet told with a highly moralistic gloss. Although most of the fables do not center on the fox, the author sometimes uses the fox as a spokesperson. Much as the Jews often had to look to monarchs for protection, the fox of these stories has to cultivate a relationship with the lion king. The fox of ha-Nakdan is highly pragmatic but, unlike that of the Renard cycle, rarely vicious. In one fable the fox gnawed the bones of goats that a lion had killed. When the lion rebuked the fox, the fox said it was ashamed and promised not to take from the lion again. Ha-Nakdan concludes with the moral that we should forgive those who wrong us.

As the peasants were gradually emancipated from serfdom and the Jews from the ghettos, the traditional elites sometimes took out their anger at these groups on the fox. When hunting stags and boars ceased to be an aristocratic privilege, the nobility, especially in England, began to pursue the fox instead. Through the Middle Ages, the fox had been considered unworthy to be hunted by a lord. During the modern period, however, foxhunting became a ritualistic affirmation of the feudal order, conducted in the most ceremonious way with elaborate calls, rituals, and uniforms. Modern sportsmen such as John Mansfield and Siegfried Sassoon wrote passionate accounts of the foxhunt, and prints of the chase often decorated living room walls. But many people were also distressed by the spectacle of so many men, ladies, dogs, and horses all arrayed against one diminutive creature; the foxhunt was sometimes used to symbolize abuse of privilege.

In East Asia, the fox of folklore has remained associated less with wit than with magic and has generally been female rather than male. Foxes in Asia are symbols of marital fidelity, and the vixen is also an icon of maternal love. Early Chinese writings on the sanctity of marriage often invoked the model of the vixen in urging mothers not to practice female infanticide. But in their dealings with human beings, foxes are not necessarily bound by the same loyalties. As shape shifters, they often assume the form of beautiful women to seduce men. They frequently carry out their seductions to draw the life force from men, yet sometimes they truly fall in love with their partners. While they may fool human beings, fox maidens are sometimes recognized by other animals. They can also be identified because they do not leave any reflection in a mirror or otherwise show their true vulpine countenances.

Among the earliest recorded stories about these shape shifters is "Jenshih, the Fox Lady," written in China by Shen Chi-chi around the end of the seventh century A.D. A poor soldier named Cheng Liu once saw a lovely lady, Jenshih, walking through the streets and gallantly offered her his donkey as a mount. They fell in love, and one day Jenshih confessed to him that she was truly a fox, but she offered to remain with him in human form if he would not reject her on that account. On his acceptance, she not only proved to be a loving wife but also brought him prosperity by managing his affairs with tact and skill. At the marketplace one day, however, some dogs caught scent of her. Jenshih immediately fell to the ground, assumed the form of a vixen, and began to run. Cheng Liu followed as best he could but was unable to save her from the hounds. More than anything else, the fox maiden in Asia represents the female realm, enticing and frightening men through its secrets. Among the few unequivocally benign foxes in Asian lore are the messengers of Inari, the Japanese god of rice, who himself is often depicted as a fox.

Much like Renard the Fox, the coyote of folklore is both a sage and a buffoon. The biggest difference, perhaps, is that the coyote of Native American legend is far more of a cosmic figure than any of the foxes or jackals of folklore, at least since ancient Egypt and

Frontispiece by Paul Meyerheim to a nineteenth-century collection of tales about Renard the Fox.

Mesopotamia. Known simply as Coyote, his (the folkloric coyote is invariably male) vocation is divine play rather than social satire. His gifts are almost endless, but they are usually flawed. According to the Zuni Indians, Coyote and Eagle once stole the sun and moon in a box from the world of spirits so that there would be light, but Coyote opened the box out of curiosity. The heavenly bodies then flew away, so there is winter as well as summer. The Klamath tell how Coyote won fire from Thunderer by cheating at dice. The Pueblo Indians report that Coyote once helped a great magician to make human beings of clay and then bring them to life by baking them in an oven. Unfortunately, most people were flawed because Coyote took them out of the oven either too early or too late. Coyote is also widely credited with bringing death into the world. It should surprise nobody that the European legends of Renard and the Native American myths of Coyote have blended in the tales told in the pueblos of Mexico and the American Southwest.

Capitalist society always loves tricksters, and Coyote remains very popular today. Some Indians have complained that white interpreters of their traditions emphasize the undignified and amoral aspects of Coyote at the expense of his holy qualities. One inheritor of that tradition is Wile E. Coyote, a cartoon character who entertains people with his fanatic, but usually futile, pursuit of a bird called Road Runner. Wile often ends up falling off a cliff or being run over by a car. At first he might appear to be too much of a loser to be a successor to the Native American trickster. On the other hand, whether Coyote won or lost was always less important than that he always survived, and that is something that Wile does remarkably well.

Selected References

Dobie, J. Frank. *The Voice of Coyote.* Lincoln: University of Nebraska Press, 1961.

Erdoes, Richard, and Alfonzo Ortiz. *American Indian Trickster Tales.* New York: Penguin, 1988.

Ha-Nakdan, Berechiah ben Natronai. *Fables of a Jewish Aesop.* Trans. Moses Hadas. New York: Columbia University Press, 1967.

Johnston, Johanna. *The Fabulous Fox: An Anthology of Fact and Fiction.* New York: Dodd, Mead and Co., 1979.

Lambert, W. G., ed. and trans. *Babylonian Wisdom Literature.* Oxford: Clarendon Press, 1960.

Mourning Dove [Humishuma]. *Coyote Stories.* Lincoln: University of Nebraska Press, 1990.

Ryder, Arthur W., ed. *The Panchatantra.* Chicago: University of Chicago Press, 1964.

Sax, Boria. "Bestial Wisdom and Human Tragedy: The Genesis of the Animal Epic." *Anthrozoös* 11, no. 4 (1998): 134–141.

Schochet, Elijah Judah. *Animal Life in Jewish Tradition: Attitudes and Relationships*. New York: KTAV Publishing House, 1984.

Terry, Patricia, ed. and trans. *Renard the Fox*. Boston: Northeastern University Press, 1983.

Wang, Chi-Chen. *Traditional Chinese Tales*. New York: Columbia University Press, 1944.

Frog and Toad

> *The old pond—*
> *A frog jumps in,*
> > *Sound of water.*
> —Basho (trans. Robert Hass)

Frogs and toads have always seemed to be close to the mythic origin of life. When relaxed, they have almost the form of a ball, the most primeval of shapes. They are found mostly in ponds or in moist areas that suggest the chaos out of which living things were created. People have long believed that frogs were generated spontaneously out of earth and water and that they could survive for centuries in stone. Frogs also seemed to embody fertility when people observed their copulation, which can last for several days. The female frog will often lay tens of thousands of eggs every year. The Egyptian hieroglyphic sign for "one hundred thousand" was a tadpole (Houlihan, p. 122). The transformation of a tadpole into a frog has been a model for all of the myriad metamorphoses in myth and legend. That is why traditional stories so often contain frogs that are transformed into men or women. Evolutionary theory partially confirms the intuition of early mythologists about the primal origin of frogs, since fossils of frogs have been found going back at least 37 million years.

The popular distinction between frogs and toads is not fully recognized by professional biologists. Both groups of amphibians are members of the order Anura, and they are almost interchangeable in myth and legend. The word *toad* is generally, though not always, used for creatures of the family Bufonidae, which have short legs, rough skin, and spend much of their time on land. Toads are generally associated with cultivated places such as gardens, as well as with dark magic. But *frog* and *toad*, as the terms are often used, seem almost like words for different aspects of a single creature.

The economy of ancient Egypt was centered on the Nile River, which teemed with frogs. The frog was particularly identified with Heket, a deity of fertility and childbirth. When the waters of the Nile receded, innumerable frogs would be heard croaking in the mud, the sort of event that may have influenced many myths. In one Egyptian creation myth, Heket and her ram-headed husband, Khnum, made both gods and human beings. According to another Egyptian creation myth, the original eight creatures were frogs and snakes that carried the cosmic egg.

The Hebrews, who reacted violently against their Egyptian captors, found the frog unclean. The Bible tells us that when the pharaoh refused to let the people of Israel leave Egypt, Yahweh sent Moses to him with the following threat, which he later carried out: "Know that I will plague the whole of your country with frogs. The river will swarm with them; they will make their way into your palace, into your bedroom, onto your bed, into the houses of your courtiers and of your subjects, into your ovens, into your kneading bowls. The frogs will even climb all over you, over your courtiers, and over all your subjects" (Exod. 7:27–29).

Though most of Hebrew tradition treats these animals as repulsive, some rabbinical interpreters during the Diaspora have viewed the frogs in Egypt as heroic defenders of the faith, willing to embrace martyrdom by being burned alive.

Since frogs generally are seen after a deluge, it may be that the biblical plague of frogs once referred to a storm. In mythologies throughout the world, frogs are associated with the primeval waters out of which life arose. Among the Heron Indians and other Native American tribes, the frog is often a bringer of rain. The scriptures of the Zoroastrians mention the frog as among the first creatures to emerge from dark waters as part of a plague created by the demonic Ahriman. In the New Testament, demons in the form of frogs spring from the mouths of the Dragon, Beast, and False Prophet (Rev. 16:13–14).

Among the aborigines of Queensland, Australia, there is a story about a frog that once swallowed all of the waters on the earth. There was a great drought, and the animals decided they could save themselves only by making the frog laugh. But the frog remained unmoved by their comic routines until the eel danced, awkwardly twisting and turning. Then the frog began to chortle hysterically, thus releasing the lakes and rivers.

The croaking of frogs around a pond has often suggested an assembly, which is a frequent theme in fables attributed to Aesop. In one of the most famous, the frogs were content in their swamp but longed for a conventional government. They asked Zeus to give them a king, and he laughingly threw down a log. After recovering from their awe at the splash, the frogs began to dance on the log. After a while, however, they decided the log was not a proper king and asked Zeus for another. The god, irritated, sent down a stork, and the new monarch immediately began to gobble up the frogs.

The classical Greek poem "The Battle of the Frogs and Mice" is a burlesque of the martial epic. A mouse fleeing a cat took refuge in a pool. A frog offered to carry the mouse to safety but drowned the mouse, setting off a war between frogs and mice that was filled with reckless acts of courage and bombastic rhetoric. Finally, the mice appeared on the point of victory, but Zeus, looking down with pity on the frogs, sent crabs to drive the mice back in confusion. For a long time the poem was attributed to Homer, but most scholars now date it from the third century B.C. The story may have been a satire on the Peloponnesian War in which the frogs represented Athens, the great sea power, and the mice represented Sparta, the dominant military force on land. The crabs, then, would have represented the city of Thebes, which finally broke the power of the victorious Spartans. No doubt somebody who had grown tired of the grandiloquent speeches that always accompany bloody rampages wrote "The Battle between Frogs and Mice," and it is not very hard to guess why he or she may have wished to remain anonymous.

In *The Frogs* by the Athenian dramatist Aristophanes, frogs actually did not play much of a role in the story. They provided a chorus by croaking in the River Styx as the god Dionysus visited the underworld—"bre-ke-ke-kex-koax, koax!" Just as the chorus in Greek tragedy tended to provide the perspective of ordinary people as counterpoint to the grand dramas being enacted, the chorus of frogs was a reminder of a mundane reality that not even the gods can escape.

In Greco-Roman culture, frogs often had a reputation for coarseness because of their wide mouths and muscular bodies. In his *Metamorphoses,* Ovid told how Latona, exiled from Heaven by Juno, wandered about the earth with her children, the god Apollo and the goddess Diana. She knelt down to drink water at a stream, but some country bumpkins tried to stop her. When she pleaded with them, the rough fellows responded with threats and insults, and they muddied the water with their feet. At last, Latona cursed them, saying, "Live forever in the foul puddle!" and the ruffians turned into frogs (book 6, lines 310–381). The story anticipated the frequent depiction of toads and frogs in Hell by many artists of the late Middle Ages and Renaissance.

Frogs and toads were used in innumerable medicines and magical formulas. The Renaissance zoologist Edward Topsell reported a superstition that held that if a man wished to know the secrets of a woman, he first had to cut out the tongue of a living frog. After releasing the frog, the man had to write certain charms upon the tongue and lay it on the woman's heart. Then he could begin to ask questions and would get nothing but the truth. This, however, was a bit much even for the normally credulous Topsell, who remarked, "Now if this magical foolery were true, we had more need of frogs than of Justices of the Peace . . . " (vol. 2, p. 723).

Many who used anurans, especially toads, in magical charms in the early modern period were not simply ridiculed but tried for witchcraft. Toads were frequently mentioned in witch trials as familiars. They were also frequently ingredients in the brews of witches. Hieronymus Bosch depicted a damned woman copulating with a toad in his painting *The Seven Deadly Sins*. Many painters of the early modern period showed demons forcing the damned to eat toads in Hell. Others depicted anthropomorphic toads or frogs cooking and devouring human beings. There were many reports of frogs or toads emerging from the mouth of a woman, an event that might sometimes be understood as evidence of witchcraft and at other times simply as a noteworthy phenomenon.

The number of superstitions connected with frogs and toads was virtually endless. At least since the time of Pliny and Aelian, toads have been widely considered poisonous. In William Shakespeare's *Richard III*, the wicked king was called a "poisonous hunch-backed toad" (1.3). It has, however, also been popularly believed that toads had a precious stone inside their heads. This stone has been avidly sought by alchemists for its magical properties, especially for use in detecting or neutralizing poison. Up through most of the nineteenth century and even afterward, many books of natural history reported that frogs could survive for many centuries encased in stone.

In China, toads were one of the five venomous animals, mentioned together with the scorpion, centipede, spider, and snake. A three-legged toad was often depicted on the moon, with one leg representing each of three lunar phases. According to legend, the hermit Liu Hai decontaminated a pool by luring out the toad Ch'an with a string of gold coins. He killed the toad, thus punishing the sin of avarice. Nevertheless, Liu Hai has often been painted with Ch'an sitting affectionately at his side as a sort of pet, and a toad with a coin in its mouth is a symbol of good fortune.

Sometimes people have envied the ability of frogs and toads to find contentment in a humble pond. The eighteenth-century Japanese philosopher Shoeki Ando, a relentless critic of human arrogance, wrote that the toad once prayed to walk upright like a person. This was granted to him, but then he found that, with his eyes focused only on Heaven, he could no longer see where he was going. When he regretted his request, Heaven returned him to his original state. He had, the toad explained, been like the sages such as Sakyamuni or Lao-tzu, for "looking only to the heights, they failed to see the eight organs of their own senses . . . " (pp. 75–76).

In the modern period, people often found the perceived homeliness of frogs and toads endearing. An old story of a witch with a frog as her demonic companion evolved in the oral tradition to become "The Frog King" (or "The Frog Prince"), the first tale in the famous collection of German fairy tales by the Grimm brothers. It told of a talking frog that was disenchanted, became a prince, and married a lovely young girl. "Frog Went A-Courting" became one of the most popular of British and American folk songs. It told of a wedding feast of a frog and his mouse-bride, together with all the animals invited as guests. In *The Call of the Toad*, a novel written by the German Günter Grass as a sort of epitaph for the twentieth century, the primeval voice of a toad served much the same role as the chorus of frogs did for Aristophanes—an admonition against hubris.

Selected References

Degraaff, Robert M. *The Book of the Toad: A Natural and Magical History of Toad-Human Relations.* Rochester, VT: Park Street Press, 1991.

Grass, Günter. *The Call of the Toad.* Trans. Ralph Manheim. New York: Harcourt, Brace and Janovich, 1993.

Hine, Daryl, trans. *The Homeric Hymns and the Battle of the Frogs and the Mice.* New York: Anthenium, 1972.

Houlihan, Patrick F. *The Animal World of the Pharaohs.* New York: Thames and Hudson, 1996.

Ovid. *Metamorphoses.* Trans. A. E. Watts. Berkeley: University of California Press, 1954.

Robbins, Mary E. "The Truculent Toad in the Middle Ages." In *Animals in the Middle Ages: A Book of Essays.* Ed. Nona C. Flores. New York: Garland, 1996.

Sax, Boria. *The Frog King: On Legends, Fables, Fairy Tales, and Anecdotes of Animals.* New York: Pace University Press, 1990.

Shoeki Ando. *The Animal Court: A Political Fable from Old Japan.* Trans. Jeffrey Hunter. New York: Weatherhill, 1992.

Toperoff, Shlomo Pesach. *The Animal World in Jewish Thought.* Northdale, NJ: Jason Aronson, 1995.

Topsell, Edward, and Thomas Muffet. *The History of Four-Footed Beasts and Serpents and Insects* (3 vols.). New York: Da Capo, 1967 (facsimile of 1658 edition).

Warner, Rex. *Encyclopedia of World Mythology.* New York: Galahad Books, 1975.

G

Goat
See Sheep and Goat

Goose
See Swan, Goose, and Duck

Gorilla
See Ape and Monkey

Grasshopper, Locust, Cricket, Cicada, and Mantis

> *The poetry of earth is ceasing never:*
> *On a lone winter evening, when the frost*
> *Has wrought a silence, from the stove there shrills*
> *The cricket's song, in warmth increasing ever,*
> *And seems to one in drousiness half lost,*
> *The grasshopper's among some grassy hills.*
> —John Keats, "On the Grasshopper and the Cricket"

Entomologists place grasshoppers, locusts, crickets, and mantises in a single order, the Orthoptera, while cicadas belong to the order Homoptera. But modern taxonomies do not necessarily reflect popular perception of animals today, much less the ways in which creatures have been regarded over the centuries. For the ancient Greeks, grasshoppers, locusts, crickets, and sometimes mantises went under the single name of *akris*, and modern translators of their works have to determine which insect seems most appropriate from the context. All of these insects were usually difficult to see and were known to people primarily through their sounds in open fields. These noises, produced by the insects' rubbing parts of their bodies together, are often amazingly loud for the tiny creatures that generate them, and they are often synchronized. They are mating calls, produced almost exclusively by males, and some ancient myths suggest a surprising aware-

129

ness of this fact. In the case of the orthopterans, people also knew the insects through the enormous damage they inflicted on crops, which was only partially compensated for by their popularity as food.

The Bible tells us that when the pharaoh refused to let the people of Israel leave Egypt, locusts were the eighth plague sent by Yahweh in punishment: "The locusts invaded the whole land of Egypt. On the whole territory of Egypt they fell, in numbers so great that such swarms had never been seen before, nor would be again. They covered the surface of the soil till the ground was black with them. They devoured all the greenstuff in the land and all the fruit of the trees" (Exod. 10:14–15).

In North Africa and the Near East, plagues of locusts have continued to occur up through the twentieth century, sometimes darkening the sky and confirming the general accuracy of the biblical descriptions. In similarly vivid terms, the prophet Joel compared locusts in their vast numbers and their destructiveness to an invading army (2:25). The same imagery was used by the Egyptians and in an inscription commemorating the deeds of Ramses II, the very pharaoh who was defied by Moses, at the battle of Kadesh, where the armies of the Hittites are said to have covered the mountains like locusts. For all the trouble such insects caused, however, the Egyptians do not seem to have hated or despised them, and one text from the Old Kingdom speaks of a ruler ascending to Heaven in the form of a grasshopper.

According to an Islamic folktale from Algeria, the Devil looked scornfully on the newly created world and said, "I can do better than God." "Very well," replied God, "I will give you the power to bring to life whatever creature you create. Stroll about the world and return in a hundred years." The Devil took up the challenge and put together a creature with the head of a horse, the breast of a lion, the horns of an antelope, the neck of a steer, and parts from several other animals. Since the parts did not fit properly, he began to whittle away at the creature, until all that was left was a tiny locust. The Lord said, "Oh, Satan . . . What is this! To show your impotence and my power I will send swarms of this creature around the earth, and thus I will teach people that there is only one God" (Dähnhardt, pp. 10–12).

Perhaps because locusts in the Bible were always a scourge of God, the insects have usually not been heavily stigmatized. People will hardly ever eat creatures that they find repugnant except in times of severe hunger, but locusts and grasshoppers are eaten in much of Africa. They are also mentioned as a possible food in the Bible (Lev. 11:20–23). The New Testament states that John the Baptist lived on "locusts and wild honey" (Matt. 3:4; Mark 1:6).

Grasshoppers are very similar to locusts in appearance, but they do not breed as quickly and are solitary. In ancient Egypt the grasshopper was a popular motif, often appearing on festive items, cosmetic boxes, or jewelry. Grasshoppers do not seem to have shared the fearsome reputation of their close relatives. The song of grasshoppers, which is rhythmic, if not conventionally musical, charmed people.

The prophet Isaiah said of Yahweh, "He lives above the circle of the earth; its inhabitants look like grasshoppers" (11:24). These insects have continued to be used as symbols of insignificance, in ways that may be either endearing or contemptuous. It is possible to see a bit of each response in the Greek myth of Tithonus, a prince of Troy who was loved by Eos, goddess of the dawn. The deity asked Zeus to grant her lover immortality, but she forgot to ask for eternal youth. As Tithonus grew old, Eos left him, and eventually he withered away to become a grasshopper or cicada.

Cicadas, especially, are generally known only through their sound, since they dwell in trees and are seen only when they die and fall to the ground. For the Greeks, they seemed to be incorporeal beings and symbolized immortality. In Plato's dialogue "Phaedrus," Socrates and the young man Phaedrus had been engaged in a passionate discussion of philosophy when the former remarked that the cicadas, while singing and conversing among themselves, must surely also be observing the two men's dialogue.

Socrates explained that the cicadas had been men in a remote, primitive age. Then the Muses, goddesses of the arts, appeared, and a few people were so ecstatic that they would do nothing but sing. They would not even pause to eat or drink, and, without being aware of what was happening, they died. They returned to earth as cicadas. In gratitude for their devotion, the Muses decreed that they would sing from the moment of their birth until the day of their death, without need of food and drink. When their time on earth had expired, they would return to Heaven and report to the Muses, saying who had honored their mistresses and how.

Socrates assured his young pupil that the two of them might expect a good report from the cicadas for discoursing on the theme of love. These insects have traditionally had a similar meaning among the Chinese, who believed that cicadas lived only on dew. From the late Chou through the Han dynasties (ca. 200 B.C. through ca. A.D. 220), the Chinese would place jade cicadas in the mouths of their dead to ensure immortality.

For cultures of the Far East, the songs of insects such as cicadas and crickets also represent the chanting of Buddhist priests. Cicadas and crickets are sometimes kept in cages, and their songs are often esteemed more than those of birds. The Chinese also value crickets for their martial spirit. Gladiatorial combats between crickets have remained a popular sport in China since ancient times.

The repeated sounds of crickets have not always impressed Westerners as unequivocally beautiful. In Germany somebody with a neurotic obsession is said to have crickets in his head. On the other hand, repetitions can represent the sometimes irritating, yet essential, lessons of conscience.

One variety of cricket is known as the "house cricket" for its habit of frequently entering homes. Because these crickets are drawn to warmth, they are symbols of the hearth. To have such a visitor is traditionally considered good luck throughout Europe, and killing it can bring ill fortune. In Carlo Collodi's classic for children *Pinocchio* (first published in Italy in 1883), the hero, a wooden doll that has come to life, smashes a cricket named Jiminy with a mallet but, after many misfortunes, regrets the evil deed. Disney Studios later made Jiminy Cricket into one of their most popular animated characters and even had him introduce the television show *Walt Disney Presents*.

The word "mantis" is Greek for "seer," and the praying mantis certainly looks the part. Its long front legs are constantly moving. For ancient people this suggested a conventional posture of supplication, with hands upturned toward the sky, while Christians have sometimes thought of its claws as hands folded in prayer. The wings of a mantis suggest the flowing robes of a priest, but the most noticeable feature of the insect is its enormous eyes. People in the ancient world believed that the mantis had the power to curse with its gaze. People in the Far East have been impressed by the aggressiveness of the praying mantis, which is willing to attack creatures several times its size. A traditional saying in Japan goes, "Like a mantis raising its arms to stop the wheel of a passing cart" (Shoeki, p. 81).

Like other religious figures, the mantis of folklore seems to veer between extremes of good and evil. There is a widespread legend that the praying mantis can divine the goal of a traveler at a glance, as well as any possible dangers along the way. When asked by a wanderer, the mantis will point in the direction he should take. In the nineteenth century, however, when females of the species were observed to eat their mates after copulation, people were disillusioned and even began to demonize the mantis.

Selected References

Arnold, Dorothea. *An Egyptian Bestiary.* New York: Metropolitan Museum of Art, 1995.

Charbonneau-Lassay, Louis. *The Bestiary of Christ.* Trans. and ed. D. M. Dooling. New York: Parabola Books, 1991.

Dähnhardt, Oskar. *Naturgeschichtliche Volksmärchen* 1. Leipzig: B. G. Teubner, 1909.

Davies, Malcolm, and Jeyaraney Kathirithamby. *Greek Insects.* New York: Oxford University Press, 1986.

Eckholm, Eric. "China's Little Gladiators, Fearsome in the Ring." *New York Times* (October 4, 2000): 4.

Houlihan, Patrick F. *The Animal World of the Pharaohs.* New York: Thames and Hudson, 1996.

Plato. "Phaedrus." Trans. R. Hackforth. In *The Collected Dialogues of Plato.* Ed. Edith Hamilton and Huntington Cairns. New York: Pantheon (Bollingen Series), 1961, pp. 475–525.

Shoeki, Ando. *The Animal Court: A Political Fable from Old Japan.* Trans. Jeffrey Hunter. New York: Weatherhill, 1992.

Griffin

See Eagle

Gull

See Seagull, Albatross, and Other Seabirds

H

Hare and Rabbit

*What is it—a hopper of ditches, a cutter of corn, a little brown cow without
any horns? Answer: A hare.*

—Irish riddle

The hare and rabbit, members of the family *Leporidae*, are rodents, yet
they usually have a far more benign reputation in folklore than does
their close relative the rat. While rabbits are highly social, hares often
tend to be solitary. Hares are also larger than rabbits and have smaller
litters. Nevertheless, the two are often confused in folklore, and much
the same stories are told of both. Like most other animals that are
prominent in myth and legend, leporids are dramatically distinguished from other animals by a single feature—their long ears.
Though not terribly fast runners, they are remarkably agile, and their
ability to elude predators by changing direction instantly has doubtless contributed to their reputation as tricksters. Even more than most
other rodents, they reproduce prolifically, a characteristic that has
made leporids, especially rabbits, symbols of fertility throughout the
world. They are endearingly timid, arousing an affection that often
makes it hard for farmers to shoot them, even when they ravish
planted fields. The most remarkable feature of their lore, however, is
the notion that a hare may be seen in the moon, a belief shared by
many cultures across the globe, including the Chinese, Hottentots,
and Maya Indians.

The widespread association of the hare with the moon cannot be
due simply to the contours of lunar landscapes, since people envisage
the hare in the moon in very divergent ways. One reason for the association is that the act of a hare leaping suggests the rising moon.
Also, the patterns of white, gray, and brown on the bodies of hares
are suggestive of the lunar surface. But the most important reason is
probably the extreme watchfulness of hares, which at attention stand
almost completely still with their eyes wide open and their ears

raised. This suggests the moon, especially when full, which appears to be continually watching events on earth.

The Jatakas, early Buddhist animal fables from India, tell one of the many stories created to explain the hare-moon relationship. The future Buddha was once a hare and lived together with three wise animals, a monkey, a jackal, and an otter. He preached to the other creatures of the forest, telling them to give alms. Sakra, the god of thunder, heard him and came down to the forest in the guise of a Brahman. The monkey offered him fruit, then the jackal offered meat, and the otter offered fish. Finally, the Brahman came to the hare, who directed him to gather wood and start a fire. When the fire was blazing, the hare hopped in, for he had resolved to offer his own body as food. The flames, however, would not burn. The Brahman revealed that he was truly a god. Then he squeezed a mountain to make ink, and he drew an image of the hare in the moon.

The Chinese see a hare with a mortar and pestle, grinding the elixir of life, in the moon, an idea inspired by the reproductive powers of the animal. This vision comes from the story of Chang-O, the beautiful wife of the famous archer King Ho-Yi. The Queen Mother of Heaven once gave Ho-Yi a pill containing the elixir of immortality at a festivity. The king had drunk much wine and wished to sleep before swallowing the pill, so he entrusted it to Chang-O. She swallowed the pill, immediately felt very light, and soon discovered that she had the gift of flight. On awakening, Ho-Yi asked for the pill, and Chang-O flew away to the moon. One day she coughed up the pill, which immediately changed into a white hare. Chang-O demanded that the

The fable of "The Tortoise and the Hare," as illustrated by J. J. Grandville.

hare restore the elixir, and she gave the rabbit a mortar and pestle to grind it. But since she was now subject to the ravages of age, Chang-O turned into a three-legged toad as she looked on and waited for the hare to finish.

A story in the third book of the Hindu-Persian *Panchatantra* may affectionately poke fun at the association between the leporids and the moon, though it also shows the rabbit (in some versions, a hare) in the familiar role of trickster. A herd of elephants discovered the paradisial Lake of the Moon, and in their eagerness to drink, they crushed many rabbits to death. A rabbit named Victory went the next day to the king of the elephants, saying he was an envoy of the moon and protected by the laws of diplomacy. He rebuked the king and his herd for killing rabbits, who were under the protection of the moon, and he spoke so eloquently that the monarch wished to find the moon and beg forgiveness. Victory led the king to a place where the full moon shone brilliantly in the water of the lake. When the elephant tried to bow down before it, his trunk touched the water, breaking the image into thousands of pieces. At that Victory said, "Woe, woe to you, O King! You have doubly enraged the moon." The elephant then promised never to return, and the rabbits once again had the lake to themselves (Ryder, pp. 308–315).

In the fables of Aesop, the hare is also a trickster, though, like most other tricksters, he often becomes a victim of his own cleverness. Perhaps the most famous fable of all is "The Tortoise and the Hare." The hare had mocked the slowness of a tortoise, which then challenged him to a race. The hare agreed, and as the race began, he spurted ahead and gained a big lead. Supremely confident, the hare dawdled, rested, and played until the slow but steady tortoise overtook him to claim victory.

Julius Caesar stated that the hare was sacred to the early Britons. According to the Roman historian Dio Cassius, Queen Boudicca, who led the Britons in revolt against Roman rule, would release a hare from the folds of her dress before each campaign. The direction in which the hare ran would be used to predict the outcome of the battle. The Easter Bunny, originally a hare, was probably a sacrificial animal offered to the gods at the start of spring. Closely associated with the Easter Bunny are colored eggs, which hark back to pre-Christian celebrations of spring in Slavic lands. At one time eggs may have accompanied the hare not only in games but also in festive meals.

In the European Middle Ages, hares were both familiars and the guises under which witches ran about at night. One confessed witch, Isobel Gowdie, told how she had taken the form of a hare when hounds surprised her. She managed to evade them by running into a house and hiding long enough to say the rhyme that disenchanted her, though she still carried a mark on her back where a hound had nipped at her. In *Precious Bane* (first published in 1924), a novel by Mary Webb set in the countryside of early-nineteenth-century Shropshire, the heroine, Prudence Sarn, had a harelip, a slit upper lip like that of a hare. Her mother thought that the deformity had been caused by a hare's running across her path shortly before Prudence was born. Fellow villagers constantly suspected the young woman of a connection with the Devil.

All across Africa, the hare is an important trickster figure, and he often matches his cleverness against the size and strength of a hyena or a lion. In one Hausa story from Nigeria, the lion had so terrified the other animals of the forest that they made a deal with him. One animal would come to the lion and sacrifice itself every day if the king of beasts would no longer hunt. After a gazelle, an antelope, and many other animals had given their lives, it was the turn of the hare. The hare told the lion that he had brought a special present of honey but that another lion, who was even fiercer, had demanded the gift. When the king of beasts demanded to know where his challenger was, the hare pointed to a well. The lion looked into the well, saw his own reflection, pounced, and drowned. All animals acclaimed the hare as the new king of beasts.

Master Rabbit is a trickster well known to several Native American tribes. The Ute tell how Rabbit once became angry because the sun had burned his back. He tested his skills by killing all the people and animals that crossed his path until he felt mighty enough to duel the sun. When he hurled a magic ball at the sun, fire spread all over the earth, and Rabbit was seared so badly that he began to cry. When his tears had finally put out the flames, Rabbit realized that killing could not solve problems. In the lore of the Lenape Indians of the Northeast, Hare, also called Tschimammus, was one of the twins born to the earth mother after she had fallen from the clouds. He ascended to Heaven, and since he was expected to return to earth, Indian converts to Christianity identified Hare with Jesus.

But perhaps the best-known, and certainly the most controversial, leporid of modern times is Brer Rabbit, from the tales that Joel Chandler Harris put in the mouth of an old black man named Uncle Remus toward the end of the nineteenth century. Brer Rabbit is as ruthless as he is clever, and he continually matches wits with larger predators such as the fox, the wolf, and the bear. His adversaries often end up not only defeated but cuckolded, roasted, flayed, or otherwise horribly punished. When Brer Fox has been killed through trickery, Brer Rabbit gives the unfortunate animal's head to the wife of Brer Fox as a steak.

The tales are as controversial as they are popular. Perhaps the most intense debate in the entire study of American folklore is the relative contributions to these tales of European, African, and Native American traditions. The aesthetic and cultural debates about the tales are no less vehement. While some critics admire the cleverness of Brer Rabbit, others consider him a racist caricature, portraying blacks as shiftless and amoral. But the Brer Rabbit tales remain, in any case, an important part of African-American folklore, and those who find the versions by Harris inaccurate or patronizing may prefer those of Zora Neale Hurston and others.

The most famous story told by Harris is that of Brer Rabbit and the Tar Baby. Brer Fox had made a little figure out of tar, left it in the bushes, and watched until Brer Rabbit came down the road. When the Tar Baby failed to return his greeting, Brer Rabbit became angry and struck the figure. His paw stuck to the tar, so Brer Rabbit struck again and again, until finally all his limbs were bound together by the pitch. Brer Fox had the culprit completely at his mercy and was trying to choose the most dreadful punishment, when the clever rabbit begged not to be thrown in the briar patch. Brer Fox promptly tossed the rabbit in the brambles. "Bred and bawn in a briar patch," shouted Brer Rabbit as he ran away (Harris, p. 19). Very similar stories are told of Hare by the Hausa and other tribes in Africa, as well as of Master Rabbit by the Apache and other Native Americans.

In the nineteenth century, rabbits and hares became favorite figures in books for children. Peter Rabbit, created by Beatrix Potter, is perhaps the most beloved, but just about everybody is also familiar with the White Rabbit and the March Hare from Lewis Carroll's *Alice's Adventures in Wonderland*. Potter turns the traditional trickery of leporids in folklore into childish misbehavior, while Carroll turns it into the insanity, from a child's point of view, of adults. Far less appealing yet in some ways closer to folk traditions is Bugs Bunny, a cartoon character created by Warner Brothers in the 1940s. An amoral trickster, Bugs outwits the dim-witted hunter Elmer Fudd, who often ends up falling from a cliff or being run over by a truck. In the 1970s Richard Adams tried to give greater dignity to rabbits in *Watership Down*, his novel about a group of male rabbits who set out to establish a new warren. Although rabbits and hares are not patriarchal, virtually all of these popular images are male.

In *Playboy Magazine*, young girls are referred to as "bunnies." In the *Playboy* clubs, the hostess bunnies wear skimpy costumes with long ears and white tails, and every issue of the magazine features a bunny of the month. These practices build on the reputation of rabbits for being cute and cuddly. The use of fertility symbolism is paradoxical, however, since the male clientele supposedly wish to remain unattached and certainly do not want to have a lot of children. This suggests that the decoupling of sex and reproduction may be far less complete in contemporary society than people usually acknowledge.

Selected References

Bierhorst, John. *Mythology of the Lenape.* Tucson: University of Arizona Press, 1995.

Erdoes, Richard, and Alfonso Ortiz. *American Indian Trickster Tales.* New York: Penguin, 1999.

Ezpeleta, Alicia. *Rabbits Everywhere.* New York: Harry N. Abrams, 1996.

Harris, Joel Chandler. *Uncle Remus: His Stories and His Sayings.* New York: A. Appleton, 1928.

Hughes, D. Wyn, ed. *Hares.* New York: Congdon and Lattès, 1981.

Hurston, Zora Neale. *Mules and Men.* New York: HarperPerennial, 1990.

Parrinder, Geoffrey. *African Mythology.* London: Paul Hamlyn, 1973.

Rowland, Beryl. *Animals with Human Faces: A Guide to Animal Symbolism.* Knoxville: University of Tennessee Press, 1973.

Ryder, Arthur W., ed. *The Panchatantra.* Chicago: University of Chicago Press, 1964.

Santino, Jack. *All around the Year: Holidays and Celebrations in American Life.* Chicago: University of Illinois Press, 1995.

Sun, Ruth Q. *The Asian Animal Zodiac.* Edison, NJ: Castle Books, 1974.

Webb, Mary. *Precious Bane.* New York: The Modern Library, ca. 1960.

Hart and Hind

Just as we think of the male lion in terms of his luxurious mane, we think of the stag in terms of his enormous horns. These also define the female, the deer, through their absence or, in some species, their relatively small size. Deer and stag each have a distinct mythology and symbolism, and our language does not even have a common word to encompass both. Most of the time we use the word "deer" as a plural to include both male and female, suggesting that the species is primarily feminine. Together, hart and hind represent nothing less than the primordial division into male and female. Through this symbolism they are also intimately associated with the forests where they live. They move among the trees silently, blend in perfectly, and have a way of suddenly appearing—all of which makes deer seem the very soul of the woods.

One of the earliest possible mythological creatures is a muscular, bearded human figure known as "Sorcerer," bearing antlers of a stag and painted about a millennium before the birth of Christ in the French cave of Trois Freres. His head is disproportionately large, and the lines of his body are sharply angular. Perhaps he is doing a sort of dance. This figure could be either a nature spirit or a shaman who wears the antlers and mask of a stag. For those who created the image, the two alternatives were perhaps not so far apart since the spirit of a stag would have possessed a shamanic dancer.

No creature is more quintessentially masculine than the stag, with its large shoulders, impressive size, athletic stride, and propensity to fight. The doe seems comparably feminine, with its relatively modest size and delicate stride of cautious steps. Furthermore, does tend to remain in a herd, suggesting the traditionally feminine role of women as guardians of the home. Stags, by contrast, tend to be solitary except during the mating season. One may choose to call the contrast either archetypal or stereotyped, but it is hard not to think of the division of roles along lines of gender in human society. Their separation can almost make deer and stag appear to be distinct species, but similar things have been said of the differences between men and women.

The solitary life is why the stag has been associated with many holy anchorites. Saint Hubert, for example, was once a pleasant but

Shou Hsing, a Chinese god of longevity, mounted on a stag.

shallow courtier at the court of King Pepin in France. His great passion was the chase, and he even skipped the service of Good Friday to hunt the stag. When he finally came in sight of the stag, he saw a vision of the crucifix between its antlers, and the voice of Christ warned Hubert that he must either accept God or end up in Hell. Hubert repented his frivolous ways, became a hermit, and devoted himself to God. He is now the patron of hunters, and a festival in his honor is still held every year in the forests of France. Christ also took the form of a stag in the vision of Saint Eustace, about whom very similar tales are told. The anchorite Saint Giles once sheltered a deer from one of King Charlemagne's hunting parties, and an arrow intended for the stag hit the saint instead. In gratitude, the deer brought him milk every day, while the king built a monastery in his honor. Saint Cairan, one of Saint Patrick's followers, had several deer among his earliest disciples when he became a missionary in Ireland. A stag accompanied Saint Cannic, an Irish hermit, and offered the holy man his antlers as a book stand.

The stag has not only been a common symbol of Christ, the resurrected God, but has also represented the entire natural world, subject to cycles of germination, growth, death, decay, and resurrection. Deer, like plants but unlike most other animals, clearly reflect the seasons in their appearance. Their fur acquires a richer color in summer. Even more significant, the males of many species shed their horns every year. Up through Elizabethan times, it was widely believed that the sex organs of stags were shed and rejuvenated every summer as well. Enormous life spans, like those of large trees, were often attributed to stags. One popular medieval legend concerned a stag that was given a golden collar by Alexander the Great (Julius Caesar, King Charlemagne, or King Alfred in other versions). This animal was reportedly found hundreds of years later, still fully vigorous, with folds of skin grown around the gold.

Tradition grants even greater longevity to deer in Asia. According to Chinese tradition, deer can live at least 2,500 years if never killed. During the first 2,000 years, the skin of the deer gradually turns white; its horns turn black in the next five hundred. From that time on, the deer becomes immortal, yet it may subsist only on clear streams and lichens in the mountains.

The identification of the stag and the forest was so intimate that it guided scientific opinion until around the end of the eighteenth century. The horns of the stag were, throughout the Middle Ages, understood as the branches of a tree, and the skin covering them as a kind of bark. Georges-Louis Leclerc de Buffon, a foremost zoologist of the eighteenth century, theorized that since the stag nibbles so much on trees, branches eventually grew out of its head.

Its association with the forest is partly responsible for another important feature of the stag in folklore. While the earth is traditionally perceived as feminine, people generally view trees, with a few exceptions, as masculine. The ash was sacred to Odin, the oak to Zeus and Thor. Deer have frequently been depicted around the base of a tree of life in ancient Mesopotamia and several other regions. According to Norse mythology, stags nibbled at the base of the world tree, Yggdrasil.

The horns of the stag have been worn by many highly masculine heroes and gods in folklore and mythology, for example, the Celtic god Cernunnos. Stags sometimes drew the chariot of Dionysus, the Roman Bacchus. Neopagans of today celebrate the stag as a symbol of the male. In European folklore, the sexuality associated with this animal is fierce and unrestrained yet also completely chaste. Neither fundamentally romantic nor promiscuous, it is more the undifferentiated sexuality of the vegetable realm than the sexuality of either animals or human beings.

By about the time of Charlemagne, the hunt of the stag was a sport and thus a privilege of princes and aristocrats forbidden to the peasantry, often on pain of death or mutilation. It was set apart from the everyday world by elaborate costumes, vocabularies, and rituals. A solemn rite reminiscent of Holy Communion followed the slaying of the stag. The body of the stag was divided among participants, from the dogs to the horsemen, and the head was finally presented to the lord of the manor.

A doe traditionally accompanies Artemis, goddess of the hunt and protector of animals. King Agamemnon, commander of the Greeks in their assault on Troy, once killed a hind sacred to Artemis and boasted that he was greater than she in the hunt. The goddess sent a calm, forcing the Greek ships to remain in port. An oracle told the Greeks that there would be wind only when Agamemnon sacrificed his daughter Iphigenia to Artemis. Under pressure from the other Greek princes, Agamemnon finally complied. When Iphigenia was led to the altar, Artemis substituted a hind and carried away the young girl in a cloud to the island of Crimea, where she became a priestess.

In his *Metamorphoses*, Ovid tells how the young hunter Actaeon once came upon Diana, the Roman form of Artemis, bathing with her nymphs at a stream. He was so overwhelmed by the sight that he stood transfixed, until the goddess became aware of him and called out to him as she splashed water in his face, "Tell people you have seen me, Diana, naked! Tell them if you can!" Acteon looked into the water and saw, with horror, that he was being turned into a stag. He was soon torn apart by his own hounds (book 3, lines 136–250). Some interpreters believe that Diana here represents Julia, daughter of Emperor Augustus, while Acteon represents Ovid himself, who was banished for witnessing one of Julia's affairs. The unfortunate hunter may also be a man who intrudes on women's mysteries.

The deer was also sacred to many other archaic goddesses, including the Mesopotamian Ninhursag, the Egyptian Isis, and the Greek Aphrodite. The nurturing quality of a hind is shown in the Greek myth of Telephus, son of Hercules and Auge. His mother, to conceal her affair, hid the infant Telephus in the temple of the goddess Athena, which caused a blight. When this was discovered, the infant was exposed on a mountain to die, but he was saved by a hind that suckled him.

The Old Testament often celebrates the hind as a symbol of feminine virtue. For example:

> Find joy with the wife you married in your youth,
> Fair as a hind, graceful as a fawn.
> Let hers be the company you keep,
> Hers the love that ever holds you captive. (Prov. 5:19)

Psalm 42 begins, "As the doe longs for running streams, so longs my soul for you, my God."

Stag and hind share an importance as divine messengers throughout most of Europe. In countless epics and fairy tales, deer appear to the hero or heroine and guide him or her through the woods. The search for the Holy Grail begins as knights of King Arthur follow a white stag into the woods. According to legend, Louis the Pious, son

of Charlemagne, was once so intent on pursuing a stag that he became separated from his hunting party, fell from his horse while crossing a stream, and became lost in a vast forest. When his men found him the next morning, daylight revealed a bush of roses blossoming in the snow, a miraculous sign that he should build a cathedral in that place. In Celtic myth deer are guides to the Other World, while in the lore of Ireland they are also sometimes the cattle of fairies.

In medieval and Renaissance culture, the hunt of deer provided a frequent metaphor for courtship. Imagery taken from the chase was used to express the fear, longing, concealment, and tension that are often part of erotic intrigues. In Shakespeare's *Twelfth Night,* Curio tried to divert the melancholy Duke Orsinio:

> *Curio:* Will you go hunt, my lord?
> *Duke:* What, Curio?
> *Curio:* The hart.
> *Duke:* Why, so I do, the noblest that I have.
> O, when mine eyes did see Olivia first,
> Methought she purg'd the air of pestilence!
> That instant was I turn'd into a hart,
> And my desires, like fell and cruel hounds,
> E're since pursue me. (1.1)

Even more frequently, a woman was viewed as a hunted deer. The horns of a stag were often used as a symbol of cuckoldry, a constant preoccupation in literature of the age.

But for the more humble social orders, the deer were often bitterly resented as a symbol of oppression. In the stories of Robin Hood, the merry men living in Sherwood Forest constantly defied the Sheriff of Nottingham by feasting on the "king's deer." When the prohibitions against deer hunting by the peasantry were finally lifted, many commoners asserted their new freedom by pursuing the chase with enormous vehemence and cruelty. The British pastor Gilbert White complained, "Unless he was a hunter, as they affected to call themselves, no young person was allowed to be possessed of manhood or gallantry" (p. 21).

In *Bambi: A Life in the Woods* (first published in 1928), Felix Salten protested this indiscriminate hunting in his beloved Vienna Woods. It tells the story of a young stag named Bambi from his birth in a clearing. He learns the ways of the woods, fights off rivals, and mates with a hind named Filene. The tale ends with the death of Bambi's father, whereupon Bambi goes off by himself to become a guardian of the forest. In this book, the poacher who killed Bambi's mother and allowed the deer no rest is a figure of awe and terror. Salten, himself an avid sportsman, later tried to draw a sharper distinction between the poacher and the legitimate hunter in a sequel. The enormously popular movie (first issued in 1942) by Disney Studios that was based on the book, however, further anthropomorphized Bambi and Filene, while it made "man," known only through fires and bullets, seem like a brutal force of nature.

A close association between deer and the landscape is also found in the cultures of Native Americans. Several tribes in Mexico and the American Southwest, including the Aztecs, Zuni, and Hopi, traditionally perform a deer dance to influence the elements and bring bountiful crops. The Yaqui Indians today generally follow a Catholicism that is heavily influenced by traditional tribal religion, and they have incorporated the deer dance into an Easter ritual that is performed every year. In all of these ceremonies, the chief dancer will wear either the head of a deer or horns and will imitate the motions of the animal, which looks cautiously about while moving amid the woods.

With the increasing suburbanization of North America and Europe, many deer have lost their fear of human beings. White-tailed deer of North America, which live on browse at the forest's edge, are now actually far more common than they were in the time of Columbus. Many suburbanites consider deer "pests" or "overgrown rats" and complain that they cause traffic accidents or destroy gardens. Perhaps it is only in the Far North, where many of the remaining wildernesses may still be found, that the ancient symbolism of the deer (and, in particular, its relative the moose) as guardians of the woods retains something of its vividness.

Selected References

Bergman, Charles. *Orion's Legacy: A Cultural History of Man as Hunter.* New York: Dutton, 1996.

Klingender, Francis. *Animals in Art and Thought till the End of the Middle Ages.* Trans. Evelyn Antal and John Harthan. Cambridge: MIT University Press, 1971.

Ovid. *Metamorphoses.* Trans. Rolfe Humphries. Bloomington: Indiana University Press, 1955.

Salten, Felix. *Bambi: A Life in the Woods.* New York: Simon and Schuster, 1928.

Sax, Boria. *The Frog King: On Legends, Fables, Fairy Tales, and Anecdotes of Animals.* New York: Pace University Press, 1990.

Shakespeare, William. *Twelfth Night or, What You Will.* New York: Dover, 1966.

Sun, Ruth Q. *The Asian Animal Zodiac.* Edison, NJ: Castle Books, 1974.

White, Gilbert. *The Natural History of Selborne.* New York: Frederick Warne, ca. 1895.

Hawk

See Falcon and Hawk

Hedgehog

Not the phoenix, not the eagle, but the he'risson [hedgehog], very lowly, low down, close to the earth.

—Jacques Derrida, "Che cos' è la poesia?"

The Greek poet Archilochus wrote in the latter seventh century B.C. that "the fox knows many tricks; the hedgehog knows only one. A great one" (Atchity, p. 43). Everybody understood that Archilochus meant the hedgehog's ability to elude predators by rolling into a ball so that spikes would be facing in every direction. The broader meaning of the epigram, however, has puzzled readers for millennia. The poet had fought as a soldier, so perhaps he was thinking of a defensive military formation in which several soldiers with spears stand back to back in a circle. Perhaps the hedgehog may also have represented the poet's native Sparta, where people specialized in war, while the fox represented more cosmopolitan cities such as Athens. At any rate, Archilochus clearly considered the defense of the hedgehog to be at least the equal of the wiles of the fox. The twentieth-century

British philosopher Isaiah Berlin divided thinkers into foxes, distinguished by breadth of understanding (Tolstoy, for example), and hedgehogs, distinguished by depth (Dostoyevski, for example).

Such thinkers were doubtless also fascinated by the singularity of hedgehogs, which resemble no other animal. They are small, nocturnal insectivores that burrow in the earth and, as already noted, are covered with spines. They sleep beneath the ground for long periods when food is not plentiful, then eventually reemerge, a characteristic that made the ancient Egyptians associate the hedgehog with the renewal of life. The Egyptians, who constantly had to contend with the bites of snakes and the stings of scorpions, also admired the resistance of hedgehogs to poisons. They often carried amulets in the form of a hedgehog for protection against venomous creatures.

But people have feared as well as admired the powers of this diminutive animal. In Europe, hedgehogs have often been taken for companions of witches. In China as well, the hedgehog has had a reputation for necromancy; people believed that it lay concealed near roads to cast spells on unsuspecting travelers.

Human beings are, like hedgehogs, unique among animals, and so the strangeness of hedgehogs could make these animals easy for people to identify with. Aristotle reported in his *Historia Animalia* that hedgehogs copulate belly to belly like human beings, since the spikes make it impossible for the male to mount the female from behind. Aristotle, Pliny, and Aelian reported that hedgehogs can anticipate changes in the direction of wind; accordingly, they block and open entrances to their burrows. In the Byzantine Empire, people sometimes attempted to predict the weather by observing the burrows of hedgehogs.

In European fairy tales, the hero is often a simpleton, a child who at first seems too odd to participate in normal life. A fairy tale, from the collection of the Brothers Grimm, entitled "Hans My Hedgehog," began with a farmer complaining, "I want to have a child, even if it's a hedgehog." Soon his wife gave birth to Hans, human to the waist and a hedgehog above. Hans's behavior was as strange as his appearance. He rode around on a rooster, played the bagpipes, and tended pigs in a forest. Though scorned and mistreated by people, Hans eventually managed to marry a beautiful princess and become fully human (tale no. 108).

The hedgehog often appears as the proverbial underdog who manages to defeat a seemingly invincible opponent. In another tale from the Grimms, the hedgehog challenges an arrogant hare to a race. After a few steps the hedgehog slips beneath the ground. His wife, however, waits at the finish line, pretending to be her husband, and claims victory when the hare approaches. The tale concludes with a moral: "No person, no matter how superior he believes himself, should ever make fun of another, even if that other person is a hedge-hog" (tale no. 187).

In an essay entitled "What Is Poetry?" ("Che cos' è la poesia?"), contemporary French philosopher Jacques Derrida compared a poem to a hedgehog that is thrown onto a street and curls up into a ball. In a similar manner, he maintained, a poem creates a self-contained world, which, however, exists amid terrible dangers. It may well be that Derrida, who is often accused of being solipsistic, identified with the proverbial hedgehog more than he cared to admit.

Once famed for its formidable defense, the hedgehog has now come to symbolize the vulnerability of nature in a technological world. Crushed or wounded hedgehogs are a regrettably frequent sight on European roads. The Prickly Ball Farm in southeast England near Exeter has established a hospital and a network of volunteers to care for and rehabilitate these animals.

Selected References

Arnold, Dorothea. *An Egyptian Bestiary.* New York: Metropolitan Museum of Art, 1995.

Atchity, Kenneth J., ed. and trans. *The Classical Greek Reader.* New York: Oxford University Press, 1996.

Berlin, Isaiah. *The Hedgehog and the Fox: An Essay on Tolstoy's View of History.* New York: Simon and Schuster, 1993.

Derrida, Jacques. "Che cos' è la poesia?" In *Points: Interviews, 1974–1994.* Trans. Peggy Kampuf et al. Ed. Elizabeth Weber. Stanford: Stanford University Press, 1992, pp. 288–300.

Fontenay, Elizabeth de. *Le silence des bêtes: La philosophie à l'épreuve de l'animalité.* Paris: Fayard, 1998.

Grimm, Jacob and Wilhelm. *The Complete Fairy Tales of the Brothers Grimm.* Trans. Jack Zipes. New York: Bantam Books, 1987.

Hen

See Cock and Hen

Heron, Ibis, Crane, and Stork

Whither, midst falling dew,
While glow the heavens with the last steps of day
Far, through their rosy depths, dost thou pursue
      Thy solitary way?

      Vainly the fowler's eye
Might Mark thy distant flight to do thee wrong

Long-legged wading birds that thrive in wetlands are noted for their watchfulness and their ability to stand still for long periods as they search for prey. They have been almost universally regarded as benign, in part because they attack only snakes and other small reptiles. The Egyptians, like other peoples of the ancient world, saw cosmic patterns reflected in the behavior of animals, and the head of a bird hovering over water could suggest heavenly bodies above the earth. Accordingly, Egyptians identified the heron with the sun, the ibis with the moon. When the birds rose and flew out of sight, it could have appeared that they had gone to the divine spheres.

According to one Egyptian creation myth, when the cosmic egg broke open, the sun god Ra flew out in the form of the Bennu bird. This avian landed on the Benben Stone, an obelisk representing a ray of the sun, created from the fire at dawn on a tree in the city of Heliopolis. The Bennu bird was depicted in paintings and hieroglyphics as a crane, sometimes with features of a falcon as well. In *The Egyptian Book of the Dead*, a guide to the next world written around the middle of the second millennium B.C., the Bennu bird was described as "keeper of the book of things which are and of things which shall be" (Budge, chap. 17).

The Greek historian Herodotus visited Egypt and identified the Bennu bird as a phoenix, which had plumage of red and gold. This bird, he reported Egyptian priests as saying, lived in Arabia and came to Egypt only once in five hundred years when its father had died. Then the phoenix encased his father in an egg made of myrrh, which he brought to the temple of the sun in Heliopolis for burial. According to Horapollo, when a phoenix was about to die, it cast itself to the ground, creating a fire from which a new phoenix would be born. According to other writers of antiquity, including Pliny the Elder and Claudian, the Phoenix (capitalized since there is only one) immolates itself. The most detailed description came from Lactantius, an early Christian author, who wrote that a phoenix lived only on dew and summoned each new day with a melodious song. After a life of a thousand years, this phoenix built its own funeral pyre from aromatic spices in Arabia. It immolated itself, but the ashes congealed with the

In this Aesopian fable, retold by La Fontaine and illustrated by J. J. Grandville, Zeus sends a crane to be king of the frogs. The story could well be of Egyptian origin.

moisture of its body to form an egg from which the magical bird would be reborn. The reborn bird would take the remains of its former body to be buried in the temple of the sun. In medieval bestiaries the phoenix became a symbol of resurrection and of Christ.

The legend of the phoenix moved north to Russia, where it became the "firebird," and east to China, where it became the "*fenghuang*," always growing more splendid as it blended with indigenous tales. The Chinese phoenix came to represent the empress and was a favorite motif on porcelain and embroidery. It is, of course, in every respect a long way from the heron of Egypt, with its simple plumage, to these elaborate creations, but the phoenix always retained its basic form and association with the sun.

The ibis of Egypt could easily represent the moon because of the bright white of its plumage and, perhaps, the gentle curve of its bill. It was associated with the moon god Thoth, who was also the scribe of the gods and the inventor of the sciences. In *The Egyptian Book of the*

Dead, Thoth was portrayed with the body of a man and the head of an ibis as he wrote down the judgments of the gods at the weighing of a soul. He had no mother or father but had created himself, and in some cosmologies he laid the cosmic egg (something also attributed to the sky god Geb) at the beginning of the world.

The crane sometimes assumed the symbolism of both the heron and the ibis. What has distinguished cranes, above all, has been their mating dances, in which males bow, leap, and turn suddenly to impress their prospective mates. The vigor of their movements could easily suggest a war dance, and this must have contributed to the legend, first found in Homer's writings, that every winter the cranes migrate to a distant country and do battle with tiny men known as pygmies. After slaying the monstrous Minotaur, Theseus, the legendary founder of Athenian civilization, performed a "crane dance" together with the youths who had accompanied him, and the dance was reenacted every year to commemorate their deliverance. The rhythmic steps imitated not only cranes but also the twisting and contortions of a man walking through the passages of the labyrinth that housed the Minotaur.

Medieval bestiaries later described flocks of cranes in martial terms, as flying in military formations, for example, with commanders shouting orders and reproving laggards. At night, sentries were sent to keep watch so that the cranes would not be ambushed. The animated call of a crane could even rouse people to new activity. Hesiod wrote in *Works and Days* that the cries of the crane meant that the time for the winter rains had arrived and the farmers should begin to plow.

In China and Japan, however, cranes are symbols of peace, and they are believed to live a thousand years or longer. As monogamous birds, they are, together with mandarin ducks, also symbols of conjugal fidelity. Cranes have often been depicted beside elderly couples against a background of aged pines.

The popular Japanese tale usually called "The Crane Wife" has many similarities with the swan maiden tales of northern Europe. A young man named Karoku rescued a crane from a trap, and the bird immediately flew away. That evening a lovely young woman came to his house for shelter, and the two soon married. Since Karoku did not have much money, his wife would periodically lock herself in a cabinet, asking him never to intrude. After three days she would emerge with rolls of cloth splendidly woven of crane feathers, which fetched a high price at the market. One day, however, Karoku was overcome with curiosity and opened the cabinet door before his wife had finished her work, only to find that she had become a crane and plucked her own feathers for the cloth. Unable to remain after her secret had been revealed, the bird sadly flew off to rejoin her flock. According to some scholars, the crane-wife may originally have been a manifestation of Ameratsu, the Japanese goddess of the sun and the patron of weaving.

Storks, which have been frequently conflated with cranes, have little fear of humankind and often nest in chimneys or in abandoned buildings. The Greeks and Romans took them as models of parental love and filial piety. Aelian, for example, reported that when no other food was available, parent storks would disgorge what they had eaten to feed their young. When they reached old age, storks would not die but would cross the ocean to islands where they would assume the form of human beings. This, according to Aelian, must be because the gods desired "there if nowhere else to uphold a human model of piety . . . " (book 3, section 23). Also praised for familial devotion was the pelican, said to feed its young with its own blood, which became a symbol of Christ during the Middle Ages.

The Muslims later also considered storks holy birds, since they made a pilgrimage to Mecca once a year. To have a stork nest on your land has traditionally been a sign of good luck, and to kill one invited disaster. In their collection of German legends, the Grimm brothers wrote that when Attila was besieging the city of Aquileia, the Romans had held out valiantly, and so the Huns were considering moving on. One day Attila saw storks carrying their young from the city to the countryside. "Behold," he said to his followers, "these birds can foresee the future. They are forsaking the city, which will soon be subdued, and the house, which will soon collapse." The invaders redoubled their efforts and destroyed Aquileia so completely that hardly a trace of it remained (vol. 2, legend no. 382).

In northern Europe, a stork flying over a house has traditionally been an omen that an infant will be born there soon. The idea that storks bring babies goes back very far but was popularized by a story entitled "The Storks," written by Hans Christian Andersen in the mid-nineteenth century. Unborn children lay dreaming inside a pond in Egypt as they waited for the storks to bring them to families. Those people who made fun of storks and other animals received infants who had died, but those who protected other creatures were given living sisters and brothers.

When animals become rare, the legends about them are usually transmuted into symbol and allegory, and that is what has happened with the stork. The image is certainly not what Andersen had in mind, but today a bundled-up infant hanging from the beak of a stork in flight often represents birth. People have sometimes regarded the idea that storks bring babies as a means of concealing from children the realities of sex and reproduction. Perhaps it has been used that way in modern times, when, for the first time, many people had sufficient privacy to be able to shelter their children. The legend, however, reflects an ancient conception of fertility as not simply offspring but the ability of the earth to constantly generate new life.

Selected References

Adams, Robert J., trans. "The Crane Wife." In *Folktales of Japan.* Ed. Keigo Seki. Chicago: University of Chicago Press, 1973, pp. 77–80.

Aelian. *On Animals* (3 vols.). Trans. A. F. Scholfield. Cambridge: Harvard University Press, 1972.

Andersen, Hans Christian. "The Storks." In *Fairy Tales and Stories.* Trans. H. W. Dulcken. New York: Hurst, ca. 1900, pp. 115–119.

Budge, E. A. Wallis, trans. *The Egyptian Book of the Dead: The Papyrus of Ani.* New York: Dover, 1967 (1895).

Grimm, Jacob and Wilhelm. *The German Legends of the Brothers Grimm* (2 vols.). Ed. and trans. Donald Ward. Philadelphia: Institute for the Study of Human Issues, 1981.

Herodotus. *Herodotus* (4 vols.). Trans. A. D. Godley. New York: G. P. Putnam's Sons, 1926.

Horapollo. *The Hieroglyphics of Horapollo.* Trans. George Boas. Princeton: Princeton UP, 1993.

Ions, Veronica. *Egyptian Mythology.* New York: Peter Bedrick Books, 1982.

Miller, Alan L. "The Swan Maiden Revisited: Religious Significance of 'Divine Wife' Folktales with Special Reference to Japan." *Asian Folklore Studies* 46 (1987): 55–86.

Nigg, Joseph, ed. *The Book of Fabulous Beasts: A Treasury of Writings from Ancient Times to the Present.* New York: Oxford University Press, 1999.

Pollard, John. *Birds in Greek Life and Myth.* New York: Thames and Hudson, 1977.

White, T. H., trans. *The Book of Beasts: Being a Translation from a Latin Bestiary of the Twelfth Century.* New York: Dover, 1984.

Hind

See Hart and Hind

Hippopotamus

So he lies beneath the lotus,
And hides among the reeds in the swamps.
The leaves of the lotus give him shade,
And the willows by the stream shelter him.

Should the river overflow on him, why should he worry?
A Jordan could pour down his throat without his caring.
                                        —Job 40:21–23

For most of history, people outside of central and southern Africa have known the hippopotamus mostly through vague rumors and a few Roman mosaics. A conception of the animal, however, had been firmly implanted in the collective imagination through the words spoken by Yahweh in the Bible:

> Now think of Behemoth;
>   He eats greenstuff like the ox.
> But what strength he has in his loins,
>   what power in his stomach muscles!
> His tail is as stiff as a cedar,
>   The sinews of his thighs are tightly knit.
> His vertebrae are bronze tubing,
>   His bones are hard as hammered iron.
> His is the masterpiece of all God's work. . . . (Job 40:15–19)

The identity of Behemoth remains a matter of perennial debate, and tradition has sometimes made the creature an elephant, a rhinoceros, or even a crocodile. The passage went on to describe Behemoth as living beneath the lotus, something that best fits the hippo. When the book was written, the Hebrews, living in Mesopotamia, probably had little or no contact with any of those animals, and they may well have confused the various creatures already. An engraving of Behemoth by

Illustration of a hippopotamus from a nineteenth-century book of natural history.

the British poet William Blake gave the monster features of both hippopotamus and elephant, an idea that may be close in spirit to the biblical inspiration.

For those in more intimate contact with the hippopotamus, the animal has seemed almost as awe inspiring but less forbidding. For all their bulk and power, hippos can move with surprising agility and even a sort of grace. The Egyptian goddess Tawaret was generally depicted with the head of a hippopotamus and the body of a pregnant woman. Her image was found on several amulets and symbolized the fierceness of maternal love. The Egyptians, however, regarded the hippo with ambivalence, perhaps because it would often trample crops. The villainous god Set took the form of a red hippopotamus in his unsuccessful battle with the god Horus for control of Egypt.

In many places in Africa, people have venerated a hippopotamus goddess who resembled Tawaret. The Ronga of southern Mozambique told of a woman who gave her son to a hippopotamus goddess for protection. The deity raised the boy beneath the river yet brought him up every evening to be suckled by his mother.

In the middle of the seventeenth century, British clergyman Edward Topsell wrote that the hippopotamus, or "sea-horse," was "a most ugly and filthy beast, so called because in his voice and mane he resembleth a horse, but in his head an ox or a calf, in the residue of his body a swine . . . " (vol. 1, p. 256). Though he had little trouble accepting the existence of such creatures as the unicorn or satyr, Topsell was skeptical about that of the hippo.

In 1849 a hippo named Obaysch, the first hippopotamus seen in Europe since Roman times, was brought to the London Zoo, where he promptly generated a craze known as hippomania. Thousands of people lined up to see him every Saturday, newspapers chronicled every detail of his life, and there was even a dance named the Hippopotamus Polka. People have continued to be fascinated by the surprising agility of these enormous animals, and the film *Fantasia*, released in the 1950s by Disney Studios, features hippos dressed as ballerinas. Whether the creators of the film were aware of it or not, these animals were not entirely unlike the hippopotamus goddess of ancient Egypt.

Selected References

Knappert, Jan. *African Mythology: An Encyclopedia of Myth and Legend.* London: Diamond Books, 1995.

Root, Nina J. "Victorian England's Hippomania: From the Nile to the Thames they loved Obaysch." *Natural History* (February 1993): 34–38.

Topsell, Edward, and Thomas Muffet. *The History of Four-Footed Beasts and Serpents and Insects* (3 vols.). New York: Da Capo, 1967 (facsimile of 1658 edition).

Horse

Are you the one who makes the horse so brave
*   And covers his neck with flowing hair?*
Do you make him leap like a grasshopper?
*   His proud neighing spreads terror far and wide.*
Exultantly he paws the soil of the valley,
*   And prances eagerly to meet the clash of arms.*
                    —Job 39:19–21

The experience of riding a horse may be the closest thing to union with an animal that people have ever known. The rider may determine the direction; the horse sets the rhythm. The rider rises and falls in a sort of trance as landscape passes beneath. The union of animal and man is commemorated in myths of the centaur, human to the waist and equine beneath.

For the most part, centaurs were dominated by animal instincts. Perhaps the fierce horsemen of the Eurasian steppes, glimpsed from a distance by people who did not yet know how to ride, inspired the legends of centaurs. The drinking and lechery of centaurs were notorious. Centaurs were invited to the marriage feast of Pirithous, king of the Lapiths, and Hippodamia, where they became drunk and tried to carry off the bride. The Lapiths finally defeated them in a ferocious battle, which is usually interpreted as the triumph of civilization over barbarism. The story was a favorite subject of painters during the Renaissance.

There are several colorful myths about the origin of centaurs. According to one, it all began as Ixion, king of Lapithea, was invited to Mount Olympus to dine with Zeus. He tried to seduce Hera, the wife of his host, but made love only to a cloud. From that union the centaurs were born. The tale is, perhaps, about the power of imagination, which centaurs have symbolized ever since. The story, however, does not have a happy ending. Zeus fastened Ixion to a fiery wheel that revolved endlessly in Hades.

Apollonius of Rhodes wrote that the deity Cronos was once having an affair with Philyra, daughter of Oceanus, when his consort Rhea surprised him. Cronos leaped out of bed, changed himself into a stallion, and galloped off. Philyra wandered away in shame but later gave birth to Chiron. Among centaurs, only Chiron had a reputation for great wisdom. His students included the warrior Achilles and the physician Asclepius.

Sometimes the wildness of centaurs proved more powerful than civilization. Ovid told the story of Canus, a young girl who made love to the god of the sea. When the deity promised to grant any wish she might have, she asked to become a man so that she might take part in battle. The god granted her request, but fearing for her safety, he added the gift of invulnerability to any weapon made of metal. Canus proved invincible in battle until he encountered a band of centaurs. Not having learned to melt metal, they killed Canus with their primitive weapons such as rocks and sticks.

In the mythology of northern Europe, the giant horse Svadilfari was a sort of centaur. The Norse gods once commissioned the giant Fafnir to build the walls of their city, Asgard. If he could finish the work by spring, he would receive the goddess Freya in marriage, together with the sun and the moon; if not, he would forfeit all pay. Svadilfari helped the giant by not only drawing the stones but also setting them into place. Loki, the god of fire, changed himself into a mare. Svadilfari ran after Loki, so the wall remained unfinished. From the union of Svadilfari and Loki, the eight-legged steed Sleipner was born, on which the god Odin journeyed through the sky and to the realm of the dead.

In the time of Homer, horses drew chariots but did not yet carry riders. After the Trojan War had dragged on for ten years, the Greeks pretended to sail away, leaving behind on the shore a giant horse made of wood. The Trojans, thinking the horse an offering to the gods, took it inside the city walls. The Greeks, who had only temporarily withdrawn to a nearby island, had concealed warriors inside the wooden image. When night came, they slipped out and opened the city gates for the invaders. Apollodorus wrote that Helen of Troy had walked around the horse imitating the voices of the wives of men inside. One of the men wished to call out in reply, but Odysseus clamped his hand over the soldier's mouth. Perhaps this incident records an imperfectly remembered rite of fertility, an offering to a horse deity that eventually granted victory to the Greeks.

For all their practical use to human beings, horses represent above all the power of imagination. They have been found in graves, from the Ukraine and Scandinavia to China, buried to carry their masters in the world to come. Shamans, especially in the Arctic Circle, have sacrificed horses to accompany them on ecstatic journeys to other worlds. Apollo, the Roman god of the sun, rode across the sky in a chariot drawn by horses; so did the Persian Mithras. Perhaps the most popular symbol of transcendence is Pegasus, a horse with wings, which sprang from a drop of blood of the monster Medusa after she was decapitated.

Though primarily vegetarian, horses have always been closely associated with war. Plutarch, in "Of Isis and Osiris," told an Egyptian legend of how Osiris, god of the dead, once instructed his son Horus. The father asked what animal would be most useful in battle, and Horus replied that it was the horse. Osiris asked why his son had not picked the lion, to which Horus replied, "A lion might indeed be very serviceable to one that needed help, but a horse would best serve to cut off and disperse a flying enemy." On hearing this, Osiris realized that his son was ready to become a warrior (vol. 4, p. 76).

Poseidon, the Greek god of the sea, was another deity associated with horses. He moistened a stone with his semen (that is, the foam of a wave), thus fertilizing the earth, and out leaped the horse Scyphius. Creatures with the head of a horse, the body of a serpent, and the tail of a fish drew Poseidon's chariot. Horses rise and fall like waves as they gallop along, while their manes look like foam. In a herd, they move to the rhythm of flowing water. When Poseidon and Athena, the goddess of wisdom, were competing to be patron of the largest city in Attica, the immortals decided that the role would go to whoever gave the greatest gift. The deity of the sea struck the ground with his trident and made a horse spring forth. Athena, however, created an olive tree, and her gift was judged finer, so the city was named Athens after her. The contest records a conflict between the nomadic life, in which the horse is absolutely central, and the settled life of agriculturalists.

One Greek myth recounts the fate of King Diomedes of Thrace, who fed strangers to his land to his mares. The eighth labor of Hercules was to capture the man-eating monsters. After a terrible struggle, he killed Diomedes and fed the lifeless body to the horses. The tale shows the fear that horses inspired at a time when they were not yet fully domesticated and might still be seen roaming in the wild. The Romans knew horses only as domestic animals, but they admired the way the animals remained spirited even in the service of human beings.

In the latter fourth century A.D., the Greek mercenary Xenophon wrote the earliest book on horsemanship that has come down to us. He approached horses without awe but with a remarkable concern and respect. The horse, he understood, was the soldier's companion in battle and shared his hardships. Much of Xenophon's treatise was devoted to detailed descriptions of such matters as how to place the halter about the neck of a horse. Xenophon's foremost rule was never to deal with a horse thoughtlessly or in a fit of passion.

The Roman emperor Caligula talked of naming his favorite horse Incitatus as consul. The Romans adopted the Celtic horse-goddess Epona. She was even displayed on Roman coins, riding sidesaddle upon a mare. The Romans would race two chariots, each drawn by two horses, at the festival of Mars in the middle of October. The finest of the horses, the one that drew the winning chariot on the inside of the track, would be sacrificed to Mars. The head and tail of the horse would then be cut off and decorated. Sometimes the head would be affixed to the house of a prominent farmer or other citizen.

The horse was also the only animal to set apart an entire social stratum—that of equestrians, or horsemen in Rome, the class that eventually became the knights of the European Middle Ages. This was a class of warriors, for riding was a privilege generally reserved for officers in the Roman army. Finally, however, superior horsemanship enabled barbarian tribes to conquer Rome. In contrast to the Romans, who made riding a privilege of class, the invaders had entire mounted armies. The Roman historian Ammianus Marcellinus, writing in the fourth century A.D., described the Huns as primitive, bestial people who were almost one with their horses; they would not dismount even to eat or sleep. Until the two world wars, battles were usually won or lost by gallant cavalry charges.

The biblical prophet Elijah ascended to Heaven in a fiery chariot drawn by horses (2 Kings 2:11). The horse is also a figure of the Chinese zodiac. The last incarnation of Vishnu, when he comes to bring salvation to the world, is to be the horse Kalki. Mohammed rode a horse named Al-Borak from Mecca to Medina and up to Heaven. Al-Borak, who was generally painted with the face of a woman, could predict danger and see the dead.

The terrifying Russian witch Baba Yaga was probably originally a horse-goddess. She lived in the depths of the woods in a house on chicken legs, surrounded by a fence made of human bones topped with skulls. She ate people like chickens, but the heroes in fairy tales often risked death by visiting her in search of help through magic or sage advice. Baba Yaga had a herd of mares, which were her daughters, and sometimes Baba Yaga herself became a mare. In the story of "Maria Morevna," recorded by Aleksandr Afanas'ev, Prince Ivan went to Baba Yaga and asked for a horse fast enough to escape Koschei, the spirit of death, who had stolen his bride. Ivan obtained this by tending the horses of Baba Yaga with the help of friendly animals for three days. With the help of the horse from Baba Yaga, Prince Ivan rescued his bride. His beloved, Maria Morevna, was a spirit of vegetation who had to spend part of the year in the underworld, much like the Greek deity Persephone. Koschei was a ruler of the underworld, similar to the Greek Hades or the Roman Pluto. Baba Yaga, though far less benevolent, has some of the traits of Persephone's mother, Demeter, who was also the mistress of horses.

A similar myth may be the origin of the famous English story of Lady Godiva. Lord Leofric had taxed people beyond what they could bear. His wife, Godiva, spoke in their defense, and he agreed to reduce his taxes if she would ride naked through the streets. She did so, covered only with her long hair. The people turned away except for one Tom, who peeped and was struck blind. Leofric, in shame, revoked all taxes except those on horses. The horse was also sacred to Freya, the Norse goddess of love. An image of the goddess was drawn through the streets in spring. Like both Persephone and Maria Morevna, Godiva here was a personification of vegetable life. Leofric was a spirit of winter, while Peeping Tom may originally have been a human sacrifice that accompanied the rites of Freya.

Horses had often been associated with fertility even before domestication, and so, as the story of Lady Godiva illustrates, the intimacy of horse and rider seemed to have a sexual side. People worried that grooms might mate with horses, producing who-knows-what dreadful progeny, and such unnatural unions were often punishable by death in the late Middle Ages and Renaissance. Since horses were most closely associated with masculine power, women had to be especially careful. Modesty required that they not place their legs around the animal. Sir Thomas More had a ribald as well as saintly side. Once he rebuked his daughter, who did not wish to ride sidesaddle as befitting a lady, by saying, "Well, my girl, no one can deny that you are ready for a husband, since your legs can straddle so large a horse" (Smith, pp. 151–152). In William Shakespeare's *Othello*, when the young Venetian girl Desdemona has eloped with the Moor Othello, the villainous Iago says to her father, "You'll have your daughter covered with a Barbary horse; you'll have your nephews neigh to you; you'll have coursers for cousins . . . " (1.1). Enemies of the Russian empress Catherine spread rumors, which circulate to this day, that she copulated with her horses. The horse was often considered a disguise for the Devil or a companion for a witch.

The sexuality of horses was sacralized in the figure of the unicorn. This fantastic animal had, in the course of a long intricate history, taken on features of the ass, rhinoceros, narwhal, goat, and many other creatures. In medieval Europe the unicorn was thought of primarily as a horse with a single horn. That protuberance, clearly phallic, seemed to absorb and transform all that was disturbing in equine sexuality, leaving the animal divinely chaste. According to legend, the unicorn could not be caught by force, but it would come to a young girl and lay its horn in her lap. Then it might be captured without difficulty. This story reflected archaic mythology of the sacred hunt, as the young girl came to symbolize Mary and the unicorn to symbolize Christ. The capture and slaying of the unicorn became an allegorical crucifixion acted out not with malice but with solemnity in the tapestries and paintings of the Middle Ages. Nobody has entirely reconstructed the meaning of this elaborate parable, but it seems to be about domestication. Our sexuality, like the unicorn, may not be overcome through force of discipline, yet, like the unicorn, it can be tamed.

Archaic beliefs about horses show up frequently in European fairy tales. In "Faithful John" by the Grimm brothers (tale no. 6), ravens tell the servant that a horse will trot up to the young king and take him up into the sky forever. The king may be saved only if somebody jumps on the horse and shoots it quickly. This probably alludes to an archaic horse sacrifice that accompanied many shamanic journeys. In another Grimm's tale, "The Goose Girl" (no. 89), a princess speaks to the head of a beloved horse that has been sacrificed. The animal offers sympathy but no sage advice, showing that the old magic will not work in the modern world.

Many Catholic saints are patrons of horses, no doubt a legacy of pagan times. One is Saint Éloi, who was a blacksmith to the Frankish kings. Once, he was asked to shoe a horse possessed by the Devil. He blessed the animal, took off its legs, placed shoes on its feet, and then returned the limbs to their rightful places. Another patron of horses is Saint Stephen, the Church's first martyr. On his feast day, December 26, parishioners in Poland shower their priests with oats as a gift from their horses.

But horses, like most animals that had once been sacred, were often demonized in the late Middle Ages and Renaissance. The long association of horses with the poles of fertility and death did not always make them beloved; neither did their association with goddesses and with death. Horses became familiars of witches and, at times, even a disguise for the Devil. One example is from *The Quest of the Holy Grail*, an anonymous medieval romance from Britain in the early thirteenth century. Sir Perceval, the holy fool of Arthurian legend, found himself alone by a vast forest. A woman appeared mysteriously and offered him a horse in exchange for his service, and Perceval accepted with delight. She went for a moment into the depths of the woods and returned leading an enormous black horse. Perceval could not look on the horse without fear, but he mounted it and galloped on until the trees ended and a wide river crossed the path. No bridge was to be seen, yet the horse continued onward. Unable to stop, Perceval made the sign of the cross. At that instant the horse threw him to the ground and plunged into the river. Perceval heard howling and shrieking, as flames rose from the water. The woman and the horse had both been devils.

Jonathan Swift, in the fourth book of his novel *Gulliver's Travels* (1726), tells of being left by pirates on an island ruled by civilized horses. The horses are extremely clean and gracious, and their society is ruled entirely by reason. They practice agriculture, for which they have domesticated cattle. They call themselves "houhynhnms." Alongside them live hairy creatures known as "yahoos," that is, human beings. The yahoos swing from trees and love to wallow in filth. The houhynhnms cannot believe it when the hero tells them of his native England, where horses are bridled and people are free.

The equestrian or knightly tradition lasted longest on the American continents, where there was plenty of open space and large herds of feral horses roamed the plains, in the United States and Argentina, for example. In stories of the American old West, wandering cowboys were a bit like the knights-errant of the European Middle Ages, moving from one town to the next in search of fortune and adventure. Even today, some police departments use horses, which are more maneuverable than motorized vehicles. But the role of horses in battle was steadily reduced as the world industrialized, and horses came to be associated more with recreation than with work.

They also became more closely associated with women than with men. The novel *Black Beauty* by Anna Sewell, first published in 1876, started a tradition of horse stories primarily for young girls. The book is a fictive autobiography of a stallion that draws carriages, starting with his childhood in open meadows, going through his adventures with several masters, and ending with a pleasant retirement on a farm. Horses now represent a gentle aspect of male sexuality, which contrasts with the brutal masculinity that is so often celebrated in the mass media of today.

The horse may be less empathetic than the dog and less mysterious than the cat, but it has probably done more to form human society than either canines or felines. Today, however, horses are becoming nostalgic reminders of our past. Horses are still a common means of transportation in remote areas where there are few roads. Their maneuverability still makes them helpful to police, and they have been trained to enter apartments and walk up stairs. But urban horses are rare enough to make many bystanders stare in surprise and admiration whenever they appear in public.

The horse race is now a gathering point for many who seem in some way to have been bypassed by the modern world, from aristocrats to the Mafia. Though horses are far slower and less powerful than our motors today, the horse still provides the ultimate model for our locomotives, automobiles, and rocket ships—for anything that is fast and sleek. Today, the word "horsepower" is still used to denote a unit of force in motors. The metaphor of the Trojan Horse is more widely used than perhaps any other image from the ancient world. It can refer to just about anything, from internal subversion in a government to a computer virus. In the late 1970s a nuclear power company was called Trojan and had a horse as its logo. Demonstrators against nuclear power in California built a large wooden horse. As they paraded it around, out popped a person dressed as the Grim Reaper with his scythe.

Selected References

Afanas'ev, Aleksandr, ed. *Russian Fairy Tales.* Trans. Norbert Guterman. New York: Pantheon, 1973.

Clutton-Brock, Juliet. *Horse Power: A History of the Horse and the Donkey in Human Societies.* Cambridge: Harvard University Press, 1992.

Dent, Anthony. *The Horse: Through Fifty Centuries of Civilization.* New York: Holt, Rinehart, and Winston, 1974.

Eliade, Mircea. *Shamanism: Archaic Techniques of Ecstasy.* Princeton, NJ: Princeton University Press, 1974.

Grimm, Jacob, and Wilhelm. *The Complete Fairy Tales of the Brothers Grimm.* Trans. Jack Zipes. New York: Bantam Books, 1987.

Hyland, Ann. *Equus: The Horse in the Roman World.* New Haven: Yale University Press, 1990.

———. *The Medieval Warhorse from Byzantium to the Crusades.* Conshohocken, PA: Combined Books, 1994.

Matarasso, Pauline Maud, trans. *The Quest of the Holy Grail.* New York: Penguin, 1969.

Plutarch. *Plutarch's Morals* (4 vols.). Trans. Robert Midgley et al. London: Thomas Bradyll, 1704.

Sewell, Anna. *Black Beauty.* New York: Dover, 1999.

Shakespeare, William. *Othello the Moor of Venice.* New York: Dover, 1996.

Smith, Lacey Baldwin. *Fools, Martyrs, Traitors: The Story of Martyrdom in the Western World.* New York: Knopf, 1997.

Swift, Jonathan. *Gulliver's Travels.* New York: Penguin, 1996.

Hummingbird

See Ostrich, Hummingbird, Parrot, and Peacock

Hyena

I will neither yield to the song of the siren nor the voice of the hyena. . . .
—George Chapman, *Eastward Ho* (act 5, scene 1)

If hyenas are "laughing," what is the joke? Maybe it is our efforts to put everything into neat categories. As intermediate creatures somewhere between felines and canines, hyenas have always filled people with consternation. Legends also make their gender indeterminate, and this has some basis in observation. In contrast to the pattern found in most animals, the female hyenas tend to be a bit larger than the males. More remarkable, the females have a bulge of skin that resembles a male sex organ. The Greco-Roman author Aelian claimed that the hyena changed its sex every year. According to Aelian, the hyena could send the power of sleep with a mere touch of its left paw. The shadow of a hyena cast against the full moon reduced dogs to silence, so they could be carried off without resistance. The hyena imitated the human voice so as to lure dogs and even men to their doom. In seventeenth-century England, Edward Topsell reported a rumor that hyenas could be impregnated by the wind.

From Africa to Europe, the hyena has usually been considered treacherous, stupid, and cowardly. One possible reason is that hyenas occupy roughly the same habitats in Africa as lions, and they often live by scavenging. Lions are symbols of kingship, making hyenas seem like venial courtiers. According to medieval European bestiaries, the hyena (sometimes called the "yena") lived in tombs and devoured dead bodies. Bestiaries also reported that the hyena had a stone in its head. When this was taken out and placed under the tongue of a person, it would enable the man or woman to see the future.

One rare legend makes the hyena not only gentle but also motherly. Saint Macarius of Alexandria lived as a hermit in the desert, where his skill in healing was known even to the animals. One day a mother hyena came to him bearing her baby in her mouth. Saint Macarius picked up the infant, looked it over, and realized that it was stricken with blindness. He made the cross over the baby hyena's eyes, whereupon the baby immediately went to its mother's breast and began to suck. Later, in gratitude, the mother hyena brought Saint Macarius the skin of a freshly killed sheep. Saint Macarius, troubled by the mother's having killed the sheep, refused to accept the gift. The mother bowed her head and begged him. Finally the holy man agreed, but only if the mother would promise henceforth not to hurt the poor by taking their sheep and to take only meat that was already dead. When the mother assented, he took the sheepskin and slept upon it until his death.

In the twentieth century, other maligned animals such as wolves have been redeemed, but the reputation of the hyena has changed little. In the 1994 Disney film *The Lion King*, the evil lion who wishes to claim the throne aligns himself with the hyenas. The makers of the film wished to be ecologically sensitive and to avoid condemning any animal, so they usually made the hyena leaders more goofy than malign. Nevertheless, the hyenas advancing in step against the lions seemed like Nazi soldiers. Several naturalists, perhaps beginning with Saint Macarius, have pleaded with the public without success to redeem the reputation of the hyena.

Selected References

Aelian. *On Animals* (3 vols.). Trans. A. F. Scholfield. Cambridge: Harvard University Press, 1972.

Glickman, Stephen. "The Spotted Hyena from Aristotle to the Lion King: Reputation Is Everything." *Social Research* 62, 3 (fall 1995): 501–539.

Topsell, Edward, and Thomas Muffet. *The History of Four-Footed Beasts and Serpents and Insects.* New York: Da Capo, 1967 (facsimile of 1658 edition).

Waddell, Helen, trans. *Beasts and Saints.* Grand Rapids, MI: William B. Eerdmans, 1996.

White, T. H., trans. *The Book of Beasts: Being a Translation from a Latin Bestiary of the Twelfth Century.* New York: Dover, 1984.

I

Ibis
See Heron, Ibis, Crane, and Stork

J

Jackal
See Fox, Jackal, and Coyote

Jackass
See Ass, Mule, and Camel

Jaguar
See Lion, Tiger, Panther, and Jaguar

Kingfisher
See Seagull, Albatross, and Other Seabirds

L

Lark

See Nightingale, Cuckoo, Lark, and Other Musical Birds

Leopard

See Lion, Tiger, Panther, and Jaguar

Lion, Tiger, Panther, and Jaguar

> *For he is of the tribe of Tiger.*
> *For the cherub cat is a term of the Angel Tiger.*
> —Christopher Smart, "My Cat Jeoffrey"

The big cats are all notable for their ability to fight and kill, yet in legend they are as various as our feelings about power. Lions are social animals that live in prides, in which the females do most of the hunting. They live on open plains, though their once vast range is now reduced to the savannas of Africa. Lions are often followed by scavengers, from vultures to hyenas, which has given rise to the idea that they are kings attended by a court. The male has an enormous head and a luxuriant mane, which suggests the sun sending forth rays. Tigers, by contrast, are usually solitary, and they are found in the jungles of Asia and the forbidding hillsides of Siberia. They are the only large mammals that will occasionally attack human beings, a feature that can make them seem like either bandits or simply untamed forces of nature. Panthers, which are almost identical to leopards except for the color of their skin, are smaller than either lions or tigers, and they rely more on stealth and speed in hunting. They are able to climb trees, where they can hide meat from scavengers and go unnoticed themselves while they observe their surroundings, and from where they can pounce suddenly upon their prey. Panthers and leopards are solitary, nocturnal hunters, often associated with chthonic realms.

Even in Paleolithic times, the great cats seem to have had a special religious significance, and they were given a place of honor among the cave paintings of Lascaux in a cavern known as the Chamber of Felines. At the dawn of urban civilization, people thought of these animals as primarily feminine. Our words "female" and "feline" both ultimately come from the Latin *"felare,"* meaning "to suck." Several figurines of women, possibly goddesses, accompanied by great cats have been found at Çatal Hüyük in Turkey, the earliest known walled town.

In early pantheons, the great cats are most closely associated with feminine deities. Among the foremost of these was the Egyptian Hathor, who was the goddess of love, dance, and feminine arts but was also capable of great fury. When men rebelled against the sun god Ra, she attacked them as a lioness and soon developed an insatiable thirst for blood. When Ra himself was satisfied that the rebellion had been defeated, she continued to kill, and the gods feared that she would destroy all of humankind. They left out vats of red wine, and mistaking the liquor for blood, she drank it, fell asleep, and finally awakened with her anger appeased. Hathor in her incarnation as a furious avenger was known as Sekmet and was depicted with the body of a woman and the head of a lioness. The Babylonian goddess Ishtar, in her capacity as a deity of war, was depicted standing upon a lion. Lions were harnessed to the chariot of Cybele, the Syrian goddess who was adopted by the Romans as a mother-goddess, their "Magna Mater."

Male lions, however, are just as common as lionesses in the visual arts of the ancient world. Both the Egyptians and Mesopotamians placed stone lions as guardians on each side of the doorways to temples and palaces, a practice that eventually spread eastward all the way to China. In Sumero-Babylonian animal proverbs, which are among the very earliest literary works to have survived, the lion had already been recognized as the king of beasts. This motif soon became one of the most widely established literary conventions and can be found in the fables attributed to the Greek Aesop. The lion often appears as a figure of brute power that terrorizes other animals, and the sly fox in one fable observes that many tracks lead into the lion's cave but none lead out. The lion is not always dominant, however, and in another fable is beaten by the ass and other animals it once tormented. In African legends as well, the majestic lion frequently falls victim to weaker but cleverer creatures such as the hare. The motif of a lion as monarch has been used in the Hindu-Persian *Panchatantra*, the medieval European stories of Renard the Fox, the Narnia stories by C. S. Lewis, and countless other works throughout the world.

To kill a lion was a supreme achievement for a warrior in the ancient world, and kings of Egypt and Mesopotamia frequently had

Illustration by Julius Schnorr Carolsfeld from the mid-nineteenth century to the story of Daniel, who was thrown to the lions but remained unharmed.

themselves depicted hunting lions. Many heroes of the ancient world, including Gilgamesh, Hercules, and Samson, were conventionally depicted wearing the skin of a lion. The Greco-Roman fable attributed to Babrius told of how a lion and a man were once traveling together when they passed a sculpture of a hero strangling the king of beasts. The man pointed to it as proof of human superiority, to which the lion replied that if lions had done the carving, "You would see many men victims of lions" (Perry, p. 479). Even the Hebrews, who generally despised predators, could not help feeling some admiration for these animals. The lion became a symbol of the biblical Judah and later of Saint Mark the Evangelist and even of Christ himself.

Romans imported vast numbers of lions for their gladiatorial games, where the animals represented the emperor as they devoured criminals before a raucous audience. Since lions do not readily attack human beings, the animals were starved or specially trained for the job. One popular story that may have had a historical basis tells of a runaway slave named Androcles who had been recaptured and placed in the arena with a lion. Instead of devouring him, the lion licked his feet. A leopard was immediately let loose, but the lion killed it. The emperor Drusus ordered the slave to come forward and asked why the lion had spared him. Androcles told how, after extreme mistreatment, he had escaped his master and taken refuge in a cave. The lion had come to Androcles and held up a bloodstained paw, from which the fugitive pulled out a thorn. From that time on the lion had fed him, bringing part of every kill. Moved by the story, Drusus granted both Androcles and the lion their freedom. The circuses relied on theatrics almost as much as they did on blood, and this incident could have been staged. The Romans did have remarkable skill in training lions. According to Pliny, Mark Anthony harnessed lions to his chariot and rode around with a courtesan, an event that shocked his contemporaries and may have contributed to his eventual downfall. The emperor Caracalla later had a pet lion that sat by his table, slept in his bedroom, and even was kissed by him in public. At any rate, Saint Jerome, who lived as a hermit in a cave, was later reputed to have tamed a lion in the same way as Androcles, and a lion was traditionally painted at his feet.

In heraldry, the lion has always represented royalty and is often depicted wearing a crown. This symbolism was even adopted in areas that had been free of lions since Paleolithic times, such as China and western Europe. Precisely because actual lions were unknown outside a few royal menageries, it was easy to stylize these animals into symbols. King Richard I, known as the Lion-Hearted for his courage in battle, chose three golden lions against a red background for the coat of arms of England. The English lion and the Scottish unicorn now flank the heraldic emblem of Great Britain.

Eventually the lion became so deeply associated with the institution of kingship that it was next to impossible for most Europeans to think of the animal in any other context. Monarchists liked to imagine the lion as dignified to the point of blandness, and they excused the predatory nature of the beast by saying it would kill only as much as it needed to eat. In the modern era, however, democratically inclined people often stigmatized lions as vicious.

The nineteenth-century French Romantic Eugène Delacroix was one of the very few who tried to imagine the animal behind the icon, though he may have celebrated the lion's ferocity too exclusively in his paintings of bloody battles between lions and Arabs. In the same era, the lion tamer became a feature of any large circus. He would be a burly man, often wearing leopard-skin trunks, who, by cracking a

whip, would compel lions or other big cats to obey him. The spectacle dramatized the ability of humanity to control nature, as well as the dominance of men over women.

The tiger was a more unequivocally romantic beast and has always been admired almost as a powerful natural force, as one might admire a storm or volcano. Malaysian myths tell of a city that tigers have built entirely from human skin, bones, hair, and other body parts. The Hindu Kali, goddess of time, who wears a necklace of skulls and holds a sword of destruction in one of her many hands, has often been portrayed riding upright upon a tiger. In his aspect as a destroyer, the god Siva wears the skin of a tiger. We should remember, however, that the annihilating power of these figures was viewed less as evil than as simply part of the cosmic cycle.

In China the tiger, ruler of the earth, has often been paired with the dragon, ruler of the sky, as the greatest primordial powers. The dragon creates clouds, while the breath of the tiger becomes wind, and together they bring rain. The tiger is associated with autumn, since it resembles that season in its violence and destruction. The tiger, rather than the lion, is called "king of beasts" in Asia (Sun, p. 57). It is the third sign of the Chinese zodiac and is often depicted with wings. Patriarchs of Taoism have been represented riding upon tigers, signifying their ability to live in harmony with the elements.

The tiger entered Western imagination as Alexander the Great invaded India. The god Dionysus, who was sometimes identified with

Alexander, occasionally was shown in a chariot pulled by tigers, especially crossing the Tigris River on the way to India. The Romans, who were attracted to exoticism as much as they were to violence, may have had tigers in their circuses. Pliny the Elder reported how people accomplished the seemingly impossible task of capturing tiger cubs. The captor would steal several cubs, jump on a fast horse, and race away. When the tigress would start to overtake him, he would drop one cub, forcing the tigress to pause and take it back to her lair. She would then start off again after the captor, and this cycle might be repeated several times until at last the man would reach his ship with a single cub. This story was frequently repeated in medieval bestiaries but with an additional twist. The horseman steals only one cub, but he throws glass balls to the tigress, and she mistakes her reflection for a cub.

Medieval depictions of Eden usually included the lion but almost never the tiger. The tiger was also too unequivocally frightening to be used in heraldry, but it again entered Western awareness when India became part of the British Empire. Thomas Bewick wrote toward the end of the eighteenth century that the tiger "fears neither the sight nor the opposition of man . . . and it is even said to prefer human flesh to that of any other animal" (p. 206). For the British colonists and many of their Indian supporters, extermination of tigers became a humanitarian mission, and many boasted of killing hundreds. Meanwhile, the most intense opposition to British rule in southern India came from Tipu Sultan, who believed that it was "better to live two days as a tiger than two hundred years as a sheep" (Courtney, p. 48). He sat on a tiger throne, had the stripes of a tiger placed on the uniforms of his soldiers, and emulated a tiger's reputed cruelty.

It was at this time that William Blake wrote "The Tyger," perhaps the most famous animal poem of the modern era, which began:

Tyger! Tyger! Burning bright
In the forests of the night,
What immortal hand or eye
Could frame thy fearful symmetry?

In what distant deeps or skies
Burnt the fire of thine eyes?
On what wings dare he aspire?
What the hand dare seize the fire?

Tales of the cruelty of Tipu Sultan, which were filtering back to England, probably influenced Blake, and he might have seen the tigers on display in the menagerie at the Tower of London. The illustration that Blake painted to accompany the poem, however, shows far more affection than awe. It is clearly a domestic housecat, though perhaps he intended to show how every pussycat has a tiger inside.

The beauty and terror that are inextricably blended in the tiger are expressed in the parable called "The Lady and the Tiger," which anonymously passes through our culture like a legend—everybody has heard it, yet hardly anybody knows from where it has come. It was actually first published by Frank Stockton in the *Century Magazine* of 1882. The king had decreed that justice for a serious crime was to be decided by a test in which the accused would be placed in a large arena and, before spectators, forced to choose between two doors. Behind one door would be a tiger that would rip him apart with its claws. Behind the other would be a lady, carefully chosen as a match for him and whom he would have to marry. The king heard that his daughter and a common man were in love, and he ordered the young man sent to the arena to be judged by providence. The princess found out what lay behind the doors and made a secret signal to her lover. The story ended with the famous question: "Which came out of the opened door—the lady or the tiger?" (Weinberger, p. 45). Victorians were obsessed by this sort of choice: bourgeois domesticity or unadulterated passion? But the beautiful lady, as Sigmund Freud recognized, is really an aspect of the tiger, and marriage to her is a sort of annihilation.

In the twentieth century the tiger took over many symbolic values previously associated with the lion. In his poem "Geronition," T. S. Eliot used the tiger as a symbol of Christ. Advertisers have constantly exploited the primitive energy associated with the tiger. Esso Petroleum, for example, has since the mid-1960s advertised gasoline with the slogan "Put a tiger in your tank!" (Courtney, p. 64). Symbolic importance in human culture, however, often makes animals more vulnerable in the wild, since it means that people will be more drawn to hunt them for folk remedies or sport. The Caspian tiger became extinct in the 1970s and the Javan tiger a decade later, while the few surviving species continue to hold on very precariously.

In the legends of Africans, who had direct experience with both lions and leopards, the lion may often have been the ruler of animals, but the leopard generally inspired greater awe. The black color of the panther enables it to blend into forests, while the spots of the leopard suggest innumerable eyes. The legendary ancestor of the kings of Dahomey and other African lands is a leopard that came out of a river to lie with a woman, and the ferocity of the beast explained its penchant for war. The biblical prophet Jeremiah, frustrated by the inability of the Hebrews to put aside their wicked ways, asked, "Can . . . the leopard change his spots?" (13:23).

The leopard or panther was sacred to Osiris, god of the dead, in ancient Egypt. The Greeks identified Osiris with Dionysus, and the priests of both gods wore the skins of a panther. Panthers generally drew the chariot of Dionysus, and they were sometimes depicted in his entourage. Both of these deities, in turn, often came to be identified with Jesus, and writers of the Middle Ages often praised the panther. Medieval bestiaries told how other animals would follow the panther drawn by the sweetness of its breath. Only the dragon would flee and take refuge in a cave, much as the Devil would run in fear from Christ.

With the end of the Middle Ages, however, many people strove to cleanse Christianity of pagan elements, and the panther, so important in pre-Christian religions, was consequently condemned for viciousness. At the beginning of Dante's *Divine Comedy*, the narrator encounters three predators in a dark wood: a panther, a she-wolf, and a lion. The panther is the first to threaten him, but he is saved from the beasts by the intercession of the poet Virgil.

In the early twentieth century, the poet Rainer Maria Rilke lamented the loss of primeval wildness in his poem "The Panther." It describes a panther pacing ritualistically in a zoo, where it can see little besides bars, and concludes:

> From time to time, the curtain of the pupils
> is raised without a sound. . . . An image flows inside
> and ripples through the stillness of his limbs
> to enter in his heart and disappear. (trans. Boria Sax)

The iconographic use of the panther in recent times has veered between anger and nostalgia. A militant African-American group that supported armed revolution in the 1960s and 1970s was known as the Black Panthers.

Perhaps the most mysterious big cat of all is the jaguar, which is native to Latin America. The motif of the jaguar appears so often in the arts of early Native American communities that historians of religion believe it may have been the master of animals or even the supreme god. In tribes in Bolivia at least until very recent times, to kill a jaguar with a wooden spear has been a test of manhood used in the initiation of a warrior. Shamans are believed to be able to turn themselves into jaguars. During an eclipse, people howl to scare the jaguar that is trying to devour the sun. The cult of the jaguar may well be felt more viscerally precisely because it has never, as far as anybody knows today, been systematized into a formal mythology. In historically recent times, however, machines have increasingly taken over the symbolism of animals, and for most people today the "jaguar" is a luxury car.

Selected References

Auguet, Roland. *Cruelty and Civilization: The Roman Games.* New York: Barnes and Noble, 1972.

Bewick, Thomas. *A General History of Quadrupeds.* Leicester: Winward, 1980 (1790).

Blake, William. "The Tyger." In *The Oxford Book of Animal Poems.* Ed. Michael Harrison and Christopher Stuart-Clark. New York: Oxford University Press, 1992.

Courlander, Harold. *A Treasury of African Folklore: The Oral Literature, Traditions, Myths, Legends, Epics, Tales, Recollections, Wisdom, Sayings, and Humor of Africa.* New York: Marlowe, 1996.

Courtney, Nicholas. *The Tiger: Symbol of Freedom.* New York: Quartet Books, 1980.

Johnson, Buffie. *Lady of the Beasts: Ancient Images of the Goddess and Her Sacred Animals.* San Francisco: Harper and Row, 1981.

London, H. Stanford, et al. *The Queen's Beasts: An Account with New Drawings of the Heraldic Animals Which Stood at the Entrance to Westminster Abbey on the Occasion of the Coronation of Her Majesty Queen Elizabeth II.* London: Newman Neame, 1953.

Osborne, Harold. *South American Mythology.* New York: Hamlyn, 1975.

Perry, Ben Edwin, ed. and trans. *Babrius and Phaedrus.* Cambridge: Harvard University Press, 1990.

Pliny. *Natural History* (10 vols.). Trans. H. Rackham, W. H. S. Jones, et al. Cambridge: Harvard University Press, 1953.

Rilke, Rainer Maria. "Der Panther." Deutsche Geidchte: Von den Anfängen bis zur Gegenwart. Ed. Beno von Weise. Düsseldorf: August Bebel Verlag, 1956, p. 566.

Rybot, Doris. *It Began Before Noah.* London: Michael Joseph, 1972.

Schrader, J. L. *A Medieval Bestiary.* New York: Metropolitan Museum of Art, 1986.

Sun, Ruth Q. *The Asian Animal Zodiac.* Edison, NJ: Castle Books, 1974.

Weinberger, Eliot. "Paper Tiger." In *Works on Paper, 1980–1986.* New York: New Directions, 1986, pp. 44–57.

Lizard

See Snake, Lizard, and Related Animals

Locust

See Grasshopper, Locust, Cricket, Cicada, and Mantis

Louse

See Fly, Louse, and Flea

M

Mantis
See Grasshopper, Locust, Cricket, Cicada, and Mantis

Merpeople
See Salmon and Carp

Monkey
See Ape and Monkey

Moth
See Butterfly and Moth

Mouse
See Rat and Mouse

Mule
See Ass, Mule, and Camel

Octopus

See Starfish, Clam, Octopus, and Other Creatures of the Sea Floor

Orangutan

See Ape and Monkey

Ostrich, Hummingbird, Parrot, and Peacock

> *Remember that the most beautiful things in the world are the most useless, peacocks and lilies for instance.*
> —John Ruskin, *The Stones of Venice*

The brilliant plumage of some birds, like the singing of others, tends to be a means by which the males attempt to attract females. From the point of view of contemporary human culture, this may seem paradoxical, since human beings today tend to place more emphasis on feminine than masculine appearance. It is primarily women who wear the brilliant plumage of birds, whether on hats or in jewelry, but this has not always been the case. Among Native Americans, for example, male warriors have usually worn the most opulent feathers.

Perhaps, however, the association of women with plumage does go back to ancient times, specifically to Egypt. Maat, the goddess of cosmic harmony, was one of the few deities who were generally depicted in fully human form, and she wore a large ostrich feather in her hair. Though styles of dress and appearance are notoriously fickle, she still appears elegant, dignified, and remarkably contemporary about three millennia after the paintings were executed. When souls were to be judged in the next world, to decide whether the person would join the immortals or be devoured by demons, the heart of the deceased would be weighed against Maat, who was sometimes represented by an ostrich feather.

Nevertheless, the fashionable plumes often received more respect than the birds they came from, which were often described in

Adam and Eve by Albrecht Dürer (1504). The first man and woman are living peacefully among the animals before the Fall, when the cat does not even seem to notice the rat in front of it. Note especially the parrot on a sprig in the hand of Adam, probably a branch from the Tree of Life, which the first man will carry with him when exiled from Paradise. (Metropolitan Museum of Art, Fletcher Fund, #MM2218B)

very bizarre ways. Ancient writers such as Pliny and Aelian maintained the ostrich was able to eat and digest virtually anything, even stones. Pliny added that the bird buried its head in the sand to evade danger, an idea that has by no means disappeared today. According to medieval bestiaries, the ostrich could divine when to lay eggs by watching the stars. !Kung Bushmen accord the eggs of an ostrich supernatural power, since they are so hard that no animal's jaws can break them. In Europe these were often taken for the eggs of a griffin and placed in royal treasuries. Sometimes the "griffin eggs" were made into goblets in the belief that they would change color when touched by poison.

The hummingbird has been admired not only for its bright, iridescent colors but also for its speed. It is able to hover in one place, switch direction instantly, and fly backward, possessing the sort of maneuverability valued by military commanders. Despite, or partly because of, its diminutive size, this bird was an attribute of the Aztec god of war, Huitzilopochtli, whose headdress was made of hummingbird feathers. The Mayan deity Quetzalcoatl, in his incarnation as a serpent, also had plumes of a hummingbird. Battle seems to be almost universally associated with eroticism, and plumes of the hummingbird have also been frequently used in love charms.

The parrot of myth and legend is generally a peaceful bird but one that seems almost too splendid for this world. In the Hindu-Persian *Panchatantra*, the god Indra kept a parrot of extraordinary beauty and intelligence named Blossom. One day as the parrot was sitting in the palm of its master's hand, Yama, lord of the underworld, appeared. Blossom was terrified, and the deities begged Yama to spare the parrot. The dark figure replied that that was not under his control, so the gods took their petition to Death himself. On beholding the visage of the Grim Reaper, the parrot perished in terror.

The ancient Egyptians kept rose-ringed parakeets in cages as pets, but the real popularity of parrots in the Mediterranean area dates from the time of Alexander the Great, who brought back previously unknown varieties from India. They attained new popularity with the vast expansion of maritime trade at the end of the Middle Ages. Much of this exploration was motivated by a longing to find a place of primal innocence, perhaps even the original Eden. In an engraving of 1504 entitled *Adam and Eve,* the German artist Albrecht Dürer depicted a parrot perched on a sprig from the Tree of Life, held by Adam as he speaks with Eve in Paradise.

For people in the Northern Hemisphere, the visual splendor of parrots has always seemed to be heightened by their exoticism and remarkable ability to mimic the human voice. According to medieval legend, a parrot had announced the coming of the Virgin Mary, and artists often painted exotic birds beside her and the infant Jesus. One cardinal during the Renaissance reportedly paid a hundred gold pieces for a parrot that could clearly recite the entire Apostles' Creed. On the other hand, some people view innocence as an invitation to corruption; rough mariners enjoyed teaching parrots obscenities. The commerce in parrots was from the start a rather shady business, in which theft and smuggling were common, and it now threatens to drive many of the remaining species of parrots to extinction.

Perhaps the most opulent bird of all, the peacock is originally from India but was imported to the Mediterranean world in very early times. The spreading tail of the peacock is an ancient symbol of the sun,

The parrot, with its brilliant plumage, has often been associated with royalty, as in this print by J. J. Grandville.

the feathers standing for rays of light. The peacock was sacred to Zeus and, most especially, to his wife, Hera. According to one myth, after changing the maiden Io into a heifer as punishment for her affair with Zeus, Hera sent the hundred-eyed giant Argos to watch over her. Taking the form of a woodpecker, Zeus signaled the location of Argos to Hermes, who then killed the monster. Hera took the eyes of Argos and, as a memorial, placed them in the tail of a peacock. The story is a bit ironic, since the peacock spreads its tail as part of a mating dance. The eyes, then, are a warning to young ladies not to trust the macho posturing of men.

The peacock, however, became ever more a symbol of splendor over the centuries. It was the mount of Karrtikeya, the Hindu god of war, as well as the mount of Brahma and his wife, Sarasvati. The kings of Persia sat on a peacock throne, and Chinese emperors from the Ming dynasty forward bestowed peacock feathers as a sign of favor. Aristocratic gardens throughout Eurasia, which were meant to be a re-creation of Paradise, had peacocks strolling about the grass. In Christianity, the peacock became a symbol of the Resurrection, as well as of the all-seeing eye of the Church. In the modern period, however, as governments became democratic and people increasingly distrusted royalty, the peacock became a symbol of vanity. Finally, as advertisers revived the abandoned heraldic symbols of an earlier era, the peacock was used to represent the wonders of color in film and television.

Selected References

Cogger, Harold G., et al, eds. *Encyclopedia of Animals.* San Francisco: Fog City Press, 1993.

Eisler, Colin. *Dürer's Animals.* Washington, DC: Smithsonian Institution Press, 1991.

Ryder, Arthur. *The Panchatantra.* Chicago: University of Chicago Press, 1964.

Owl

Now the wasted brands do glow,
Whilst the screech-owl, screeching loud,
Puts the wretch, that lies in woe,
In remembrance of a shroud.
—William Shakespeare, *A Midsummer Night's Dream* (act 5, scene 1)

Anybody who has come across the eyes of an owl shining alone in the night will have no trouble understanding why owls have always been associated with the dead. Especially in colder regions of the Northern Hemisphere, owls are often at least partly white, and their feathers eerily reflect the moonlight. Not only does the owl look like an apparition, but its call is usually a drawn-out, wavering note that easily suggests the muffled voice of a spirit. Owls are attracted to places of burial by the smell of decaying flesh, and they could easily have been taken for the spirits of the deceased. These birds also have exceptionally fine sight at night, and in total darkness they can navigate by hearing or, with some species, even by echolocation. The ability of owls in flight to locate mice far below still sometimes impresses researchers as almost supernatural. The ancient Egyptians represented part of the soul, called the *"ba,"* as a bird with a human head, and pictures of it in *The Egyptian Book of the Dead* somewhat resemble an owl. In mythology and literature, death is intimately associated with wisdom, and the owl is an ancient symbol of both.

With most varieties of owls, the female is a bit larger than the male, which may partially explain why owls often symbolize primeval feminine power. In the Sumerian poem "The Huluppu Tree," the goddess Lilith made her home in the hollow of a tree until the hero Gilgamesh cut the tree down to make a throne for Inanna, the Queen of Heaven. Owls often nest in such places, and Lilith, who became a demon in Hebrew tradition, is referred to as a "screech owl" in Isaiah (24:14). Babylonian reliefs from the early second millennium showed a goddess-demon, probably Lilith, with the claws and wings of an owl, sometimes with owls at her side. Ever since, owls have been the frequent companions of sorceresses and goddesses. Athena, the Greek goddess of wisdom and war, is also closely associated with the owl. Homer refers to her as "owl eyed," and the earliest depictions represent her as a woman with the head of an owl. She was later portrayed holding an owl aloft in one hand. The Latin word for owl, *"strix,"* is the origin of *"striga,"* or "witch." In *The Golden Ass* by Lucius Apuleius, written in first-century Rome, a witch flies off at night in the form of an owl.

The owl is a loner among birds, a figure of both awe and revul-

Sepa, a Chthonic God of Egypt associated with the Owl.

sion. In one tale from the Hindu-Persian *Panchatantra,* the birds were so impressed by the owl's venerable demeanor that they elected him king. During the day, when the owl was asleep, the crow mocked the choice, saying the owl was repulsive with his hooked nose and huge eyes. The birds rescinded their decision, but an enmity between owl and crow has remained to this day.

In the Middle Ages the owl often represented the Jews, for, like them, the bird was said to have "scorned the light." Writers of antiquity, including Pliny the Elder and Aelian, had observed that other birds mobbed the owl when it appeared during the day. This idea was used later in Christian Europe as a justification for attacks on Jews who ventured beyond their ghetto.

For Odo of Cheriton, a clergyman writing in Kent during the early thirteenth century, the owl represented the rich and powerful who abuse their position. In his fable "The Rose and the Birds," he told how the birds came upon a rose and decided that it should go to the most beautiful bird. They then debated whether this should be the dove, the parrot, or the peacock but had come to no decision when they went to sleep. The owl stole the rose during the night, so the other birds banished him from their presence, and they still attack him if he shows himself by day. "And what will happen on judgement day?" Odo continued. "Doubtless all the angels ... and just souls will—with screams and tortures—set upon such an owl" (p. 151). It is a conclusion that anticipates the peasants' revolts and other revolutionary movements that would start to become more common toward the end of the Middle Ages.

The aristocrats, who could be contemptuous of the masses, occasionally took the solitary nature of the owl as evidence of its superiority to other birds. A shield from Hungary at the end of the fifteenth century, now in the Metropolitan Museum of Art in New York, shows an owl, perched above the coat of arms of a noble family, saying, "Though I am hated by all the birds, I nevertheless enjoy that" (Schrader, p. 38).

At the same time, the image of the various birds ganging up on the owl clearly suggested the persecution of Christ. The full ambivalence that people felt toward the owl was expressed in a Middle English poem from the early twelfth century entitled *The Owl and the Nightingale,* which presented a heated debate on many subjects between the nocturnal bird of prey and the beloved songbird. When the nightingale accused the owl of filthy habits, the latter replied that it cleaned the churches and other buildings of mice. When the nightingale taunted the owl by saying that men used its dead body as a scarecrow, the owl replied that it was proud to be of service after death. The image of the stuffed owl, however, suggested a crucifix, which was also a sort of scarecrow set up to keep demons away. The owl boasted of being able to foresee the future and warn people of impending disaster. No judgment was rendered in the poem, but most readers think the owl got the better of its adversary. Medieval artists sometimes placed a cross above the head of an owl to indicate that it represented the Savior.

The idea that the cry of an owl prophesies death is found in a remarkable range of cultures from the Greeks and Romans to the Cherokee Indians. For the Navaho, the owl was a form taken by ghosts. For the Kiowa, it was a favored form of magicians after death. The Pueblo Indians would not enter a house where owl feathers or the body of an owl was displayed. For the Aztecs, an owl symbolized the god of the underworld, Techlotl. In the Aztec rites of human sacrifice, the heart of the victim was placed in a stone container decorated with an owl. Among several West African tribes such as the Yoruba, the owl is often a form taken by evil magicians, and simply to see or hear an owl can bring ill luck. For the Chinese, the great horned owl was the most powerful symbol of death.

In the modern period, however, life expectancy expanded dramatically, and people were no longer so constantly reminded of their mortality. In consequence, literature began to emphasize the reputation of the owl for wisdom, not necessarily somber, rather than for death. Since the nineteenth century the "wise old owl" is probably most familiar as a figure in books for children. In the film *Bambi* by Disney Studios (1942), an owl is even shown benevolently instructing baby rabbits and other creatures of the forest.

In J. K. Rowling's Harry Potter stories, wizards communicate by sending letters by owl. Harry, a budding young wizard who is learning magic at Hogwarts School, has an owl named Hedwig who keeps him company during lonely evenings. When not working as his messenger, she flies freely in and out of Harry's room, sometimes bringing back dead mice, and affectionately nibbles on his ear.

Nevertheless, the fear that owls traditionally aroused has by no means vanished entirely. In the late twentieth century, a proposal to control the population of rats by importing owls was raised several times in New York City. The idea never got very far, in part because the call and eyes of an owl during dark urban nights have proved too upsetting to people.

Selected References

Medlin, Faith. *Centuries of Owls in Art and the Written Word.* Norwalk, CT: Silvermine Publishers, 1968.

Odo of Cheriton. *The Fables of Odo of Cheriton.* Trans. John C. Jacobs. New York: Syracuse University Press, 1985.

Rowling, J. K. *Harry Potter and the Sorcerer's Stone.* New York: Scholastic/Arthur A. Levine Books, 1998.

Ryder, Arthur W., ed. *The Panchatantra.* Chicago: University of Chicago Press, 1964.

Schrader, J. L. *A Medieval Bestiary.* New York: Metropolitan Museum of Art, 1986.

Stone, Brian, trans. *The Owl and the Nightingale/Cleanness/St. Erkenwald.* 2nd ed. New York: Penguin, 1988.

Weinstein, Krystyna. *The Owl in Art, Myth, and Legend.* New York: Crescent Books, 1985.

Wolkstein, Diane, and Samuel Noah Kramer. *Inanna: Queen of Heaven and Earth.* New York: Harper and Row, 1982.

P

Panther
See Lion, Tiger, Panther, and Jaguar

Parrot
See Ostrich, Hummingbird, Parrot, and Peacock

Peacock
See Ostrich, Hummingbird, Parrot, and Peacock

Pelican
See Heron, Ibis, Crane, and Stork

Petrel
See Seagull, Albatross, and Other Seabirds

Phoenix
See Heron, Ibis, Crane, and Stork

Pig

> *I am fond of pigs. Dogs look up to us. Cats look down on us. Pigs treat us*
> *as equal.*
> —Attributed to Winston Churchill

Human attitudes toward pigs may cover an enormous range, but they are consistent in one respect. We almost always perceive pigs as being very close to the earth. Perhaps this is in part because they root up the ground. They are indispensable in looking for truffles in southern France, since their ability to smell things beneath the soil exceeds that of even dogs. They also sometimes take baths in mud to escape the heat. If we see earth as a prison of the spirit, we are likely to hate pigs; if we long for contact with the earth, we may love them. For better or

worse, they represent the joys and limitations of the flesh. The pig is holy, yet perfectly at home in Hell. The pig is gentle, yet harbors such wildness that even devils are terrified. The pig is revered, hated, loved, feared, admired, exploited, laughed at, and regarded as a friend. It is as if the pig were the entire animal kingdom in a single form.

The ambivalence was already present in the earliest civilizations. Pigs have large litters, which helped to make them a symbol of fertility. Ancient Egyptian women who wished to have children sometimes wore amulets depicting a sow and piglets. Pigs would also assist in agriculture by turning over the soil so it could be more easily plowed. Nut, the beloved Egyptian goddess of the sky, was sometimes depicted as a pig. Nevertheless, Set, the evil brother who kills the god Osiris, was also sometimes given porcine form. He is a very early image of the Devil. Traditional devils in medieval times and even today have the pointed ears and tusks of a boar.

Herodotus wrote that pigs were normally considered so unclean in Egypt that swineherds were banned from temples. Should an Egyptian accidentally touch a pig, he would immediately rush to a river and jump in, not even bothering to undress. Nevertheless, revulsion alternated with reverence. Osiris, the god of the dead, was associated with pigs. At his yearly festival, swine were sacrificed during the night of a full moon. On the next day everyone would eat pork, which was otherwise strictly forbidden. Those who were too poor to afford a pig would form one of dough, which they would then sacrifice.

In India, the bloodthirsty goddess Kali was represented as a black sow, perpetually giving birth and eating her offspring in an endless cycle. The *Ramayana*, an ancient Hindu epic, recorded how the earth once began to sink into the waters of oblivion. The god Brahma took the form of a boar and raised the world up on his tusks.

In Rome and Greece, Demeter, the gentle goddess of agriculture, was also associated with pigs. On the other hand, the Babylonian Tammuz, an agricultural deity, was, like the Greek Adonis, killed by boars while hunting. In the ancient world, boars were often feared not only for their fierceness but also for the damage they could do to crops by eating and tearing up fields. When heroes—such as Meleager, Theseus, and Hercules—did manage to kill boars, they often gained great renown.

In Homer's *Odyssey*, the sorceress Circe changed the crew of Odysseus into pigs for one year, after which Odysseus forced her to return them to their original form. She symbolized any temptress who inspires men to behave in a bestial way. Nearly a millennium after the age of Homer, Plutarch wrote a delightful satire entitled "On the Use of Reason by So-called 'Irrational' Animals." In Plutarch's version, at the request of Odysseus, Circe agreed to change the pigs back into men, but only if they themselves wanted to change. She called on a pig named Gryllus to speak for the crew. When Odysseus said that human beings showed greater courage than animals, Gryllus reminded him of the Crommyum sow who, without even the use of weapons, almost defeated the hero Theseus. When Odysseus said that humans showed greater reason, Gryllus gave many examples of animal intelligence; pigs, for example, went to riverbeds and ate crabs to cure their illnesses. The debate ended abruptly and the manuscript may never have been finished, but Odysseus was so completely beaten that it is very hard to imagine a recovery.

The pig can seem very "human" in body as well as mind. The internal organs of a pig are remarkably similar to those of a human being. This feature helped make pigs a favorite animal for sacrifice to the gods, since the sacrificial victim was generally a symbolic substitute for a human being. Whenever the Roman State entered a contract, a pig would be taken to the temple of Jupiter. As he slit the animal's throat with a sacred sickle, the priest would say, "If the Roman people injure this pact, may Jupiter smite them as I smite this pig" (Lewinsohn, p. 102).

In Norse mythology, the god Frey rode in a chariot drawn by the boar Gollinborsti, whose name means "golden tusks." The boar's head, traditionally served in England at Christmastime, was originally a sacrifice to Frey. The boar Saehrimnir was killed every evening and served to the heroes in Valhalla, to be reborn the next day. In a similar way, pigs in Celtic legend were the food of the gods in other-

Illustration of
various pigs from a
nineteenth-century
book of natural
history.

worldly feasts. The pigs of Manannán, the Irish god of the sea, would reappear after being eaten.

For the Hebrews, however, pigs were not merely "unclean"; they were the most repulsive of animals. Perhaps it was because pigs were carriers of the disease trichinosis, but just about every domesticated animal was a carrier of some disease. Another possible reason was that pigs had been associated with so many pagan mother-goddesses, divinities the Hebrews abhorred. It could also be because pigs would eat just about anything, while the Hebrews were very fastidious about their food.

For the most part, Christians initially shared the Hebrew view of pigs as unclean. Matthew told us not to "cast pearls before swine" (7:6). In Mark, when Jesus cast out demons from a madman, they entered a herd of swine, which then ran out into the sea and were drowned (5:1–20). It was rare in medieval times for animals to be depicted as living on after death, but Dante in his *Inferno* described pigs as living in filth in the third level of Hell. Peasant culture of Christianity, however, sought to distance itself from Judaism and partially sacralized the pig. Throughout much of Europe, peasant families raised pigs with special intimacy. Pigs were fed scraps from the table and treated as pets. When the time finally came for a pig to be slaughtered, it was done ceremoniously; the whole family would be present. The bones and inedible parts of the pig would later be ritually buried, in expectation of resurrection.

A pig, usually immaculate, was often painted alongside the hermit Saint Anthony. An Italian tale from the Mediterranean islands, retold by Italo Calvino, described a time when all fire was in Hell so no hearths warmed families in winter. People, shivering so badly that they could barely speak, appealed to Saint Anthony for help. The holy man went down to the very gate of Hell and knocked with his staff. At his side, as always, was his faithful pig. A devil opened the door a crack, looked out, and said, "Get out of here! We know you. You're a saint. Only sinners are allowed in Hell!" The pig would not take no for an answer and forced open the door. The pig knocked down the devil, scattered a pile of pitchforks, and raised so much hell in Hell that the devils were terrified. "Come in and get your pig!" shouted the devils to Saint Anthony. The saint walked in and touched the pig lightly with his staff. The animal became completely calm. "Now get out of here, both of you, and don't ever come back again!" shouted the devils. Without a word or even a grunt, Saint Anthony and his pig walked away. What the devils didn't know was that Saint Anthony was carrying a spark of fire concealed within his staff. As soon as Saint Anthony and his pig reached earth, the holy man swung the staff above his head so that sparks flew in all directions. And so, thanks to Saint Anthony and his pig, people could tell stories in comfort around the fireplace while the ground was covered with snow (vol. 2, pp. 673–676).

The boar is the last cycle of the Chinese zodiac, and those who are born in the year of the boar are said to be courageous but stubborn. The domestic pig in Asia shared a reputation with its Western counterparts for appetite and earthy charm. The sixteenth-century Chinese epic *Journey to the West* told of a monk who undertook a pilgrimage from China to India to bring back Buddhist scriptures and save China from chaos. The animals that accompanied him included a monkey, a horse, a sea monster, and Old Hog, a pig that subdued demons with his rake. Old Hog may have been a formidable fighter, but laziness or appetite easily overcame him. As a reward for his good services, he was finally made not a Buddha but Janitor of the Altars, and he had the pleasant task of eating scraps left after celebrations.

Aristocratic families of medieval Europe took their animal symbolism far less from Christianity than from warrior religions of their pagan past. The nobles admired boars for their military virtues, and boars were among the most popular animals in heraldry. When hunted, boars charge and fight to the end no matter how many dogs and men they face. Social position in medieval times was indicated by which animals one was allowed to hunt. As a noble animal, the boar was second only to the stag in status, and it presented an even greater test of a hunter's skill and bravery. Metaphors for love were often drawn from hunting. In the late medieval British romance *Sir Gawain and the Green Knight*, the wife of his host tried to seduce Gawain several times. Once, when Gawain resolutely rejected her seductions, he was implicitly compared to a boar confronting a hunting party directly and without fear.

Meanwhile, the Jews retained their traditional abhorrence of the pig. The Old Testament told how the Greek emperor Antiochus Epiphanes tried to force Jews to eat pork, which helped set off the furious revolt of Judas Maccabeus (2 Macc. 7:1–2). Much later, the Spanish Inquisition tested Jews who claimed to have converted to Christianity by requiring them to eat the flesh of pigs.

For those outside the Jewish community, however, it often seemed that the Jewish avoidance of pork could be attributed only to worship of the pig. During the first century A.D., Petronius Arbiter wrote in a poetic fragment, "The Jew may worship his pig-god" (pp. 424–425). For many Christians, the Jewish avoidance of pork appeared to be something like a taboo against cannibalism. In numerous popular stories, Jews were turned into pigs. A chronicle of wonders published in Binzwangen, Germany, in 1575 reported that a Jewish woman gave birth to two piglets. At the end of the Middle Ages in Europe, a popular anti-Semitic motif was "the Jew's sow," an enormous pig suckling Jewish men.

The fact that pigs foraged freely in woods and were even allowed to enter homes made them particularly vulnerable during animal trials at the end of the Middle Ages. Prosecutors sometimes alleged that pigs had an infernal smell, showing their association with the Devil. Their grunts and squeals, which seemed disrespectful to the courts, made things even worse. Plenty of pigs were convicted, and some acquitted, in courts throughout Europe for such offenses as eating their own young or having sex with human beings. Those found guilty were usually either hanged or burned alive.

Since domestic pigs were allowed to roam relatively freely until around the start of the modern era, they would often interbreed with wild boars. Until the nineteenth century, they still had gray hair and tusks. It is only in recent times that what we usually think of when we think of pigs—pink, hairless, and very fat—has been created from albino varieties. The physical change brought many modifications in both the use and the symbolism of pigs. They became an image of those spoiled by the comforts and privileges of civilization.

In Berlin during the 1920s, there were several riots by veterans, working men, Nazis, and Communists. The police who were summoned to put down the violence were called "pigs." In Nazi Germany, Minister of Agriculture R. Walter Darré wished to proclaim the pig the central animal of the Aryan people, but other Nazis identified pigs with Jews. Student rebels throughout much of the world took up this epithet again in the 1960s, using it to taunt both politicians and law-enforcement officers. In 1968, protesters at the Democratic convention in Chicago held a mock convention and nominated a pig for president.

BEASTS

Domestic pigs are generally looked on with affection in books for children, in part because of their dependence and vulnerability. This illustration from the early twentieth century by W. Heath is a good example.

In his novella *Animal Farm*, first published in 1946, George Orwell used the modern farm as an allegory for the totalitarian state. Pigs, as the most intelligent of animals, led a revolt against the brutal farmer Jones. "All animals are equal," the pigs proclaimed, but they later added, "some are more equal than others" (p. 123). A Berkshire boar named Napoleon drove out his porcine rivals, learned to walk on two legs, and exploited the other animals as much as human beings had ever done.

Such a depiction of pigs may be excellent literature, but it is still rather ungracious. Pigs are among the most useful of animals to human beings. Just about every part of the body of a pig is used; pudding is made from the blood of pigs, and sausages are wrapped in the intestines; the leather of a pig's skin is highly prized. The ability of pigs to digest almost anything and convert it into edible material makes them especially helpful to farmers. For the most part, pigs receive remarkably little gratitude; they are often kept in cramped, filthy conditions until the time of slaughter arrives.

Pigs are still among the most beloved figures in books and movies for children. These include Wilbur (from E. B. White's *Charlotte's Web*), Porky Pig, and Babe, all gentle figures who show little of either the valor or the filthy habits traditionally associated with swine. Miss Piggy, the biggest star of *The Muppet Show,* is a modern heir to ancient porcine goddesses such as Nut. She has starred in feature films, written a popular book on fashion, and been featured on posters and calendars. Miss Piggy is forever flirting. She may act vain and clumsy, but you had better not laugh at her too openly. She has the superhuman strength and fierceness of her porcine ancestors, which so impressed people in ancient times.

Selected References

Calvino, Italo. *Fiabe Italiano: Raccolte e transcitte da Italo Calivino* (2 vols.). Milan: Oscar Mondadori, 1986.

Caras, Roger A. *A Perfect Harmony: The Intertwining Lives of Animals and Humans throughout History.* New York: Simon and Schuster, 1996.

Digard, Jean-Pierre. *L'homme et les animaux domestiques.* Paris: Fayard, 1990.

Fabre-Vassas, Claudine. *The Singular Beast: Jews, Christians, and the Pig.* Trans. Carol Volk. New York: Columbia University Press, 1997.

Herodotus. *Herodotus* (4 vols.). Trans. A. D. Godley. New York: G. P. Putnam's Sons, 1926.

Lewinsohn, Richard. *Animals, Men, and Myths: An Informative and Entertaining History of Man and the Animals around Him.* New York: Harper and Brothers, 1954.

Nissenson, Marilyn, and Susan Jones. *The Ubiquitous Pig.* New York: Harry N. Abrams, 1996.

Orwell, George. *Animal Farm.* New York: Harcourt, Brace and Janovich/Signet Classics, 1946.

Petronius Arbiter. *Petronius/ Sececa, Apocolocyntosis.* Trans. Michael Heseltine, W. H. D. Rouse, E. H. Warmington. Cambridge: Harvard University Press, 1997.

Sax, Boria. *Animals in the Third Reich: Pets, Scapegoats, and the Holocaust.* New York: Continuum, 2000.

Wu Ch'eng-en. *Journey to the West* (4 vols.). Trans. Anthony C. Yu. Chicago: University of Chicago Press, 1983.

Pigeon

See Dove and Pigeon

Porcupine

See Beaver, Porcupine, Badger, and Miscellaneous Rodents

R

Rabbit

See Hare and Rabbit

Rat and Mouse

> *Rats! They fought the dogs and killed the cats,*
> *And bit the babies in the cradles,*
> *And ate the cheeses out of the vats,*
> *And licked the soup from the cooks' own ladles*
> *Split open the kegs of salted sprats,*
> *Made nests inside men's Sunday hats,*
> *And even spoiled the women's chats*
> *By drowning their speaking*
> *With shrieking and squeaking*
> *In fifty different sharps and flats.*
> —Robert Browning, "The Pied Piper of Hamelin"

For the most part, rodents and people may be rivals and enemies, yet the two have a paradoxical intimacy, a bit like a married couple who cannot live in harmony yet find it impossible to separate. Rats and mice can adapt to a vast range of environments, and they are quite capable of living without human beings. Nevertheless, they thrive particularly in urban settings, where humans inadvertently provide them with great quantities of food and enclosures for shelter. As carriers of plague, rodents have killed untold millions of people in the course of human history. Even today, all our technologies cannot prevent rats and mice from devouring about a quarter of the grain grown for human consumption. In the West, rats often appear in nightmares, and they can inspire revulsion and terror. Nevertheless, their ability to survive earns grudging respect and admiration from people. In the Orient, rats are associated above all with prosperity, since they gather wherever food is plentiful. A Japanese proverb goes, "Getting rich is to invite the rat" (Sun, p. 29).

Most of folklore up through at least the Renaissance distinguishes only loosely between rats and mice. In Greek and Latin both kinds of animals were generally designated by the word "*mus*," which is the origin of our word "mouse." The word "rat" comes originally from the Vulgar Latin "*rattus*," a term that probably originated in the Middle Ages. Like they have done with other pairs of closely related animals— lions and tigers, for example—people have polarized these rodents as opposites, so in the West the mouse has become beloved while the rat has become despised. In ancient manuscripts people usually tend to translate the word "*mus*" according to whether the rodents in question seem large and aggressive, like rats, or small and passive, like mice.

It was not until the nineteenth century that new techniques of construction enabled people to make buildings ratproof, and before then rodents were found in every structure, from the barn to the royal palace. This produced a sort of intimacy with rats and mice, which must have softened the anger at the damage that they did. Rodents surely spoiled many meals and even destroyed homes, so it is remarkable that they were not often demonized in the ancient world. People might have seen rats and mice only occasionally, but they could hear them all the time, especially when falling asleep at night. They could not help but wonder, often with a certain sympathy, what transpired in the secret society on the other side of holes in the wall.

One early attempt to imagine this is the fable known as "The Town Mouse and the Country Mouse," included by the Roman poet Horace in his *Satire II*. It tells how a country mouse once received a city mouse in his humble hole, offering him a few scraps of bacon and remains of vegetables. The city mouse would hardly deign to touch such fare. He explained to his rural companion that since life was short, he should make the most of it by spending his time amid more pleasant surroundings. A short while later the country mouse accepted an invitation to dinner from the city mouse. The host brought in course after course of fine dainties left over from a banquet the evening before. The guest was rejoicing in his good fortune, when all of a sudden somebody started banging on the doors and the entire house trembled at the barking of two ferocious hounds. The terrified country mouse took his leave, saying he would rather live in peace than risk his life for sumptuous delights. The fable, a classic expression of the contrast between the city slicker and the country bumpkin, has been constantly retold, often set in contemporary urban centers such as New York or London.

People have been continually amazed at the ability of rodents to get to food no matter how carefully it seemed to be locked up. Up through the nineteenth century and even today, they have tried to explain this with countless anecdotes in which admiration for the ingenuity of rodents almost always seems to cancel any resentment of them as pests. Many authors, for example, told how one mouse or rat would lie on its back and hold an egg in its paws in order to be dragged like a sled by colleagues. Others would tell how mice stood on one another's shoulders to form a living ladder in order to reach food on a table. Many authors even maintained that rodents had customs such as burying their dead.

But no affection for rats could ever overcome the practical necessity of keeping the rodent population under control. The Egyptians sometimes depicted mice with affection, but they also kept mongooses and cats in their homes to catch rodents. The eternal rivalry between cat and mouse became a favorite theme of storytellers, from Aesop and his fables to the producers of the "Tom and Jerry" cartoons in America during the twentieth century. In one popular fable from the Middle Ages, the mice met in council to decide what they should do about the cat. They agreed that the greatest danger from the cat lay in the silence of its approach. One mouse proposed that a bell be tied around the neck of the cat to warn them of its approach. The members of the council applauded until an old mouse got up and asked, "Who will bell the cat?"

Herodotus tells of an Egyptian king named Sethos who had once alienated the warrior class by claiming the soldiers' ancestral lands. When the Assyrian Sanacharib invaded Egypt, the warriors refused to support the king, who was also a priest of the sun god Ra. Sethos entered the inner sanctuary of Ra's temple, prayed, and wept until he fell asleep. The god appeared to him in a dream and told him not to worry. He should gather whatever soldiers he could, even if they were only merchants or artisans, and go forth to face the enemy. The two armies were encamped opposite each other. On the night before the battle, a swarm of field mice entered the camp of the Assyrians. They devoured the bowstrings and quivers of the enemy, leaving them weaponless. A statue of Sethos was later erected in the temple of Ra. In his hand, the king held a mouse. The inscription read, "Look on me, and fear the gods" (book 2, section 141).

Since the lion is a symbol of kingship, it seems possible that that story may be the ultimate origin of the Aesopian fable "The Lion and the Mouse," which was retold by the Roman freedman Phaedrus and many others. A lion had caught a mouse, which begged to be let go, saying it might someday return the favor. The lion was so amused at the idea that so tiny a creature could ever help the king of beasts that he magnanimously lifted his paw and spared the mouse. A while later hunters caught the lion in a trap. The mouse passed by and, seeing its friend struggling haplessly, gnawed the ropes and set the lion free.

The Japanese tell a story about the medieval painter Sesshu, who was once tied up during his childhood as punishment for idling away his time with art. He drew pictures of rats by moving his feet in the sand. The pictures were so vivid that the rats came to life and gnawed at his bonds. A modern rendering of this theme is Edgar Allan Poe's famous story "The Pit and the Pendulum." Rats had tormented a man who had been tied up in a dungeon by the Inquisition, but they ultimately liberated him by gnawing away his bonds.

All of the stories of liberation by rats or mice may also refer to the emancipation of the soul at death. Because of their preference for human dwellings, rodents have often been taken for the souls of the departed. Because of their association with the next world, they are often credited with clairvoyance. Throughout the world, rats leaving a home or ship is a sign of impending ruin. In another Greco-Roman fable traditionally attributed to Aesop, a farmer once noticed that a mountain was rumbling, rocks were tumbling down, and dust was spewing from its summit. He decided that the mountain was in labor, and he called his companions to see what it might give birth to. As they gazed on in fear and wonder, a tiny mouse finally emerged and came running down the slope. The story may well have originally referred to the emergence of the soul from the body. Sometimes a rodent also represents the separable soul, which can run about while a person is in a trance or asleep. In the Walpurgis Night episode in the first part of Johann Wolfgang von Goethe's *Faust,* the protagonist dances with a young witch at a nocturnal revel, but he is horrified when a rat leaps out of her mouth and runs away.

This idea of rodents as the souls of human beings seems to underlie the mysterious tale of the Pied Piper of Hamelin, which was recorded in several versions during the Middle Ages. In 1284 the town of Hamelin in Germany became infested with rats, and the village council hired a brightly dressed piper to get rid of them. He played a mysterious tune that made the rats follow him, and he led them into the Weser River to drown. The Piper disappeared for a while, but he returned on Saint John's Day to demand payment. When the village refused to pay what the Piper wanted, he began to play his pipe again, and this time the children followed him. A mountain opened up to receive the procession and closed after it, so the children were never seen again. The Grimm brothers made the story famous in their collection of German legends, and Robert Browning, Goethe, and others have retold it. Various scholars have traced the tale back to the bubonic plague, to the Children's Crusade of the Middle Ages, or to a migration southward to Bohemia. In any case, the image of the Piper with the children or rats greatly resembles medieval representations of Death leading the departed in a dance.

There is also at least a very strong association between rodents and the dead in the legend of Bishop Hatto of Mainz, Germany. There was a famine, but Hatto continued to dine in luxury and refused to lower the prices on his ample store of grain. Finally, weary of hearing the starving people complain, he invited all who lacked bread to assemble in a huge barn. Then, instead of offering the people food, he set the barn on fire and burned them to death. Next morning the bishop rose and saw that rats had eaten his portrait. A servant informed him that rats had eaten everything in the granary. He looked out over his lands to see a huge army of rats descending on the palace. In terror, the bishop fled to an island in the Rhine and locked himself up in a structure known today as the Mouse Tower. The rats followed, gnawed through the door, and finally ate the villain alive.

The perspective on rats in East Asia is far more unequivocally positive. As legend has it, when the Buddha was near death all the animals came to pay their last respects. The ox was leading the way, and the rat hitched a ride upon its back. As they reached the pavilion where the Buddha lay, the rat jumped down, raced ahead, and arrived before the other animals. As a reward for piety, the Buddha granted the rat the first position in the Chinese zodiac.

Daikoku, the Buddhist god of wealth, is often depicted holding a large bale of rice that is being nibbled at by rats. These rodents serve him as messengers. The amazing fertility of rodents makes them symbolic of the way money can increase through good business, though even Daikoku has sometimes had to guard his store from rats.

In the Middle Ages, rats were sometimes familiars of witches or forms in which sorcerers ran about at night. It was not, however, until some centuries after the worst episodes of the bubonic plague that we start to see intense expressions of aversion and disgust for rats, as people gradually began to suspect their connection with disease. The reputation of rats took a drastic turn for the worse at the end of the nineteenth century, when the French missionary Paul Louis Simmond discovered that bubonic plague had been caused by a bacillus that was found on fleas carried by rats. This meant that, without being identified, rats had been responsible for the deaths of millions of people, more than were killed in all the wars throughout human history.

Bubonic plague may have been around since the advent of humankind, but the first probable reference to it is in the Bible. In the early eleventh century B.C., the Philistines had defeated the Hebrews and taken the Ark of the Covenant. "The hand of Yahweh weighed heavily on the people of Ashdod [Philistines] and struck terror in them, afflicting them with tumors" (1 Sam. 5:6). Outbreaks of the plague gradually became more common and more severe as the growth of trade increased the density of population during the Roman Empire. The plague of Justinian in A.D. 531–532 killed tens of millions, depopulating entire towns and perhaps destroying what remained of ancient civilization.

But the most terrible outbreak of all was in 1348–1350, when bubonic plague destroyed more than one-third of the population of Europe. The people of Europe then aggravated the plague by killing cats and dogs, animals that they mistakenly believed had caused the disease but that actually had helped to keep the population of rats in check. Literature and the arts seem to have gradually anticipated medical discoveries about the plague, since over the next several centuries they increasingly depicted rats, especially in packs, as diabolic.

The plague had sometimes been blamed on Jews, and thousands of them were burned alive in the Middle Ages in consequence. In the latter nineteenth and twentieth centuries, rats were often used in anti-Semitic propaganda. Cartoonists made the proverbial "Jewish nose" appear like the snout of a rat. In the Nazi propaganda film *The Eternal Jew*, directed by Fritz Hippler, the migrations of Jews were compared to the spread of rats across the world. The physician Hans Zinsser, doubtless thinking of the two world wars, has observed that the conflict between the brown rat, indigenous throughout Eurasia, and the black rat, brought to Western Europe on the boats of crusaders, was a very close equivalent to armed conflict among human beings. In George Orwell's novel *1984*, the most dreaded fate for the hero Winston is to be eaten by rats.

But as the rat has been demonized, the mouse, as though in compensation, has generally grown more beloved. In 1928 Walt Disney, then a struggling entrepreneur, introduced one of the first animated films, which starred Mickey Mouse as Steamboat Willie, a captain who raucously hooted and danced as he steered his ship. As Disney Studios grew into a giant corporation, Mickey became more subdued and, in the eyes of his critics, even bland. The Mickey Mouse Club was founded as part of the television show *Walt Disney Presents*. It featured boys and girls wearing large mouse ears, who sang, danced, and had adventures.

But if mice were identified with cute little kids in entertainment, the relations with actual rodents remained as troubled as ever. The strong identification of human beings with rodents continues to produce not only affection and respect but also hatred and exploitation. In the United States alone, at least 20 million rodents are killed every year in experiments. In 1988 the first patent ever was issued for an animal other than a microorganism, namely, the "onco-mouse," which was genetically engineered to develop cancer so it could be used in research. The scientific findings will, of course, suggest possible cures for cancer in human beings, but let us hope the exploitative attitudes are not generalized to people as well.

Selected References

Aesop. *The Fables of Aesop.* Ed. Joseph Jacobs. New York: Macmillan, 1910.

Baring-Gould, Sabine. *Curious Myths of the Middle Ages.* London: Longman's Green, 1892.

Carlson, Rev. Gergory I. "Horace's and Today's Town and Country Mouse." *Bestia* 4 (May 1992): 87–112.

Hendrickson, Robert. *More Cunning than Man: A Social History of Rats and Men.* New York: Dorset Press, 1983.

Herodotus. *Herodotus* (4 vols.). Trans. A. D. Godley. New York: G. P. Putnam's Sons, 1926.

Sax, Boria. *The Parliament of Animals: Legends and Anecdotes, 1775–1900.* New York: Pace University Press, 1990.

Sun, Ruth Q. *The Asian Animal Zodiac.* Edison, NJ: Castle Books, 1974.

Zinsser, Hans. *Rats, Lice, and History.* New York: Macmillan, 1963.

Raven

See Crow, Raven, and Other Corvids

Reptiles

See Snake, Lizard, and Related Animals

Rhinoceros

For an actress to be a success she must have the face of Venus, the brains of Minerva, the grace of Terpsichore, the memory of Macaulay, the figure of Juno, and the hide of a rhinoceros.

—Attributed to Ethel Barrymore

Sometimes the legend and symbolism surrounding an animal becomes so elaborate that the creature is completely overshadowed, and that is the case with the rhinoceros. The rhino may not, of itself, be one of the most central animals in myth or legend; it has rarely been worshipped in temples or appeared in epic poems. Nevertheless, sight-

Illustration of rhinos from a nineteenth-century book of natural history.

Rhinoceros unicornis. One horned Rhinoceros.

ings of the rhinoceros probably began and sustained the cult of the unicorn, which eventually incorporated features of the horse, ass, goat, and narwhal. The irony is perhaps best illustrated in several medieval treasuries of Europe, where the horn of a narwhal was kept as a relic of a unicorn. Alongside that horn was often that of a rhinoceros, which was believed to be a claw of a griffin. If we count the unicorn as a rhinoceros, the rhino becomes one of the most important cult animals in the world.

The lore of the unicorn has a fascinating but very tangled history from the start, and there are possible depictions of it going back to cave paintings. The first description, however, comes from the Greek Ctesias, who was the physician of the king of Persia around the start of the fourth century B.C. He considered the animal to be a giant wild ass, and nothing in nature matches his description. What suggests a rhinoceros, however, is his mention of the horn's being used by Indians as a goblet and an antidote for poison. Rhinoceros horns have been used for drinking, and folk medicine attributes to them great potency as both a medicine and an aphrodisiac.

The description of a unicorn, or "monoceros," by Pliny the Elder in the first century A.D. is more clearly suggestive of a rhinoceros: "The wildest animal [in India] is the monoceros, whose body is like a horse but which has the head of a stag, elephant's feet and a wild boar's tail. It utters a deep, growling sound, and a black horn, two cubits long, protrudes from the center of its forehead. It is said that the animal cannot be captured alive" (book 8, chap. 5). Actual rhinoceri had appeared in triumphal processions in Rome, and Pliny may have seen that animal but failed to connect it with the accounts he had heard from travelers.

From this point on, the lore of the unicorn became ever more elaborate and romantic in Europe. Medieval people believed that the unicorn could never be subdued by force yet would lay its head in the lap of a virgin and allow itself to be captured. The rhinoceros, meanwhile, was usually known only from confused reports by travelers to exotic lands and, when mentioned at all, usually seemed diabolic by virtue of its brute power. When Marco Polo saw a Sumatran rhinoceros on his voyage to China, he was able to connect it with the fabled unicorn. "All in all," he wrote, "they are nasty creatures, they always carry their piglike heads to the ground, like to wallow in the mud, and are not in the least like the unicorns of which our stories speak in Europe. Can an animal of their race feel at ease in the lap of a virgin?" (Eisler, p. 269).

One feature of the unicorn, however, which observation did not seem to contradict was its reputation for near invincibility. Manuel I of Portugal brought a rhinoceros to Lisbon, the first in Europe since Roman times, in 1517. As an experiment, the king set the rhinoceros against an elephant on a street, and the pachyderm sought refuge by crashing through the iron bars of a large window. Not very long afterward, Duke Alessandro de Medici had a rhinoceros engraved on his armor with the motto "I make war to win" (Eisler, p. 272).

In the nineteenth and twentieth centuries, people were particularly fascinated by the combination of melancholy and power in the rhinoceros. The graceful unicorn, known through the accumulation of lore over the centuries, appeared familiar and even "natural," but the rhinoceros often came across as a bizarre freak. The Romanian-French dramatist Eugene Ionescu, the leading exponent of a school known as "Theater of the Absurd," used the perceived strangeness of these animals in his play *Rhinoceros* (first performed 1958) to dramatize the arbitrary quality of social mores. The hero of the play is a clerk named Berenger who gradually discovers that all of his friends and colleagues are turning into rhinoceri. He resolves, probably in vain, to remain a human being.

There are many other versions of the unicorn throughout Eurasia and beyond. The oldest may be the Ky-lin, which emerged from the Yellow River before the emperor Fu Hsi around the start of the third millennium B.C. At least in those areas where the rhinoceros is known, it is usually at least vaguely associated with these legendary cousins. Today, as many species of rhinoceros approach extinction, governments struggle, with only limited success, to prevent poachers from killing the animals for their fabulous horns.

Selected References

Beer, Rüdiger Robert. *Unicorn: Myth and Reality.* Trans. Charles M. Stern. New York: Van Nostrand Reinhold, 1972.

Eisler, Colin. *Dürer's Animals.* Washington, DC: Smithsonian Institution Press, 1991.

Gotfredsen, Lise. *The Unicorn.* New York: Abbeville Press, 1999.

Ionescu, Eugene. *Rhinoceros; The Chairs; The Lesson.* New York: Penguin, 1996.

Pliny. *Natural History* (10 vols.). Trans. H. Rackham, W. H. S. Jones et al. Cambridge: Harvard University Press, 1953.

Rybot, Doris. *It Began before Noah.* London: Michael Joseph, 1972.

Shephard, Odell. *The Lore of the Unicorn.* New York: The Metropolitan Museum of Art, 1982.

Robin

See Wren and English Robin

Rodents

See Beaver, Porcupine, Badger, and Miscellaneous Rodents

Rook

See Crow, Raven, and Other Corvids

Salamander

See Snake, Lizard, and Related Animals

Salmon and Carp

> *Now I am swimmer who dies,*
> *Who runs with rain and moon and salt-wind tide,*
> *River and falls and sweet pebble water.*
> —Kwakiutl Indians, "Swimmer the Salmon"
>   (adapted by Gerald Hausman)

Since very archaic times, people have thought of the sea as the womb from which all life emerges. Fish have symbolized the inexhaustible fertility of nature, and they have been closely associated with mother-goddesses such as Tiamat and Atargatis. Fishermen are the last hunter-gatherers, and in ancient times they were already surrounded by nostalgia and romance. The first disciples of Jesus were fishers, and Christ told them, "Follow me and I will make you fishers of men" (Matt. 4:19). The fish was the earliest symbol of Christ, and the Hindu Vishnu has often been depicted riding upon a fish. But despite their enormous importance in religion and other aspects of human culture, fish are remarkably difficult to humanize. The reason may be a combination of their remote, expressionless eyes and their utter silence, which are such a contrast to the expressive glances and constant speech of human beings. Even in the animistic world of folklore, a talking fish is only rarely found, and when a fish does speak, it is usually in connection with some remarkable event.

The salmon, however, lives according to a remarkably "human" pattern. It is born in freshwater, migrates to the ocean, and finally returns, sometimes swimming hundreds of miles upstream, to the place of its birth to spawn. Atlantic salmon may sometimes make the journey a few times during their lives, but Pacific salmon die after laying eggs. In their determination to complete their destiny, salmon seem not only human but also very noble indeed. The entire life of a salmon may be understood as a sort of quest. It follows the mythic pattern described by Joseph Campbell in *The Hero with a Thousand Faces,* where the archetypal hero, after many adventures, returns to end his life in the place of his birth. The way the salmon crosses the boundary between freshwater and the sea suggests a passage between the realm of men and that of immortals, and the salmon is a symbol of transcendence in many cultures.

Fish carved on antlers of reindeer have been excavated in Paleolithic settlements of Spain and France, and a few of these fish are clearly recognizable as salmon. According to the Norse Eddas, Loki, the god of fire, assumed the form of a salmon to hide beneath a waterfall after he had offended the other deities with his taunts. The salmon is most central in the cultures of the Celts and the Indians of North America. The salmon of wisdom, which has superhuman knowledge, appears often in the myths and legends of the Celts. In the tale "The Marriage of Culhwch and Owlen," this is the salmon of Llyn Llyw, one of the oldest animals in the world. When King Arthur and his knights seek the hunter Mabon, they consult this salmon, who not only tells them where Mabon is imprisoned but then ferries two men to the place upon its back.

According to one Irish legend, a giant had once caught the salmon of wisdom and told the hero Finn MacCumhail to roast it for him. A blister arose on the salmon, and Finn pressed the burn with his thumb, which he placed in his mouth to ease the pain. He immediately was filled with wisdom, and he knew exactly how to defeat the giant. In other versions of the tale, Finn was asked to roast the salmon by an old poet named Finnegas.

Several tales place five salmon of wisdom in Connla's well near Tipperary. Above the well were nine hazel trees, and their purple nuts would fall into the well to feed the salmon. The hazelnuts represented the spirit of poetry, and the sound of their striking the water was said to be lovelier than any human song. The bellies of the salmon were purple from the nuts, and their wisdom constantly increased. Only the salmon could eat the nuts in safety, yet legend has it that the goddess Sinend was once so eager for wisdom that she defied a prohibition and approached too close to the well, whereupon the waters rose and swallowed her.

A similar tale is told of a young girl named Liban in *The Book of the Dun Cow,* from the early Middle Ages. A well overflowed and formed a lake, and Liban was swept to the bottom with her dog, but God protected them from the waters. The two stayed there for a year, when Liban saw a salmon and prayed, "O my Lord, I wish I were a salmon, that I might swim with the others through the clear green sea!" In that moment she became a salmon from the waist down, while her dog became an otter, and together they swam about for 300 years. Finally, she allowed herself to be captured by some holy men and taken to a cloister. She died immediately after being baptized and was consecrated as one of the holy virgins (Joyce, pp. 68–73).

The return of a salmon to its place of birth has suggested the coming of Christ, and the transition between Celtic religion and Christianity was probably eased by the shared symbolism of the fish. A similar significance was eventually accorded in Celtic areas to eels, which share with salmon the ability to move between pond and ocean. The salmon of knowledge could also be the ultimate origin of the wise fish in such popular fairy tales as the Grimm brothers' "Fisherman and His Wife," where it is a flounder, and Alexandr Afanas'ev's "Emilya and the Pike."

The salmon also represents rebirth among Native American tribes of the Northwest coast such as the Kwakiutl and Haida, although not so much as a unique event but as part of an eternal cycle. A salmon swimming upstream as it endeavors to elude predators such as bears represents the individual bravely endeavoring to complete his or her destiny. Finally, after spawning, the dead salmon are swept back into the ocean, representing the ultimate union with all of life.

The carp is essentially a freshwater fish, but it also swims upstream, sometimes leaping over falls, to spawn. In East Asia, the carp is a symbol of perseverance, and it is used especially to signify the scholar who studies hard to pass his or her examinations. According to ancient legends of China, a carp on reaching its destination would become a dragon. Because it suggested transcendence, the carp was also a frequent form for paper kites. The bright scales of a carp resemble armor, so the carp was often used as a symbol of samurai warriors. Oriental gods and goddesses have often been depicted riding upon a carp.

The first recorded versions of the enormously popular fairy tale "Cinderella" came in the early ninth century in China, and the helper of the young girl—that is, the equivalent of the fairy godmother in the well-known version by Charles Perrault—was a fish. The young girl took the fish home from a well, to be kept in a pond. Her wicked stepmother killed the fish out of spite, but the heroine prayed to its bones, which would grant her every wish. The kind of fish was not specified, but, since it was brightly colored and kept as a pet, it certainly appears to have been a carp.

While the cultural importance of the salmon probably derives largely from its gastronomic value, that of the carp is largely ornamental. Carp were introduced to Europe from the Far East in about the fifteenth century, and they have greatly extended their range throughout the world with the growth of trade. Salmon, by contrast, are now everywhere endangered, partly because of excessive fishing but mostly because of dam construction along their migratory routes. They are produced for the market in hatcheries, in varieties that are artificially bred and even genetically engineered. These are sometimes inadvertently released into the wild, where they interbreed with wild salmon, often further endangering the original inhabitants of streams. In terms of contact with human beings, it would seem to be safer for animals to be beautiful than useful.

Selected References

Campbell, Joseph. *The Hero with a Thousand Faces*. Princeton, NJ: Princeton University Press, 1990.

Davis, Courtney, and Dennis O'Neil. *Celtic Beasts: Animal Motifs and Zoomorphic Design in Celtic Art*. London: Blandford, 1999.

Glassie, Henry, ed. *Irish Folk Tales*. New York: Pantheon, 1985.

Grantz, Jeffrey, trans. *The Mabinogion*. New York: Dorset Press, 1976.

Hausman, Gerald. *Meditations with Animals: A Native American Bestiary*. Santa Fe: Bear, 1986.

Jameson, R. D. "Cinderella in China." In *Cinderella: A Casebook*. Ed. Alan Dundes. Madison: University of Wisconsin Press, 1988, pp. 71–97.

Joyce, P. W., ed. *Old Celtic Romances: Tales from Irish Mythology*. New York: Devin-Adair, 1962.

Larrington, Caroline, trans. *The Poetic Edda*. New York: Oxford University Press, 1996.

Netboy, Anthony. *The Salmon: Their Fight for Survival*. Boston: Houghton Mifflin, 1973.

Wentz, W. Y. Evans. *The Fairy Faith in Celtic Countries*. London: Colin Smythe, 1977.

Scorpion

Do not forget Yahweh your God who brought you out of the land of Egypt, out of the house of slavery: who guided you through this vast and dreadful wilderness, a land of fiery serpents, scorpions, thirst . . ."

—Deuteronomy 8:14–15

Since the scorpion is found in cracks, crevices, holes, and enclosed places, it is associated with chthonic powers. Much like a snake, it can strike unexpectedly. Its sting can be very painful and sometimes deadly. Though often a symbol of evil, the scorpion can also be an instrument of divine retribution.

This dual symbolism was already apparent in ancient Egypt. It was in the form of a scorpion that the god Set, evil brother of Osiris, attacked the infant Horus—no doubt an experience familiar to the ancient Egyptians since children were particularly vulnerable to the sting of this creature. The divine infant was saved by the medicine of Thoth, god of knowledge. Selket, a goddess of marriage, fertility, and the underworld, could, however, also use the power of the scorpion to fight demonic powers. She was often depicted with the body of a scorpion and the head of a woman, sometimes also as a scorpion holding an ankh, the Egyptian cross. In addition, she was painted as a woman with a scorpion on her head or in her hand, an image that the Romans eventually began to use as an allegorical representation of the African continent.

The Babylonian equivalent of Selket is the goddess Ishara, who is associated with love and with motherhood. In her honor, the scorpion first became a constellation of the zodiac among the Semitic peoples of Mesopotamia. Scorpion-men frequently appear in the art and literature of Mesopotamia. They usually have the heads of human beings, the wings and talons of birds, a serpent for a penis, and the tail of a scorpion. Sometimes they are associated with Tiamat, the sinister mother-goddess, but they are also attendants of the sun god Shamash and guard his realm against demons. In the epic of Gilgamesh, a scorpion-man and scorpion-woman guard the mountain where the sun rises.

According to a Greco-Roman legend, the great hunter Orion boasted that he would kill all animals. On hearing that, the earth-mother Gaia sent a scorpion, which bit his heel and killed him. Asclepius (or Ophiuchus), the divine physician, restored Orion to life, but Zeus would not accept this interference in the process of life and

Scorpion-man from an inlaid harp found in excavations of Ur, circa 2600 B.C.

Selket, a scorpion-goddess of ancient Egypt.

death. The supreme god sent a thunderbolt, which killed Orion a second time. Placed in the zodiac, the scorpion and Orion now represent death and life, whose eternal battle is enacted as the sun moves between the two constellations.

In China the scorpion was one of the five venomous animals, but images of it could help keep at bay demons or illness. In Zoroastrian religion, the scorpion was a creation of the power of darkness, or Ahriman. In Mithraic religion, however, the scorpion became one of the animal companions of Mithras as he sacrificed a great bull to regenerate the world.

In Christianity, the scorpion was often a symbol of the Devil, waiting in ambush for unsuspecting travelers. Jesus told his followers, "Yes, I have given you power to tread underfoot serpents and scorpions . . . " (Luke 10:19). In the late Middle Ages and Renaissance, the tempter in Eden was sometimes depicted not as a serpent but as a creature with the face of a woman and the tail of a scorpion, an image that goes back to Selket. Some moralists misogynistically compared the scorpion's habit of hiding in holes to a woman who would hide perfidious intent behind a beautiful face.

Selected References

Black, Jeremy, and Anthony Green. *Gods, Demons, and Symbols of Ancient Mesopotamia: An Illustrated Dictionary.* Austin: University of Texas Press, 1992.

Flores, Nona C. " 'Effigies Amicitiae . . . Veritatas Inimicitiae': Antifeminism in the Iconography of the Woman-Headed Serpent in Medieval and Renaissance Art and Literature." In *Animals in the Middle Ages: A Book of Essays.* Ed. Nona C. Flores. New York: Garland, 1996, pp. 167–196.

Houlihan, Patrick F. *The Animal World of the Pharaohs.* New York: Thames and Hudson, 1996.

Staal, Julius D. W. *The New Patterns in the Sky: Myths and Legends of the Stars.* Blacksburg, VA: McDonald and Woodward, 1988.

Sea Creatures

See Starfish, Clam, Octopus, and Other Creatures of the Sea Floor

Seagull, Albatross, and Other Seabirds

At length did cross an Albatross,
Through the fog it came;
As if it had been a Christian soul,
We hailed it in god's name.
—Samuel Taylor Coleridge, "Rime of the Ancient Mariner"

Mariners traditionally observe seabirds closely, since the behavior of these creatures can tell them about subtle changes in the weather or the distance from land. Interpreting the flight and calls of birds, however, is a fairly intuitive art, and it is still often hard to distinguish reasonable calculation from superstition. The lore of mariners, especially those from the British Isles, is full of superstitions about seagulls and related birds.

Three gulls flying overhead together are an omen of death. To kill an albatross or gull brings bad luck, and the fisherman should immediately release any bird caught in his net. Should a seagull fly against the window of a sailor's house while he is away, it is a sign that the master is in danger. Seagulls are remarkable flyers, able to ascend to great heights or hover on the wind. The ability of seagulls and related birds to glide on currents of the wind while remaining almost motionless makes them appear as a cross when seen from below, and so they have sometimes been held in religious regard. These birds follow ships, as though drawn by some kinship with human beings. Their calls are loud and confident yet also plaintive. Gulls and other seabirds can also easily appear to be spirits, especially when their white feathers are seen at night against a dark sky. Sailors from at least medieval times to the present have believed that gulls, albatrosses, and stormy petrels were the souls of people drowned at sea.

Ovid told the story of how the impetuous Greek hero Diomed had wounded the goddess Venus, the Greek Aphrodite, when she appeared in the fields before Troy. Later, as he returned home after victory, his boat was tossed about by terrible storms. The sailors knew this was the vengeance of Venus. One hotheaded crewman named Acmon heaped his scorn on the goddess and challenged her to do her worst. His companions rebuked him, and he tried to answer. The words would not come, for his voice grew thin, his mouth became a beak, and his arms were covered with feathers. He first and then his companions were turned into white birds, gulls and their various relatives. In *The Golden Ass* by Lucius Apuleius, a gull flew about the world to bring back news to Venus.

Ovid also wrote in his *Metamorphoses* that when Ceyx, king of Thrace, was preparing to journey by sea to consult an oracle, his wife

Alcyone was seized with foreboding. She pleaded with him to remain. She reminded him of the shards of ships washed up on the shore. When Ceyx insisted on leaving, she begged to accompany him. That way, she said, should the ship go down in a storm, at least they would lie together. After a long pause, Ceyx refused, promising to be home again within two months' time. The premonitions of Alcyone proved true, and the ship went down in a terrible storm. Juno, the goddess of marriage, sent a dream of Ceyx to Alcyone. He appeared naked and pale, and water flowed through his hair and beard. Alcyone woke and ran to the sea by the light of dawn. In the distance she could see a body. As it floated toward her, she slowly recognized her husband. When Alcyone ran toward him, her feet skimmed over the surface of the sea. Her arms changed into wings, her nose into a beak. Ceyx rose from the sea, and they became a pair of birds. Since that time the winds and sea stay calm for seven days in winter as Alcyone broods on her nest on the surface of the waters. Ovid does not identify the birds, but tradition makes the wife a halcyon, a half-legendary bird mentioned by many authors from Homer on, which scholars believe was a mythologized kingfisher. The name Ceyx means "tern," but Ovid was far more interested in vivid tales than in ornithology, and he probably thought of both husband and wife simply as birds of the sea.

The albatross is reportedly able to predict the weather. In Japan the albatross is a servant of the sea god and, therefore, auspicious. In the West, however, an albatross following a ship has been considered a herald of storms. In Samuel Taylor Coleridge's poem "Rime of the Ancient Mariner" (1800), the narrator kills an albatross that accompanies his ship, apparently on a perverse impulse but probably also in an attempt to evade a tempest. The ship is then stopped by a terrible calm, and the crew drapes the dead albatross about his shoulders as a cross. Only when he learns to love his fellow creatures does the bird fall from his neck.

Selected References

Beck, Horace. *Folklore of the Sea.* Mystic, CT: Mystic Seaport Museum, 1973.

Hole, Christina, E. Radford, and M. A. Radford. *The Encyclopedia of Superstitions.* New York: Barnes and Noble Books, 1996.

Ovid. *Metamorphoses.* Trans. Rolfe Humphries. Bloomington: Indiana University Press, 1955.

Pollard, John. *Birds in Greek Life and Myth.* New York: Thames and Hudson, 1977.

Seal and Dolphin

> That dolphin-torn, that gong-tormented sea.
> —W. B. Yeats, "Byzantium"

Dolphins and seals are aquatic mammals that seem to have a special affinity for human beings. Seals spend a good deal of time sunning themselves on coastal rocks, and they will stare at people in the distance. They will usually scatter into the water if somebody approaches, although in heavily populated coasts, they sometimes lose their fear of human beings. Dolphins are confined to water, but they follow ships at sea, often leaping into the air. There are many stories, some probably true, of dolphins rescuing people from drowning. People have long viewed the upturned mouth of the dolphin as fixed in a perpetual smile.

Mermaids and mermen have been part of myth and legend at least since ancient times in Babylon, where they were depicted on walls. Many cryptozoologists believe that the legends about mermaids first originated from observation of seals. Others, however, believe that the objects of observation were manatees, relatives of seals that appear far less human in form but more human in their locomotion. At any rate, it has not been difficult for sailors to interpret the gaze of female seals as one of amorous longing. The Selkie, figures of British and Irish folklore, are seals that slough off their coats to become human and dance together for an evening on the shore. Sometimes a man will manage to steal the skin of a Selkie maiden and win her as a bride, though she will generally find the skin eventually and rejoin her tribe. Many families along the northern and western coasts of Britain and Ireland trace their ancestry to seal people, and people in some families can even show webbed hands to prove their origin.

Dolphins have been particularly beloved in Greece, where they were sacred to Poseidon, god of the sea. They often drew Poseidon's chariot and accompanied the Nereids and Tritons in his entourage. Pliny the Elder wrote, "Dolphins are not afraid of humans as something alien but come to meet vessels at sea and play and leap around them; they try to race ships and overtake them even when they are in full sail" (p. 130).

Apollo was known also as Delphinus, or Lord of the Dolphin. The Homeric hymn "To Pythian Apollo" relates how the god of the sun was once looking for priests for his temple when he caught sight of a boat containing pirates from Crete. Apollo changed himself into the form of a giant dolphin and leaped from the sea into the ship. The sailors were too frightened to lower their sail, and a wind drove their

ship until it reached the shrine at Delphi. Then Apollo took the form of a young man and told the pirates that he had brought them to be keepers of his sanctuary.

The dolphin was also sacred to Dionysus, a sort of shadow image of Apollo, who shared the shrine at Delphi. According to Apollodorus, Ovid, and others, Dionysus once chartered a pirate ship to the island of Naxos, not far from Crete, which was to be a center of his worship. The pirates, not realizing Dionysus was a god, sailed past his destination, planning to sell him as a slave. The mast and the oars suddenly turned into snakes, the craft filled with ivy, panthers appeared, and the wild music of flutes drove the pirates mad. The men leaped from the boat in terror and became dolphins.

In part because their leaps are so rhythmic, dolphins are reputed to be fond of music. Herodotus told a popular story in which Arion, a peerless musician on the harp, hired a boat to take him to Corinth. Once they were on the open sea, the sailors decided to kill Arion and steal his wealth. Arion entreated them to allow him to sing for one last time on the quarterdeck, after which he promised to end his life. The sailors, delighted at the opportunity to hear his song, quickly agreed. When he had finished his song, he jumped from the boat and landed upon the back of a dolphin, which then took him to his destination. Christians would later think of Arion as a martyr, while the dolphin that bore him away became a symbol of Christ the Savior.

The salvation of Arion was commemorated at Corinth with a bronze statue of a man riding upon a dolphin, and this became a popular motif in Greco-Roman art. Since very early times, the dolphin has been a favorite symbol of port cities in heraldry and on coins. Roman coins since the time of Emperor Titus showed a dolphin, considered the fastest of animals, entwined around an anchor with the motto "*Festina lente*," or "Make haste slowly" (Hall, p. 19).

The lore of the dolphin belongs mostly to maritime culture, in which the ways of many nations have always blended. Because they seem to have such an affinity for human beings, dolphins have often been carefully watched by sailors, who use their motions to forecast weather and, occasionally, fortunes in war. In *The Tale of the Heike*, a medieval Japanese epic of the war between the mighty Heike and Genji clans in the late thirteenth century, a school of about two thousand dolphins suddenly appeared before start of the decisive sea battle of Dan-no-ura. "The Genji will be destroyed if the dolphins stay on the surface and then turn back; we will be endangered if they dive and pass us," an oracle predicted. As soon as the words were out, the dolphins passed under the Heike boats and the commanders realized that they were doomed (McCullough, p. 375).

Occasionally, however, people have interpreted the attraction dolphins appear to feel for human beings as a longing for a tragically departed love. The sounds of the dolphins as they play become a bittersweet lament. The Indonesians tell a story about a man who once beat his wife for giving one of his fish to her son. She went down to the sea to wash off the blood and found herself changed from the waist down into a dolphin. Her husband later mended his ways, set out in search of his wife, and finally was transformed into a porpoise, but the two were never reunited.

With the use of larger, more mechanized ships, traditional maritime culture has declined, and even sailors no longer feel as intimate with the sea as in earlier eras. There has, however, been a revival of interest in dolphins as people have come to value mental over physical abilities. Dolphins have long been reputed to rank among the smartest of animals. Popular writers and a few scientists of the twentieth century have speculated that they might have an oral culture that rivals in sophistication that of humankind. A few science fiction writers have even wondered if dolphins might eventually challenge human supremacy.

But loneliness, far more than intellect, draws us to seals or dolphins and, perhaps, makes them interested in us. For all their well-deserved reputation for drinking, brawling, and whoring, mariners traditionally led a very austere life most of the time. Almost alone on the wide sea, any miracle of love could seem possible.

Selected References

Douglas, Norman. *Birds and Beasts of the Greek Anthology.* New York: Jonathan Cape and Harrison Smith, 1929.

Hall, James. *Illustrated Dictionary of Symbols in Eastern and Western Art.* New York: HarperCollins, 1996.

Herodotus. *Herodotus* (4 vols.). Trans. A. D. Godley. New York: G. P. Putnam's Sons, 1926.

Hine, Daryl, trans. *The Homeric Hymns and the Battle of the Frogs and the Mice.* New York: Anthenium, 1972.

Johnson, Allison. *Islands in the Sound: Wildlife in the Hebrides.* London: Victor Gollancz, 1989.

Knappert, Jan. *Pacific Mythology: An Encyclopedia of Myth and Legend.* London: Diamond Books, 1992.

McCullough, Helen Craig, trans. *The Tale of the Heike.* Stanford: Stanford University Press, 1988.

Pliny the Elder. *Natural History: A Selection.* Ed. and trans. John F. Healey. New York: Penguin, 1991.

Sax, Boria. *The Serpent and the Swan: The Animal Bride in Folklore and Literature.* Blacksburg, VA: McDonald and Woodward, 1998.

Serpent

See Snake, Lizard, and Related Animals

Sheep and Goat

I am not certain that anyone who has not spent time with shepherds can appreciate the intense involvement that exists between the shepherd and his flocks. The well being of the flock is all, everything else falls by the wayside. All that is done the whole year long is attuned to the single overriding consideration of the flock. Man's fierceness in defending his flocks and his lack of tolerance for anything he even imagines impinging on them are remarkable. To people who keep sheep, it almost seems, every other animal on earth could perish and it would be of no account.

—Roger Caras, *A Perfect Harmony*

Sheep and goats were, together with the dog, the first animals to be domesticated by human beings, around the end of the last ice age. Over the millennia, the symbolism and patterns of behavior these animals inspired have been especially intimately integrated into human culture. Sheep and goats are perhaps the only animals that have created not only an industry but also an entire way of life. Pastoral peoples must traditionally base almost every activity around their flocks, staying in one place for a time and then migrating when the edible vegetation is exhausted. Flocks inspire intense protectiveness, and they compel herders to constantly view predators such as wolves and even neighboring people as possible threats. By moving in unison and following a leader, sheep especially provide a model for understanding human society.

Sheep also provide wool, for clothing and food. They will generally eat little besides grass, but they may be kept in rough, mountainous areas that are unsuitable for farming. Goats provide less meat, but they give copious quantities of milk. What is more, they can eat almost anything that grows, and they are even able to climb trees to get at their leaves. Domestic herd animals were the earliest currency and the first measure of wealth, and contemporary expressions such as the "growth" of investments hark back to those origins. Tending flocks offered the best peaceful means to financial advancement in the relatively static societies of the ancient world, so shepherds were perhaps the first middle class.

The biblical story of Cain and Abel records an early conflict between nomadic herders and settled agriculturists. Abel the shepherd offered the firstborn of his flock to God, while Cain the farmer offered his produce. God looked with favor only on the sacrifice of sheep, whereupon Cain killed his brother (Gen. 4:1–8), perhaps as a human sacrifice. Since herding requires a larger area of land than does farming, growing density of population gradually forced more people to turn to agriculture. Nevertheless, the vocation of shepherd remained an honored one in the ancient world, especially among urban dwellers who felt nostalgic for a simpler past. It offered plenty of opportunity for solitude and contemplation. In *Theogony,* the Greek mythologist Hesiod describes how he first became a poet when the Muses appeared to him as he tended sheep on the slopes of Mount Helicon.

The Egyptian god Amun was often portrayed with the head of a ram. The Greeks identified Amun with Zeus, who they believed had taken the form of a ram when the gods fled temporarily to Egypt in their war against the titans. To commemorate his escape, Zeus later placed the ram in the zodiac, where it became the constellation Aries. Zeus was also identified with a domestic herd animal in his own right. When the goddess Rhea, his mother, hid the infant Zeus on the island of Crete to escape the wrath of his father Cronos, the fairy goat Amalthea suckled him. Later one horn of Amalthea broke off, and Zeus turned it into the cornucopia, or horn of plenty.

Perhaps because sheep and goats seem to integrate themselves so well into otherwise forbidding landscapes, the Greeks constantly associated the two animals with flight and hiding. Odysseus, according to Homer, hid himself from the cyclops Polyphemus by clinging

Illustration by Julius Schnorr Carolsfeld from the mid-nineteenth century showing God looking with favor on the sacrifice of Abel while Cain looks on in anger.

to the wool on the belly of a sheep. When the children Phrixus and Helle were in danger of being sacrificed by their wicked stepmother, a golden lamb sent by Zeus swooped down from the sky to carry them away on its back. Helle fell into the sea, but Phrixus was taken to Colchis, where he sacrificed the ram. Its golden fleece was placed upon a tree and guarded by a dragon until it was stolen by the hero Jason, assisted by the princess Medea; today it is used to symbolize the goal of a mystic quest.

The Hebrews were largely a nation of herders, and many patriarchs of Israel, including Abraham, Moses, Jacob, and David, tended flocks. Abraham was commanded by God to sacrifice his son Isaac but was stopped at the last moment by an angel, who directed him to a ram struggling in the bushes, which he was to kill instead of the boy (Gen. 22). This story is usually interpreted as a test of faith, though some thinkers also see it as a rejection of human sacrifice. At any rate, it illustrates the close identification, almost to the point of being interchangeable, between Israel and a flock. According to Jewish legend, Moses tended flocks for forty years, not allowing a single sheep to be hurt by wild beasts or lost. As a reward for his care, God made Moses the leader of Israel.

When Moses had placed a curse on Egypt that the firstborn in every home would be slain, Yahweh directed that every household sacrifice a one-year-old male sheep or goat without blemish and smear some of the blood on the doorposts or lintel, so that Israel might be spared (Exod. 12). The Jews commemorate this event in spring at the feast of Passover, during which a lamb is eaten with unleavened bread and bitter herbs. The Last Supper of Christ, commemorated in the mass, was probably a Passover meal.

The one other herd animal that has had a comparable role in the religious history of humanity is the scapegoat. In a passage from Leviticus, Aaron was directed to take two goats, one of which was to be sacrificed to Yahweh and the other, the scapegoat, driven into the desert for the demon Azazel (16:7–10). This event probably reflected a residual paganism among the Hebrews, which was very promptly repudiated. A slightly later passage in Leviticus states that the Hebrews "must no longer offer their sacrifices to the satyrs [that is, goats and associated deities] in whose service they once prostituted themselves" (17:7). The goat consecrated to Azazel has become a symbol of all who are made to suffer for the sins of the community, for example, Jews in Nazi Germany.

Both the Old and New Testaments also constantly used metaphors drawn from herding to speak of religious matters. Psalm 23, known as "The Lord's Prayer," begins:

> Yahweh is my shepherd
>   I lack nothing.
> In the meadows of green grass he lets me lie.
> To the waters of repose he leads me;
>   There he revives my soul. (1–3)

When John the Baptist first saw Jesus, he exclaimed, "Look, there is the lamb of God that takes away the sins of the world" (John 1:29). Jesus also compared God to a good shepherd (John 10), and the metaphor is commemorated in a bishop's crosier, a ceremonial shepherd's crook. In Revelations, the "Lamb" is used as a code word for Christ, who is to return for a final battle against the forces of evil. Matthew compared the Last Judgment, in which people are sent to

Heaven or Hell, to a shepherd separating the sheep from the goats (25:32–33).

The growing antipathy toward goats in the Judeo-Christian tradition came in reaction to their veneration in other cultures of the ancient world. The Greek god Dionysus took the form of a goat when fleeing to Egypt to escape the serpent Typhon. A goat was sacrificed at the annual festival of Dionysus in a ceremony out of which Greek tragic drama eventually emerged.

According to some myths, the nature spirit Pan was the offspring of the god Hermes and a goat. For the other figures of the Greek pantheon, he was a sort of country bumpkin. They banished Pan from Mount Olympus for his ugliness, and so he wandered the fields and forests. When fleeing from the serpent Typhon, he tried to turn himself into a fish but was so terrified that he could not complete the transformation. He is pictured in the zodiac as a goat with the tail of a fish, the sign Capricorn, and the tale is the origin of the word *panic*. Pan himself could inspire terror, the dreadful solitude of remote places, in any traveler who would disturb his midday sleep. Also goatlike were the Greco-Roman satyrs, though they had human bodies with only the ears, and sometimes horns, of a goat. They were often depicted pursuing nymphs, usually without much success, and they were lecherous enough to mate with animals as well.

The Greek historian Herodotus reported that the Egyptians considered Pan (that is, their god Khem) the most ancient of their gods. The historian also wrote that the people in the Egyptian province of Mendes venerated goats, especially the males, and held goatherds in great honor. To his revulsion, the people of that town reportedly allowed a woman to publicly mate with a goat. Two magical goats, which could be sacrificed, eaten, and then resurrected, accompanied the Norse god Thor. In northern Europe, goats were admired not so much for their fecundity as for their ability to thrive in severe, mountainous landscapes. In the Middle Ages, however, painters often depicted the Devil with the horns of a goat.

In summary, sheep and goats were increasingly used throughout the ancient world to express various polarities: sheep were generally thought of as feminine, goats as masculine; sheep were civilized, goats natural; sheep were Judeo-Christian, goats pagan. This basic symbolism changed very little throughout the Middle Ages and the modern world, but the way in which these various qualities were valued varied greatly. In the eighteenth century, bucolic poetry often nostalgically celebrated the simple shepherd tending his flock. Among Romantics of the nineteenth century, who were fascinated by the idea of primeval wildness, the goat-god Pan became by far the most popular figure in the Greco-Roman pantheon. It was a rather ironic choice, since goats actually do prodigious damage to forests by nibbling at young trees. But, as in so many other contexts from hunting to exploration, people often seem to celebrate the natural world most when engaged in destroying it.

By contrast with the West, the Chinese have never made such a great symbolic distinction between sheep and goats; in fact, the two are often interchangeable. The goat, with its preference for remote solitary places, can often represent the anchorite, and the beard of a male goat resembles the beard often depicted on a Chinese sage. The half-legendary Huang Ch'u P'ing, who lived in the fourth century A.D., was a goatherd who decided to withdraw from the world. He had been meditating for forty years when his brother found him in a cave. After greeting him, the brother asked what had become of the goats. Huang Ch'u P'ing pointed to several white stones that lay scattered around the cavern, and he began to touch them, one by one, with his staff, whereupon each rock jumped up and became a goat. Sheep were introduced in East Asia later than goats, and in oriental art the two herd animals have often been pictured grazing together. The eighth sign of the Chinese zodiac may be depicted as either a goat or ram.

Selected References
Caras, Roger. *A Perfect Harmony: The Intermingling Lives of Animals and Humans throughout History.* New York: Simon and Schuster, 1996.
Herodotus. *Herodotus* (4 vols.). Trans. A. D. Godley. New York: G. P. Putnam's Sons, 1926.
Hesiod. *Theogony/ Works and Days.* Trans. M. L. West. New York: Oxford University Press, 1988.
Hutton, Ronald. *The Stations of the Sun: A History of the Ritual Year in Britain.* New York: Oxford University Press, 1997.
Sun, Ruth Q. *The Asian Animal Zodiac.* Edison, NJ: Castle Books, 1974.

Snake, Lizard, and Related Animals

Now the serpent was more subtle than any beast of the field which the Lord God had made.

—Genesis 3:1

Snakes can have dozens of young at a time, and so they are often symbols of fertility. They resemble vegetation, especially roots, in their form and frequently in the green and brown of their skins. The form of a snake also suggests a river. A point of muscular tension passes through the body of a snake and drives the animal forward, like a moment moving along a continuum of days and years. Like time itself, a snake seems to progress while remaining still. In addition, the body of a snake resembles those marks with a stylus, brush, or pen that make up our letters. Ornamental alphabets of the ancient Celts and others were often composed of intertwined serpents. It could even be that the tracks of a snake in sand helped to inspire the invention of the alphabet. The manner in which snakes curl up in a ball has made people associate them with the sun.

According to one legend, Sakyamuni, who later became the Buddha, was once walking beside a cliff when he looked down and saw a great dragon renowned for wisdom. Seeking enlightenment, Sakyamuni asked many questions, and the dragon answered all of them correctly. Finally, Sakyamuni asked the meaning of life and death. The dragon replied that it would answer only when its hunger had been stilled. Sakyamuni promised his body as food, and the dragon revealed the ultimate truth. Then Sakyamuni hurled himself into the open jaws of the dragon, which suddenly changed into a lotus flower and carried him back to the precipice. The snake, in this case a dragon, is an eternal mediator between opposites: good and evil, creation and destruction, female and male, earth and air, water and fire, love and fear.

Since the snake does not have exposed sexual organs, it is very hard to tell the male snakes from the female ones. Serpents often represent a primeval androgynous state before the separation of male and female. In the ancient world, however, serpents were associated with a vast number of goddesses. These include the Greek Athena, the Mesopotamian Ishtar, the Egyptian Buto, and the Babylonian Tiamat, a primeval goddess from whose blood the world was created. The pharaohs of ancient Egypt would wear uraeus on their heads, a protective image of the goddess Wadjet in the form of a cobra, leaning back and ready to strike.

As people turned more to patriarchal deities, there was a massive revolt against the cult of the snake. This is why serpents are so often destructive in mythologies from very early urban civilizations. Egyptians believed that the serpent Apep would try to devour the boat of the sun god Ra, who sailed through the earth every night. Serpents have been killed by just about every major god or hero of the ancient world and by many heroes in medieval times as well. The Babylonian Marduk killed the serpent-goddess Tiamat, and Zeus killed the primeval serpent Typhon. Apollo, the son of Zeus, killed the serpent Python to gain the shrine at Delphi, formerly sacred to the goddess Gaia. As an infant in his crib, Hercules killed two serpents.

Cadmus, a legendary founder of Greek civilization, killed a serpent and then planted its teeth, whereupon warriors sprang from the earth to become the ancestors of the noble families of Thebes. Sigurd, the Norse hero, killed the dragon Fafner. Saint George—patron of England, Russia, and Venice—killed a dragon, while Saint Patrick drove the snakes out of Ireland. Even today in some communities in Texas, people festively collect rattlesnakes, tease them, and finally kill them for food during annual rattlesnake roundups.

Images of the snake are often similar in cultures that appear to have little or no contact with each other. In Aztec mythology, for example, there was once a female serpent, the earth mother Coatlicue, in a primordial sea. The gods Quetzalcoatl and Tezcatlipoca made Heaven and earth from two parts of her body, an act of creation strangely reminiscent of the creation myth about the Babylonian serpentine goddess Tiamat. Quetzalcoatl, who vanquished Coatlicue, also took on ophidian features, and he was depicted as a feathered serpent of jade. Some of the mythology of serpents may go back to a time before humanity spread across the world and divided into different cultures.

After expelling Adam and Eve from Eden for eating from the Tree of Knowledge, Yahweh placed a curse on the serpent, which has ever since crept upon the ground. But just as the biblical Yahweh does not seem unequivocally good, so the serpent of Eden does not appear entirely evil. Both, in fact, are figures that appear to transcend all earthly categories. In the Middle Ages and Renaissance, the serpent of Eden was often painted with a human head, usually that of a woman. In *Paradise Lost*, John Milton describes the serpent thus:

Woman to the waist, and fair,
But ended foul in many a scaly fold
Voluminous and vast, a Serpent arme'd
With Mortal sting. (lines 2650–2653)

At times, the serpent is a mirror image of Eve. Even in paintings where the head of the serpent is bestial, the serpent and Eve often seem to be exchanging meaningful glances, while Adam simply looks confused. Eve and the serpent share a feminine wisdom. The serpent of Eden has also been identified with Lilith, the first wife of Adam, who was also a Sumerian goddess-demon.

The large, intense eyes of the snake are very mysterious. Pliny the Elder and countless subsequent writers have reported that snakes can hypnotize and even kill with a simple gaze. The basilisk, a serpent with a crown and wings, reportedly had this ability, as did the rattlesnake in the United States. Many authors, from journalists and novelists to serious natural scientists, reported that snakes could draw birds out of the sky by looking upward and could sometimes even work their powers of fascination on human beings.

The serpent has frequently been revived and even deified, especially by the Gnostics and the alchemists. What is feared as "regression" may also be celebrated as "rejuvenation." Serpents are ancient symbols of healing. In the Mesopotamian epic of Gilgamesh, the serpent steals the plant of immortality, then sheds its skin and lives forever. Ancient physicians from Greece to China realized that venom extracted from certain serpents could be used to cure ailments such as paralysis. Serpents are associated with the Greek healer Asclepius, who once raised a man from the dead. The ancient Greek physicians, or Asclepiadae, had so much confidence in the healing powers of the serpent that they would sometimes place snakes in the beds of patients with high fevers. The snakes may have served as a sort of placebo, and the coolness of the serpents' flesh could have convinced the sufferer that he was recovering. The caduceus, a wand with two serpents entwined around it, was carried by Hygeia, daughter of Asclepius, and by the god Hermes. Today it remains a symbol of the medical profession.

The alchemists saw the serpent as an animal that joined all of the four elements from which the cosmos was formed. Of all animals, serpents are the most intimately associated with the earth. This further associates them with fire, since that element escapes from the earth in volcanoes. The red tongue of many serpents, ending in a fork and flickering in and out, also suggests flame. Dragons, especially in European traditions, often breathe fire. Furthermore, serpents may also frequently be found in water, and their rhythmic motion suggests waves. Many dragons and other serpentine figures are often depicted with wings.

Among the most popular images among the alchemists was the ouroboros, a snake with its tail in its mouth, a symbol of primal unity that goes back to ancient Egypt—at least to the time of *The Egyptian Book of the Dead*, written around 1,500 B.C.—and was later taken over by the esoteric religions of Greece. An analogous figure is the serpent Mitgard of Norse mythology, which is coiled around the earth. The Chinese used the V-shaped fangs of a serpent to symbolize the essence of life, and the upside-down version represented the spirits of deceased ancestors.

From the point of view of folklore, lizards may generally be regarded as snakes, even though most (though not all) lizards have legs. Because these animals are often found lying in the desert sun, they have sometimes been associated with contemplative ecstasy. Pliny the Elder reported that the salamander, a black-and-yellow lizard found in most of southern Europe, would seek the hottest fire to breed in and would quench the flames with the coldness of its body. Paracelsus, an influential alchemist and physician of the Renaissance, believed that the salamander was a being of pure fire. The salamander sitting inside a furnace became a symbol of esoteric knowledge. The salamander was compared to the three young Hebrews in the book of Daniel who were thrown into a fiery furnace by the king of Babylon but were not harmed by the flames (3:22–97) and to Christ descending into Hell.

Even the Hebrews, who reacted so vehemently against the archaic cult of the serpent, have occasionally attributed godlike power to this animal. In the book of Exodus, Moses and Aaron were demanding of Pharaoh that the people of Israel be released from bondage. To demonstrate the power of his god, Aaron threw his staff down in front of Pharaoh and his court. It immediately turned into a serpent. At the direction of Pharaoh, the magicians of the court of Egypt took their staffs and performed the same magical act. Then the serpent that had been Aaron's staff swallowed those of the magicians (7:9–13). Later, on the journey to Canaan, the Hebrews were stricken by a plague of fiery serpents. Moses directed the people of Israel to erect a bronze serpent on a standard. All those who looked upon the brazen serpent were saved from death (Num. 21:4–9). Had these stories not been sanctioned by scripture, the bronze serpent would probably have seemed to the Jews like sorcery and idolatry. Among the most extravagant dragons of all was the one that did battle with Saint Michael in the biblical Revelation. It had seven heads, each bearing a crown, and ten horns, and it swept a third of the stars from the sky with its tail (12: 1–9).

A positive view of the serpent has also frequently been preserved in folk culture. During his wanderings after the fall of Troy, Aeneas' father, Anchises, had died. Landing on the coast of Sicily, Aeneas began the funeral rites by pouring out wine, milk, and the blood of sacrificial victims. Then he cast flowers upon the funeral mound and started his oration. He had barely begun to speak when, in the words of Virgil's *Aeneid*, translated by John Dryden:

> Scarce had he finished, when, with speckled pride,
> A serpent from the tomb began to glide;
> His hungry bulk on sev'n high volumes roll'd;
> Blue was his breadth of black, but streaked with scaly gold:
> Thus riding on his curls, he seem'd to pass
> A rolling fire along, and singe the grass.
> More various colors thro' his body run,
> Than Iris with her bow imbibes the sun.
> Betwixt the rising altars, and around,
> The sacred monster shot along the ground;
> With harmless play amidst the bowls he pass's,
> And with his lolling tongue assay'd the taste:
> Thus fed with holy food, the wondrous guest
> Within the hollow tomb retir'd to rest. (book 5)

The snake was the spirit of his father, whom Aeneas would later visit in Hades. Romans would sometimes feed snakes at household altars.

In *Zoological Mythology*, Angelo De Gubernatis wrote that the practice of keeping a snake in the home for good luck survived among Italian peasants into modern times. The Sythians, who lived by the Black Sea and were known for their fierceness, traced their ancestry to the daughter of the Dnieper River, who was a woman above the waist but whose body ended in a serpent's tail. Not only the ancient Romans but many other peoples—for example, Australian Aborigines—have believed that ancestors return in the form of snakes. Zulu kings of legend sometimes would return to this world in the form of a powerful snake.

Despite, or because of, the fact that they are not easily distinguished by gender, snakes appear highly sexual, and there are many tales of serpentine paramours. One fable from the Hindu-Persian *Pan-*

chatantra tells of a Brahman and his wife who had longed for children but were unable to conceive. One day a voice in the temple promised the Brahman a son who would surpass all others in both appearance and character. A short time later his wife did indeed become pregnant, but she gave birth not to a human being but to a snake. Her friends advised her to have the monster killed, but she insisted on raising the snake as her child, keeping him in a large box, bathing him regularly, and feeding him fine delicacies. At her urging, the Brahman even arranged for the snake to marry a beautiful girl, the daughter of a friend. The girl, who had a strong sense of duty, accepted the marriage and took over the care of the reptile. One day, a strange voice called her in her chamber. At first she thought a strange man had broken in, but it was her husband, who had climbed out of the snakeskin and taken on human form. In the morning the Brahman burned the snakeskin, so his son would not be transformed again, then proudly introduced the young couple to all the neighbors.

Both snakes and dragons are designated by the same word, *draco,* in Latin. We can generally regard dragons as snakes, just as zoologists of the Middle Ages and Renaissance did. Edward Topsell, for example, wrote in *The History of Four-Footed Beasts and Serpents and Insects* (1657), "There be some Dragons which have wings and no feet, some again have neither feet nor wings, but are only distinguished from the common sort of Serpents by the combe growing upon their heads and the beard under their cheeks" (vol. 2, p. 705). The variety and range of dragons vastly exceed those of any other mythic animal. Dragons often have features of other animals, such as the wings of bats or horns of stags, but these are set upon serpentine forms. Just as it mediates between the elements, the snake seems to combine features of all creatures in its incarnation as the dragon.

The Chinese dragon known as "lung" is among the most colorful and extravagant composites. When first born, it appears as a simple serpent. Over thousands of years of life, it acquires the head of a camel, the scales of a carp, the horns of a deer, the eyes of a hare, the tusks of a boar, and the ears of an ox. It also has four short legs with enormous claws, a mouth with long teeth, and a flowing mane running down its back. A combination of fire and steam issues from its nostrils to form the clouds, and so it controls the weather. These dragons are the most beneficent figures of the Chinese zodiac.

In European culture, opposites are generally thought of as mutually exclusive, whereas Asians tend to view them as complementary. Because of this, Western culture has alternated between admiration and scorn for the serpent, while the Chinese have expressed both at once. In very archaic times, the serpent was almost universally revered in China. Into the twentieth century, several temples in southern China have followed the tradition of keeping sacred serpents that are offered wine and eggs on the altar. Chinese culture gradually began to distinguish sharply between the snake and the dragon, yet the two are associated as contraries. The snake represents qualities opposite to those of the dragon in the Chinese zodiac, where its symbolism is remarkably close to that in the Judeo-Christian tradition; the snake is as deceitful as the dragon is exuberant.

As the modern period began, people increasingly thought of the snake as masculine. The traditional eroticism of the snake was originally considered primarily a feminine attribute, later a male one. The latter view was sanctioned especially by Freudian psychology, where people have usually interpreted the snake as phallic. In James Joyce's *Portrait of the Artist as a Young Man,* the hero, Stephen Dedaelus, calls his sexual organ "the serpent, the most subtle beast of the field" (chap. 3).

Legend usually locates fantastic beasts on the frontier of human exploration, and the serpent is a good example. With the expansion of maritime trade at the end of the Middle Ages, the Great Sea Serpent was second in importance only to the mermaid as a figure in the law of mariners. Sightings of serpentine creatures were reported everywhere from Loch Ness in Scotland to the coasts of the New World and were often attested to by persons who had reputations for good judgment and sobriety. The animals were identified with many mythological creatures, from the Norse serpent Mitgard to the biblical Leviathan. While the descriptions differed in their details, they generally described the serpent as extremely long and as moving with an undulating motion. On August 21, 1936, for example, newspapers reported that several Newfoundland fishermen had seen a monster that was at least 200 feet long, had "eyes as big as an enamel saucepan," snorted blue vapor from its nostrils, and stirred up such waves that "for days no boat dared venture out to sea" (O'Neill, pp. 194–195).

The symbolism of the snake has changed far less fundamentally than has that of other animals such as the dog or horse. It seems to surface whenever people contemplate origins, whether of humanity, of life, or even of the universe itself. Today, the DNA code that directs the development of the embryo is sometimes called "the cosmic serpent."

Selected References

Gubernatis, Angelo De. *Zoological Mythology or the Legends of Animals.* Chicago: Singing Tree Press, 1968.

Joyce, James. *A Portrait of the Artist as a Young Man.* New York: Barnes and Noble Books, 1999.

Milton, John. *Paradise Lost and Paradise Regained*. New York: Penguin, 1976.

Mundkur, Balaji. *The Cult of the Serpent: An Interdisciplinary Survey of Its Manifestations and Origins*. Albany: SUNY Press, 1983.

Nott, Charles Stanley. *The Flowery Kingdom*. New York: Chinese Study Group of America, 1947.

O'Neill J. P. *The Great New England Sea Serpent: An Account of Unknown Creatures Sighted by Many Respectable Persons between 1638 and the Present Day*. Camden, ME: Down East Books, 1999.

Roob, Alexander. *Alchemy and Mysticism*. New York: Taschen, 1997.

Rybot, Doris. *It Began before Noah*. London: Michael Joseph, 1972.

Ryder, Arthur W., ed. *The Panchatantra*. Chicago: University of Chicago Press, 1964.

Sax, Boria. *The Serpent and the Swan: The Animal Bride in Folklore and Literature*. Blacksburg, VA: McDonald and Woodward, 1998.

Sun, Ruth Q. *The Asian Animal Zodiac*. Edison, NJ: Castle Books, 1974.

Topsell, Edward, and Thomas Muffet. *The History of Four-Footed Beasts and Serpents and Insects* (3 vols.). New York: Da Capo, 1967 (facsimile of 1658 edition).

Virgil. *Virgil's Aeneid*. Trans. John Dryden. New York: P. F. Collier and Son, 1937.

Sparrow

> *The brawling of a sparrow in the eaves,*
> *The brilliant moon and all the milky sky,*
> *And all the famous harmony of leaves,*
> *Had blotted out man's image and his cry.*
> —W. B. Yeats, "The Sorrow of Love"

The sparrow is among the most familiar of animals in both urban and rural settings. The diminutive size of sparrows has often made them objects of affection, but their raucous, noisy behavior has hurt their reputation.

The Greek poetess Sappho wrote of sparrows drawing the chariot of Aphrodite, the goddess of love. The sparrow was, however, often a symbol of profane love, which was sometimes contrasted with the chaste passion of the dove. The Roman poet Catullus wrote a tender elegy beginning "Mourn ye Graces . . . " (*Lugete, o Veneres . . .*) to the pet sparrow of his mistress. The author described how the sparrow would "chirp to his mistress alone" and celebrated the great love they had for each other, clearly identifying with the bird.

Christ told his apostles, "Can you not buy two sparrows for a penny? And yet not one falls to the ground without your father knowing" (Matt. 10:29). Sparrows became symbols of the apparently inconsequential things that are significant in the sight of God.

Bede used this symbolism during the early eighth century in his *Ecclesiastical History of the English Nation,* when a noble said to King Edwin, "The present life of man, o king, seems to me, in comparison of that time which is unknown to us, like the flight of a sparrow through the room wherein you sit at supper in winter . . . " (book 2, chap. 13). He went on to compare the sparrow's flying from the warm room into the wintry storm with the passage of a soul into eternity. Christianity, the noble explained, offered promise of certainty in that precarious journey. The way sparrows nest in almost any enclosed space, including the corners of barns or porches, has also made them symbols of domesticity. Folk belief, especially in Britain, often holds that deceased ancestors may come back as sparrows.

But the sparrows of folklore can also be malignant. One European legend says that when Christ was hiding from his pursuers, sparrows betrayed him by their chirping. A similar legend says that when Christ was on the Cross, the swallows tried to prevent his enemies from inflicting further torment by saying, "He is dead," but the sparrows replied, "He is alive."

Its integration into the routines of everyday life made the sparrow a politically charged theme in the middle of the nineteenth century. Sparrows from England were imported and became naturalized in major cities of the eastern United States. An intense debate raged for several decades as to whether these birds were harmful to American landscapes. The Great English Sparrow War, as it was known, closely resembled disputes about whether the United States should welcome immigrants. In describing the sparrows, their detractors employed the same sort of rhetoric used to attack foreigners, calling the birds loud, unclean, and promiscuous. Others found the little creatures a charming addition to urban landscapes.

Selected References

Bede [Beda Vererabilis]. *Ecclesiastical History of the English Nation.* Trans. John Stevens et al. New York: Dutton, 1975.

Catullus. "Lugete, o Veneres." In *Catullus, Tibullus, Pervigilim Veneris.* Ed. C. P. Goold. Cambridge: Harvard University Press, 1962, pp. 4–5.

Hole, Christina, ed. *The Encyclopedia of Superstitions.* New York: Barnes and Noble Books, 1961.

Lawrence, Elizabeth Atwood. *Hunting the Wren: Transformation of Bird to Symbol.* Knoxville: University of Tennessee Press, 1997.

Spider

The Soul, reaching, throwing out for love,
  As the spider, from some little promontory, throwing out filament after
    filament, tirelessly
      out of itself, that one at least may catch and form a link, a bridge, a
  connection

—Walt Whitman

The spider is an image of fate in its relentlessness, as well as in its combination of terror and beauty. The image of a spiderweb gleaming in the dew suggests the stars against the Milky Way. Furthermore, spiders certainly have abilities that could move even a goddess to envy. Even today, engineers have not managed to create a filament with the same combination of thinness, flexibility, and tensile strength as that of a spider. The usual manner in which spiders devour their prey can make anybody shudder. When a fly is caught in a web, the spider will inject it with digestive juices and go away, returning later to eat the prey a little at a time. Among certain species, particularly the garden spiders of southern Europe, the female will devour the male upon mating, an eerily literal expression of the primal unity of conception and death. Spiders have not two eyes but eight, enabling them to see in almost every direction. Nobody can meet, much less read, the gaze of a spider. Two eyes are so much the rule among animals from whales to grasshoppers that any other number can impress people as grotesque. Folklore constantly exaggerates the fearsome attributes of spiders, especially the deadliness of their poisons.

Ovid traced the origin of spiders to the story of Arachne, a young girl who was so skilled at spinning and weaving that even the nymphs gazed on her with wonder. She had boasted that her skill exceeded even that of the goddess Athena. Upon hearing this, the goddess took on the shape of an old woman and went to Arachne, warning her against arrogance. When Arachne refused to retract her boast, Athena revealed herself and challenged Arachne to a contest in weaving. Even then, Arachne was not intimidated, and she accepted without hesitation. On her loom, Athena wove pictures of mortals who had dared to measure themselves against the divinities and met their doom. On her loom, Arachne wove pictures showing the follies of gods and goddesses, especially in their affairs with mortals. Athena, on seeing this, became so furious that she began to beat Arachne until the young girl ran away, placed her neck in a noose, and tried to hang herself. "Live," said Athena, "but hang forever," and Arachne was changed into a spider suspended by a thread (book 4, lines 1–145).

This tale shows the horrible fate that awaits those who would challenge the gods and goddesses. But just a moment! Take a good look at Arachne. She is every spider. Many people think she is creepy, and many others think she is beautiful. Nobody, however, really thinks she appears unhappy. Was the punishment of Athena so terrible? After all, Arachne not only eluded death but was able to continue the work she loved until the end of time.

Animals, gods, and tribal totems are far more ancient than divinities in the form of men and women. I suspect that Arachne, far from a simple mortal, was a divinity who was more powerful than even Athena. The spider symbolizes archaic mother-goddesses, the weavers of fate. This creature is associated with the Egyptian Neith, the Babylonian Ishtar, and the Germanic Holde. In Greek mythology, the three fates, to whom even the greatest of the gods and goddesses are subject in the end, resemble spiders. Perhaps in some lost version of her story, Arachne simply assumed a human appearance to trick Athena, and she revealed her true form in victory.

The spider is among the most primordial and powerful divinities in many cultures. For numerous West African tribes, the spider is a trickster and a culture hero. Among the Hausa, the spider is Gizo. Among the Ashanti and in Jamaica, he is Anansi. According to the Ashanti, the animals were once arguing about who was the oldest and deserved the most respect. Finally, they asked Anansi to be the judge. First came the guinea fowl, who told of a great fire at the beginning of the world. She had to stamp it out and her legs are red to this day. Then the parrot claimed to be the oldest. There were no blacksmiths when he was created, so he had to beat iron with his beak, and it is bent to this day. The elephant, rabbit, and porcupine all told stories from the beginning of the world, showing their great age. Finally, Anansi told them that he himself was the oldest. He was created before the earth and had nothing to stand on. When his father died, there was no earth to bury him, so Anansi had to bury his father in his head. The animals all bowed to Anansi, acknowledging that he was the most ancient.

Because spiders are unique, they seem to share something akin to human alienation from the natural world. Their ability to spin threads from their bodies is shared only by silkworms and caterpillars, and the intricacy of their webs has no parallel. It may well be that early hunters were inspired by spiderwebs to create nets and traps. By preserving food to be eaten later, spiders seem to show a human sort of foresight. By stunning prey yet not killing it immediately, they also seem to show a human sort of cruelty.

The spider is a solitary creature, and it has been an aid and inspiration to people who are isolated and pursued. When David was fleeing from the soldiers of King Saul and took refuge in a cave, a spider covered up the entrance with its web. The pursuers thought nobody could have entered and so passed on. The same story is told of Mohammed when he was hiding from his enemies in Mecca. When Robert the Bruce of Scotland was hiding from the English in a barn on the island of Rathlin, he looked up and saw a spider try six times to swing from one rafter to another. "Now shall this spider teach me what I am to do," said Robert, "for I also have failed six times." The spider made it on the seventh try. Robert returned to Scotland, rallied his men, and won a great victory over the English at Bannockburn in 1314.

But the asocial character of spiders also contributes to the fear they inspire. In the Middle Ages spiders were a frequent ingredient in witches' brew; they were also familiars of witches. The spider, lying in wait for its prey, became a common symbol of the Devil. The most feared of all are the large, hairy spiders known as tarantulas, found in Latin America, Africa, and southern Europe. In southern Italy during the Renaissance, there was an epidemic of hysteria about these spiders that was far out of proportion to the danger from their actual bite. People believed that only continual movement could overcome the poison of the spider, and thus, to stay alive, a bitten person had to dance the tarantella.

In cultures of the Far East, spiders are generally disliked because they hide in corners. Furthermore, as major predators in the world of small creatures, they seem sinister and almost cannibalistic. The Chinese novel *Journey to the West*, written by Wu Ch'eng-en in the sixteenth century, tells how the monk Tripitaka Tang was once captured by spider-women on his journey from China to India to obtain the Buddhist scriptures. He stopped at a mansion to ask for a vegetarian meal and was greeted by four pleasant young women, but the meal they offered turned out to be human flesh. When the monk tried to leave, they tied him with strings spun from their navels. Only rescue by his animal companions prevented him from becoming their meal.

In Japan there are many stories of enormous spiders that haunt abandoned castles and other ruins. They may take the form of human beings to fool the unwary. One tale collected by Lafcadio Hearn told of a samurai who went to spend the night in an old temple that villagers said was haunted. A priest came in the night and played on a stringed instrument with skill that seemed more than human. After a while the priest turned to the samurai and said laughingly, "Did you think me a goblin? I am only a priest, but I must play my instrument to keep the goblins away. Would you like to try?" The samurai carefully reached out his left hand to touch the instrument, whereupon the strings changed into a giant spiderweb and the priest became an enormous spider. The samurai drew his sword with his right hand and slashed at the goblin, which retreated. The samurai was bound in the web and could not follow. The next morning villagers came and freed him, and then they followed the trail of blood and killed the spider (pp. 13–15).

By contrast, for many Native American tribes, including the Navaho and Hopi, Spider Woman is the creator deity. According to

Navaho legend, a young girl once saw a line of smoke emerging from a hole in the ground. When she looked closely, she saw Spider Woman, who invited her to come down and learn to weave. Navaho women still place a hole in their blankets in memory of the place where the young girl encountered the goddess.

Similarly powerful but far less beneficent is Iktomi, the major trickster figure of the Sioux and other Indians of the American Midwest. According to the traditions of the Lakota Sioux, he is the creator of time and the inventor of language. He is, however, also a coward, a liar, a lecher, and constantly prone to trouble. Undisciplined though he may be, the Indians still respect his power. An offering of tobacco to Iktomi can bring success in hunting.

There could hardly be a more enthusiastic arachnophile than Thomas Muffet, the Englishman who wrote *The Theater of Insects* in 1658. He observed of the spider:

> When she sticks aloft with her feet cast every way, she exactly represents a painted star. As if nature had appointed not only to make it round like the heavens, but with rays like the stars, as if they were alive. The skin is so soft, smooth, polished and neat, that she so precedes the softest skin'd maids, and the daintiest and most beautiful strumpets, and it is so clear that you may almost see your face in her as in a glass; she hath fingers that the most gallant virgins desire to have theirs like to them, long slender, round of exact feeling, that there is no man, nor any creature that can compare with her. (vol. 3, pp. 1065–1066)

Spiders may be ruthless toward flies, but, Muffet argues, they have a vast number of uses for human beings. Not only are their webs good for binding wounds, but the spiders themselves may be used in many kinds of medicines.

Of course, not everyone agreed with his judgment. Perhaps the most famous of the Mother Goose nursery rhymes is a satire that was probably written about Patience Muffet, the daughter of Thomas:

> Little Miss Muffet
> Sat on a tuffet [a nonsense word],
> Eating her curds and whey;
> There came a big spider,
> Who sat down beside her
> And frightened Miss Muffet away. (Baring-Gould, p. 114)

By giving the spider so many feminine virtues, perhaps Thomas Muffet had made her an ironic sort of patron for girls and women.

Jonathan Swift, however, showed us a distinctly masculine spider in his story "The Battle of the Books" (first published in 1697), a satire on the dispute over which writers were better, those of antiquity or those of contemporary times: "For upon the highest corner of a large window there dwelt a certain spider, swollen up to the first magnitude by the destruction of infinite numbers of flies, whose spoils lay scattered before the gates of his palace, like human bones before the cave of some giant. The avenues to his castle were guarded with turnpikes and palisades, all after the modern way of fortification" (p. 381). Because he lived indoors and practiced a sophisticated form of architecture, this spider became the advocate of the modern writers, while a wayward bee represented the ancient ones.

Folklore not only makes spiders fearsome but also gives them protection. It is very widely believed that to kill a spider brings bad luck. Another English nursery rhyme goes:

> If you wish to live and thrive,
> Let the spider run alive. (Hillyard, p. 19)

A small black spider found in England is known as the "money spider," and if it lands on your clothes, that is an omen of wealth. You must not carelessly brush this spider off, though you are permitted to toss it over your shoulder. The spider is close to primordial powers and should be treated with care.

As chthonic figures, spiders are constantly linked with the dead and the realm beneath the earth. The Massachusetts Puritan Jonathan Edwards preached in his sermon "Sinners in the Hands of an Angry God" (first published in 1734) that "the God that holds you over the pit of Hell, much as one holds a spider, or some loathsome insect, over a fire, abhors you, and is dreadfully provoked" (p. 57). Spiders may be our most potent symbol of primeval life, yet they are associated not with expansive landscapes but with desolate crannies. This paradox is the basis of a vision by the perverse Svidrigaylov in Fyodor Dostoyevski's novel *Crime and Punishment* (first published in Russian in 1865–66). Svidrigaylov pictures eternity not as vast but as "a little room, something like a village bath-house, grimy, and spiders in every corner . . . " (p. 305).

A positive image of the spider may be found in the classic children's story *Charlotte's Web*, by E. B. White, first published in 1952. By writing messages in her web, Charlotte saves the piglet Wilbur from slaughter, but her compassion is tempered by acceptance of a natural order in which life is sustained only through killing. Even Wilbur must accept that Charlotte and her children live off other insects.

Giant spiders, sometimes created through radioactivity, have become a cliché of horror and science fiction. A popular comic-book hero today is Spiderman. He climbs buildings and throws out mechanical webs. Although Spiderman is usually a hero, his arachnid identity suggests power, mystery, and a piquant sense of menace. Today, the spider has become a symbol of technology, the gatekeeper of the Internet and the World Wide Web.

Selected References
Baring-Gould, William S. and Ceil. *The Annotated Mother Goose.* New York: Bramhall House, 1962.

Courlander, Harold. *A Treasury of African Folklore: The Oral Literature, Traditions, Myths, Legends, Epics, Tales, Recollections, Wisdom, Sayings, and Humor of Africa.* New York: Marlowe and Co., 1996.

Dostoyevski, Fyodor. *Crime and Punishment.* Trans. David Magarshak. New York: Greenwich House, 1982.

Edwards, Jonathan. "Sinners in the Hands of an Angry God." In *The Sermons of Jonathan Edwards: A Reader.* Ed. Wilson H. Kimnach, Kenneth P. Minkena, and Douglas A. Sweeney. New Haven: Yale University Press, 1999, pp. 49–65.

Hearn, Lofcadio. *Japanese Fairy Tales.* Mount Vernon, NY: Peter Pauper Press, 1936.

Hillyard, Paul. *The Book of the Spider: From Arachnophobia to the Love of Spiders.* New York: Random House, 1994.

Mullett, G. M. *Spider Woman Stories.* Tucson: University of Arizona Press, 1979.

Ovid. *Metamorphoses.* Trans. Rolfe Humphries. Bloomington: Indiana University Press, 1955.

Swift, Jonathan. "The Battle of the Books." In *The Writings of Jonathan Swift.* Ed. Robert A. Greenberg and William B. Piper. New York: Norton, 1973, pp. 373–396.

Topsell, Edward, and Thomas Muffet. *The History of Four-Footed Beasts and Serpents and Insects* (3 vols.). New York: Da Capo, 1967 (facsimile of 1658 edition).

White, E. B. *Charlotte's Web.* London: Hamish Hamilton Children's Books, 1952.

Squirrel

See Beaver, Porcupine, Badger, and Miscellaneous Rodents

Stag

See Hart and Hind

Starfish, Clam, Octopus, and Other Creatures of the Sea Floor

The Kraken sleepeth: faintest sunlights flee
About his shadowy sides: above him swell
Huge sponges of millennial growth and height;
And far away into the sickly light,
From many a wondrous grot and secret cell
Unnumber'd and enormous polypi
Winnow with giant fins the slumbering green.
  —Alfred Lord Tennyson, "The Kraken"

Though the surface of the earth has long been thoroughly explored, the floor of the ocean retains, at least for now, most of its ancient mystery. Ancient mythologies anticipated modern science by having life emerge from deep waters. Tradition makes the ocean a remnant of the primeval chaos surrounding the land and its kingdoms. The ocean impressed early people as an endlessly fertile womb from which new forms of life constantly emerged. The variety of life within the ocean is far greater than that on land. The structural similarity among most vertebrates, with their legs and arms, is easy to observe. Many invertebrates from the sea, from octopuses to clams to sea anemones, seem unlike anything else in the entire world. According to Hesiod in his *Theogony*, Aphrodite, the Roman Venus, first emerged from the ocean when it was fertilized from the sperm of the castrated Uranus.

Aphrodite was sometimes portrayed as floating toward the shore on the shell of a scallop, after she had been created from the foaming sea. Shells were later used as baptismal fonts in Christianity, and they came to be associated with the Virgin Mary, who assumed many attributes from the pagan goddesses who preceded her. The starfish is known in Latin as the "*Stella Maris*," or "star of the sea," and takes its name from the Virgin Mary in her capacity as a guardian of mariners. In secular culture, it is a positive symbol of the richness and bounty of the sea. Just as mariners navigated by the stars, starfish are often shown pointing directions with their arms.

In many cultures, shells have been used as a medium of exchange. The money originally used by American Indians of the Eastern woodlands was wampum, which consisted of strings of shells. Since the Bank of England did not allow the American Colonies to coin their own money and European currency was in short supply,

Illustration from mid-nineteenth-century America showing a man assaulted by an octopus.

the Colonists often adopted Indian currency for their own transactions, and in 1761 they even set up a factory in New Jersey to manufacture wampum. The clam seems to provide a more vivid symbol in death than in life, for living clams are often thought of as slimy. On the other hand, the phrase "happy as a clam" designates a carefree existence.

The octopus, according to contemporary researchers, is exceptionally intelligent, and it also shows an emotional expressiveness that is perhaps (at least from a human point of view) unique among invertebrates. Not only does it seem to express moods through changes in color, but also its gestures appear remarkably articulate. As might be expected, people have been disconcerted as well as charmed by these signs of internal life. The octopus is a common motif—its limbs often stylized in curvilinear patterns—on jars and artifacts from Crete and other early civilizations in the Aegean. In Christian culture, its practice of squirting black ink to blind other creatures has made the octopus a symbol of the Devil, while its many arms have sometimes made it stand for lechery. It is often depicted on top of a treasure chest from a sunken ship as guardian of the watery depths. Kupe, the legendary ancestor of the Maoris, discovered New Zealand while pursuing an octopus in his boat.

Closely related to, and often confused with, the octopus is the squid, though it does not have the same simplicity of form. The squid tends to be more aggressive, and in addition to having eight arms like the octopus, it has two tentacles that are used for seizing prey. The existence of a giant squid, so large it could pull down boats, was reported in the sixteenth century by the Swedish naturalist Olaus Magnus and by many explorers over the next several centuries. The superstitious mariners scored a remarkable triumph over skeptical scientists when several enormous squids, one about fifty-five feet long, were washed ashore on the coast of Norway in the 1870s. This creature may have been the prototype of many ancient monsters of legend, such as the Greek Scylla who seized men from the ship of Odysseus.

The ocean mirrors the sky, and many creatures of the watery depths, such as the octopus and lobster, have sometimes been seen in constellations. The crab representing the constellation Cancer was sent by Hera to harass Hercules as he battled the seven-headed Hydra. The hero, brandishing a torch in one hand and a sword in the other, still managed to crush the crab under his feet. In Japan, crabs are sometimes said to be the spirits of the Heike warriors who committed suicide by throwing themselves into the sea after losing the battle of Dan-no-Ura to the Genji clan.

All of these sea creatures are more or less anomalies, unlike anything else in the natural world. And perhaps we humans are fascinated by them because we ourselves are an anomaly, constantly troubled by our isolation from the rest of nature. Many of these creatures seem to show a glimmer of the human spirit in a paradoxical way. The crab, for example, with its zigzag walk, seems to reflect the human propensity for hesitation. The remains of these creatures are a tangible link with a mysterious kingdom, and so, in the nineteenth century, such relics as shells became favorite souvenirs for tourists of coastal towns.

Selected References

Cohen, Daniel. *The Encyclopedia of Monsters.* New York: Dorset Press, 1982.

Gibson, Claire. *Signs and Symbols: An Illustrated Guide to Their Meaning.* New York: Barnes and Noble, 1996.

Olalquiaga, Celeste. *The Artificial Kingdom: A Treasury of Kitsch Experience.* New York: Pantheon, 1998.

Stork

See Heron, Ibis, Crane, and Stork

Swallow

True hope is swift and flies with swallow's wings.
—William Shakespeare, *Henry V* (act 5, scene 2)

The swooping, gliding motion of a swallow as it catches insects in flight, together with its incessant calls, has sometimes impressed people as something resembling signs of mourning. In much of the world, however, the swallow is also a joyful bird, since its presence announces the coming of spring. Because the swallow often makes its nest in crannies of buildings, it has always been on intimate terms with human beings. In France and other parts of Europe, rural people have often believed that the nest of a swallow would protect their homes. For Romans, swallows represented the penates, or household spirits. Sometimes swallows were believed to be spirits of dead children, and people were not permitted to kill them. Swallows are almost perpetually in the air, and so medieval people thought they did not have feet. In part for that reason, they have always been considered very spiritual.

In the following ancient love poem from Egypt, a young woman is returning from a visit to her lover:

> The voice of the swallow is speaking.
> It says:
> Day breaks, what is your path?
> (The girl answers) Don't little bird!
> Are you scolding me?
> I found my lover on his bed,
> And my heart was sweet to excess. (Arnold, p. 45)

This poem shows a remarkable resemblance to the "songs of dawn" by medieval minnesingers and troubadours, in which lovers would often be awakened by a lark or other bird.

Swallows were often depicted on Egyptian mummies, suggesting they were already associated with resurrection. According to Plutarch, when Isis had retrieved the coffin of Osiris, she flew about his body and lamented in the form of a swallow. As Isis often became identified with Mary, similar tales were eventually told of the mother of Christ. An Italian legend relates that when Mary stood before the Cross, the swallows saw her distress. They swooped down and tried

The swallow and spider compete for a fly in this illustration from the mid-nineteenth century by J. J. Grandville.

to comfort her, coming ever closer until finally they began to touch her with their feathers. As they turned, Mary's tears landed on their breasts and changed them from black to white. Swallows have frequently been portrayed darting about Christ as he lay on the Cross. According to Swedish legend, they fanned him with their wings. For devout Christians, the appearance of swallows traditionally suggests the resurrection. Insects, especially flies, have often been associated with the Devil, and swallows, like agents of God, would relentlessly pursue bugs in flight.

People have always watched for swallows as a sign that winter was at an end. A fable recorded by the Hellenized Roman Babrius told of a young man who saw a swallow, thought that spring was coming, and decided to wager his winter clothes on a throw of the dice. After he had lost, a snowstorm came, and he soon saw the swallow lying dead from the cold. "Poor creature," he said, "you fooled both yourself and me." This tale may be the origin of the famous saying "One swallow does not make a spring" (Perry, pp. 171, 173).

In part because the trajectories of the birds' flights resembled those of bats, many Europeans believed swallows hibernated in caves. In a famous letter of August 4, 1767, the British pastor and naturalist Gilbert White made one of his rare mistakes. When a large fragment of a chalk cliff had fallen one winter in Sussex, England, many swallows reportedly had been found dead in the debris. Though a bit skeptical of the account, White thought the dead swallows might have been in hibernation. About six and a half years later, White observed that the first swallows of the year were usually seen near ponds and that they disappeared in the event of frost. He suggested that the birds lay dormant through the winter underwater. A few naturalists of the seventeenth and eighteenth centuries even believed that swallows sojourned on the moon. In Muslim countries swallows have traditionally been considered holy, on the ground that they make a yearly pilgrimage to Mecca. Only in the nineteenth century, however, were their migratory paths gradually mapped out.

Selected References

Arnold, Dorothea. *An Egyptian Bestiary.* New York: Metropolitan Museum of Art, 1995.

Charbonneau-Lassay, Louis. *The Bestiary of Christ.* Trans. and ed. D. M. Dooling. New York: Parabola Books, 1991.

Perry, Ben Edwin, trans. and ed. *Babrius and Phaedrus.* Cambridge: Harvard University Press, 1965.

Plutarch. *Plutarch's Morals* (4 vols.). Trans. Robert Midgley et al. London: Thomas Bradyll, 1704.

Steedman, Amy. *Legends and Stories from Italy.* New York: G. P. Putnam's Sons, ca. 1910.

White, Gilbert. *The Natural History of Selborne.* New York: Frederick Warne, ca. 1895.

Swan, Goose, and Duck

But now they drift on the still water,
Mysterious, beautiful;
Among what rushes will they build,
By what lake's edge or pool
Delight men's eyes when I awake some day
To find they have flown away?
—W. B. Yeats, "The Wild Swans at Coole"

Swans, geese, and ducks are closely related, and they have often been substituted for one another in different versions of folktales. They are aquatic birds, which appear more comfortable on water or in the air than on land. They tend, however, to congregate along the shore, since that is where food is most plentiful. If a stranger approaches a pond, they may all rise in unison. Since they often act in concert, they seem to have a sort of solidarity across lines of species. In Sanskrit, a single word, *"hansa,"* was used to designate all three varieties of birds. Nevertheless, their personalities in folklore have become quite distinct. The swan is poetic, solitary, and often tragic in myth and legend, perhaps because of its white plumage and extraordinary grace. The duck is generally not alone but found together with its mate and offspring. The folkloric goose is more gregarious and earthy, and it is often part of a noisy flock.

These birds had considerable religious significance in prehistoric times. Throughout Eurasia and the Near East, there are many myths about the world being hatched from a cosmic egg. The Egyptians, for example, thought that Ra, the god of the sun, emerged from the egg of a goose. Many figurines have been found in which the features of waterbirds, such as elongated necks and beaks, are combined with those of human females. Several scholars such as Marija Gimbutas have speculated about the worship of a bird-goddess in Neolithic times. The Aspares of archaic Hindu mythology, water nymphs that transform themselves into the form of waterfowl, are perhaps early versions of swan maidens, which are important figures of Eurasian folklore. There are countless stories, especially in Scandinavia and elsewhere in northernmost Eurasia, about waterbirds who become women and marry into human society, only to leave their husbands, resume their old form, and fly away. Jacob Grimm and many other scholars have connected the swan maidens with Valkyries, the warrior women of Norse mythology who lead those slain on the battlefield into Valhalla.

Zeus took the form of a swan to seduce the maiden Leda, who then gave birth to the heroic twins Castor and Polydeuces. Leda herself, however, may have at one time been a swan deity. According to some versions of the legend, she laid two eggs. From one egg hatched the twins and from the other, Helen of Troy. According to yet another version of the tale, given by Apollodorus, Nemesis, the goddess of fate, tried to escape the amorous attentions of Zeus by turning into a goose, but the god changed into a swan and raped her. Nemesis laid an egg; it was found by a shepherd in the woods and brought to Leda, who placed it in a chest. Helen eventually hatched from the egg, and Leda raised her as a daughter.

The swan was sacred to the Greco-Roman sun god Apollo, and it appeared on Greek coins as early as the third century B.C. In early Greek religion, people sometimes believed that swans drove Apollo's chariot across the sky each day, though horses later replaced them. The Greek philosopher Plato was known as the "swan of Apollo." Socrates, according to tradition, had once dreamed that a fledgling swan had flown to him from the altar consecrated to love, rested for a while on his knees, then flew away singing beautifully. As he finished relating the dream, Plato was introduced to him, and Socrates knew immediately that this boy had been the swan. Just before dying, Plato dreamed himself to be a swan that flew from tree to tree as people tried in vain to catch him. Simmias, a former companion of Socrates', interpreted the dream to mean that many would try to grasp Plato's spirit, yet no interpretation would capture the full meaning of his words.

A very widespread legend—found in the works of Aelian, Pliny the Elder, and many other writers of the ancient world—is that swans sing a supernaturally beautiful song as they die. In the late Middle Ages, a swan portrayed as pierced with an arrow and singing as it swam became a symbol of the house of Lusignan in France. Swans were especially linked with death in Irish mythology, where they were the form taken by lovers to cross the boundary between earthly existence and the otherworld. According to one myth, Oengus, the god of love, fell in love with a maiden named Cáer. She changed into a swan on the feast of Samhain (November 1) and flew to join him. He also became a swan, and together they flew around a village three times and sang the people to sleep.

Traditional Chinese motif of ducks as symbols of conjugal love.

One popular legend relates that when Lir had been deposed as ruler of Ireland, he married Aev, and together they had three boys and one girl. A short time afterward, however, Aev died. Lir remarried, this time to Aoife, Aev's sister. The stepmother could not bear the way everyone admired the four children, since they were not her own. One day, as the children were bathing, Aoife took a magic wand and transformed them into swans. The girl, Fionnula, eldest of the siblings, begged Aoife to give them back human form. Aoife would not relent, but eventually she agreed to place a limit on the enchantment. She let the children retain human voices and ordered that they would have to wander the desolate islands for nine hundred years before they would again become human. When the allotted time was almost up, they passed Saint Mackevig, one of Saint Patrick's followers, on the remote island of Innis Gluaire. The saint heard the children singing as they swam by, marveled at their voices, and wanted to find them for his choir. After much searching, Saint Mackevig found the children and led them into his chapel. When the bell rang for Communion, the curse ended. In place of the swans were four ancient human beings. Saint Mackevig had just enough time to bless them and baptize them before they died.

The story of Lohengrin, the swan knight, is a sort of swan maiden story with genders reversed. It was included in the epic *Parz_ifal* and many other Middle High German manuscripts, and the Grimm brothers eventually included several versions in their collection of German legends (legends no. 540–545). Though often embellished with colorful details, the essential story is as follows: Elsa, the Duchess of Brabant had been pressured to marry, but she rejected her suitors. One day the knight Lohengrin sailed down the Rhine River in a boat drawn by a swan. Else received him, and the two soon fell in love, married, and had children. Lohengrin defended the kingdom valiantly, but he warned his wife never to ask about his origins. One day, thinking that her children should know about their father, she inquired about Lohengrin's family in a moment of forgetfulness. The knight then returned to his boat, drawn by a swan, and sailed away, never to be seen again.

Perhaps people were too intimidated by the poetic magnificence of swans to ever domesticate them very successfully. The cackling of geese, however, has been heard constantly on farmyards since ancient times. Because they became excited and noisy at any disturbance, they would alert people of any threats. For this reason, they were thought of as protectors of the home. Geese were sacred to Hera, the Greek goddess of marriage, and to her Roman counterpart, Juno. They were often kept in temples. When the Gauls invaded Rome in 390 and were scaling the Palatine Hill by night, the dogs remained silent but the geese alerted the defenders and saved the city. According to Aelian, the event was commemorated yearly in Rome by a celebration in which a dog was sacrificed but a goose was paraded in a litter.

There are many tales of a goose that laid golden eggs, the best known of which comes from the fifth-century Roman fabulist Avianus. A farmer had such a bird, but he became impatient waiting every day for eggs. Finally, he decided to kill the goose, in the expectation that he could obtain the entire treasure all at once. Cutting open the fowl, he found, to his distress, absolutely nothing inside. The moral is to be thankful for what you have and not to demand more.

People have distinguished sharply, however, between domestic geese and their wild counterparts, whose migratory habits remained unknown until modern times. In 1187 Giraldus Cambrensis, who explored the coasts of Ireland, stated that wild geese hatched from shells that clung to driftwood. Later authors reported that the birds grew on trees near the edge of the sea, and they were called barnacle geese or tree geese. The famous botanist John Gerard, in his *Herbal* of 1597, related how he had come across several shells on an old, rotted tree and taken them apart to find avian embryos in various states of development. These reports enabled people of the late Middle Ages and Renaissance to classify wild geese as fish rather than as meat, which meant they could be eaten on Fridays and during Lent.

Male authors from the Renaissance through the Victorian period tended to view women as either utterly wild or completely domestic, and they had much the same attitude toward geese. Unlike swans or ducks, geese have always been thought of as feminine, in part because their incessant chatter made men think of gossipy females. Charles Perrault gave "Tales of Mother Goose" (*Contes de ma Mère l'Oye*) as an alternative title for his famous collection of fairy tales published in 1697. The frontispiece to the first edition showed an old woman spinning as she told tales to children. Since then people have debated the identity of Mother Goose and even whether there was ever such a person at all. In any case, the designation Mother Goose soon came to refer to an archetypal teller of stories, a bit like Aesop in the ancient world. From at least the latter part of the eighteenth century, English and American nursery rhymes have been known as poems of Mother Goose. This apocryphal author has been depicted as an actual goose, at times wearing a bonnet like an old-fashioned nursemaid or housekeeper.

All waterbirds are monogamous. In folklore, while swans and sometimes geese marry human beings, ducks are simply content with their own kind. This is in part because with ducks, unlike their relatives, the male and female of the species are usually very distinct in appearance. Ducks are beloved in the Orient for the variety and splendor of their plumage. Mandarins, especially, are symbols of conjugal fidelity, and to kill them brings bad fortune. Lafcadio Hearn has retold a Japanese story of a hunter named Sonjo, who once came upon a mandarin couple in the rushes, killed the male, cooked him, and ate him. That night he dreamed that he saw a beautiful woman weeping bitterly. She noticed Sonjo, reproached him for killing her husband, and told him to go again to the rushes. When he did so the next morning, the female duck swam straight toward him, tore open her breast with her beak, and died before his eyes. Sonjo was so shaken that he gave up hunting and became a monk.

In the West, ducks have become affectionate symbols of the modern bourgeoisie, who value domestic peace more than poetry or heroism. Hans Christian Andersen contrasted the traditional and modern values, to the detriment of the latter, in his famous tale "The Ugly Duckling." One egg of a mother duck was slow in hatching; the bird that finally came out was oddly proportioned and unusually big. It was not accepted by the other ducks and wandered about alone. Finally, the bird flew up to join a flock of glorious white swans. Looking at its reflection in the water, the bird finally realized that it had been hatched from a swan's egg that had been laid among the ducks. The theme, a common one during the Romantic Movement of the early nineteenth century, was the suffering of the poet in the prosaic world of the middle class.

By the latter nineteenth century, swans were featured less in literature than in the highly stylized medium of opera—for example, Richard Wagner's *Lohengrin* and Pyotr Ilyich Tchaikovsky's *Swan*

Lake—where they evoked the wonder of a heroic past. In *The Wild Duck,* a drama by the Norwegian playwright Henrik Ibsen, the barnyard confinement of a wounded wild duck that had been rescued by a young woman, symbolizes the frustrations of domestic life.

Though the swan was favored in heraldry, the duck is far more prominent in popular culture of the modern age. Rubber ducks for the bathtub are among the most beloved of children's toys, while wooden ducks often decorate the mantelpiece. The most popular duck of all is Donald, who has been the subject of innumerable cartoons and comic books since the 1930s. He displays all the neuroses and insecurities of the middle classes. He is perpetually jealous of his companion, Mickey Mouse, and is forever getting into trouble. All of this makes him easy to identify with in our relatively unheroic age, and, besides, he is usually pretty successful in the end.

Selected References

Aelian. *On Animals* (3 vols.). Trans. A. F. Scholfield. Cambridge: Harvard University Press, 1972.

Andersen, Hans Christian. "The Ugly Duckling." In *Fairy Tales and Stories.* Trans. H. W. Dulcken. New York: Hurst, ca. 1900, pp. 121–129.

Apollodorus. *The Library of Greek Mythology.* Trans. Robin Hard. New York: Oxford University Press, 1997.

Avianus. *The Fables of Avianus.* Trans. David R. Slavitt. Baltimore: Johns Hopkins University Press, 1993.

Gimbutas, Marija. *The Goddesses and Gods of Old Europe: Myths and Cult Images.* New York: University of California Press, 1992.

Giorgetti, Anna. *Ducks: Art, Legend, History.* Trans. Helena Ramsay. Boston: Little, Brown and Company/Bullfinch Press, 1992.

Grimm, Jacob and Wilhelm. *The German Legends of the Brothers Grimm* (2 vols.). Ed. and trans. Donald Ward. Philadelphia: Institute for the Study of Human Issues, 1981.

Hearn, Lafcadio. *Kwaidan: Stories and Studies of Strange Things.* Rutland, VT: Charles E. Tuttle, 1971.

Henish, Bridget Ann. *Fast and Feast: Food in Medieval Society.* University Park, PA: Pennsylvania University Press, 1994.

Nigg, Joseph, ed. *The Book of Fabulous Beasts: A Treasury of Writings from Ancient Times to the Present.* New York: Oxford University Press, 1999.

Price, A. Lindsay. *Swans of the World: In Nature, History, Myth, and Art.* Tulsa, OK: Council Oak Books, 1994.

Warner, Marina. *From the Beast to the Blonde: On Fairy Tales and Their Tellers.* New York: Farrar, Straus, and Giroux, 1994.

Woodbridge, Frederick. *The Son of Apollo: Themes of Plato.* New York: Houghton Mifflin, 1929.

Tern
See Seagull, Albatross, and Other Seabirds

Tiger
See Lion, Tiger, Panther, and Jaguar

Toad
See Frog and Toad

Tortoise
See Turtle and Tortoise

Turtle and Tortoise

> *I am related to stones*
> *The slow accretion of moss where dirt is wedged.*
> —Anthony Hecht, "Giant Tortoise"

Tortoises are generally larger than turtles and spend more time on land, but people did not make a rough distinction between the two until the sixteenth century. The word "turtle" is still sometimes used as a general term for both species, and that is how we will use it here. The folkloric reputation of the turtle as a primeval creature has, in some respects, found surprising confirmation by scientists. The animals have existed for about 230 million years, and individuals of some species can live more than two centuries.

The wrinkled features of turtles suggest age, while their silence can give the impression of wisdom. Though not very fast even in the water, turtles have great strength and stamina. Even the enormous Galapagos tortoises can raise themselves off the ground and walk on all fours. When swimming, turtles can look almost like an island, and several cultures, from the Plains Indians to the Tatars, have believed

Brer Terrapin is having a tug of war with Brer Bear, but the clever turtle ties his end of the rope to an underwater root, in this illustration by A. B. Frost to an Uncle Remus tale by Joel Chandler Harris.

that the world rests on a turtle's back. The shell of a turtle often represents the cosmos, with a dome for the sky and a flat surface beneath for the earth. A turtle emerging from its shell can be likened to a new creation, while withdrawal into the carapace can seem like reversion to the beginning of the world.

Mythologies throughout the world have associated turtles with the primordial waters out of which the earth was formed. Turtles have often been used as symbols of fertility, since they are constantly seen copulating in ponds in spring. Furthermore, the head of a turtle emerging from the shell can suggest a penile erection. On the other hand, the resemblance of the carapace to a womb has moved people in some cultures, such as the Chinese, to think of turtles as primarily feminine. Oppian believed that female turtles were always unwilling sexual partners and had to be raped by the males for the species to reproduce. Several modern observers have shared this impression, but it is hard to tell what turtles are feeling during copulation or at any other time. The apparent detachment with which turtles copulate may have later helped make them symbols of chastity in the Christian Middle Ages.

In Greek mythology, the god Hermes invented the lyre, the first musical instrument, from a carapace when he was just a mischievous infant. He saw a mountain tortoise grazing in front of a cave and, possibly thinking of the echoes in the cavern, killed the animal and strung the guts of sacrificed bulls across its shell. He later gave the lyre to the god Apollo in payment for cattle. Perhaps in lost versions of the story a nymph was transformed into a tortoise to escape amorous advances from the god, much as Syrinx was transformed into reeds when fleeing Pan. The lyre itself seems feminine, and playing it can easily suggest a sublimated sexuality. This would explain why it seemed inappropriate for Hermes to keep the instrument as his emblem.

According to legend, the *I Ching*, the Chinese system of divination, began in the early third millennium B.C. as the fabled emperor Fu Hsi was walking along the Yellow River and saw a turtle emerge from the waters. The sage ruler saw eight trigrams on the back of the turtle—that is, eight groups of three lines, either solid or broken, each. He interpreted these signs as patterns of cosmic energy that might be used to divine the future. Historians believe the *I Ching* may have actually been developed from a practice of divination that used the cracks in a tortoiseshell exposed to intense heat.

A symbol carried on banners by the imperial army in China was a serpent wound around a turtle, though this image has been variously interpreted. Sometimes it has been taken as a struggle between the might of the serpent and the indestructibility of the turtle, a struggle in which neither party can be victorious. In another view, the serpent was male, or yang, while the turtle was female, or yin, and the two were engaged in copulation. It is not unusual, however, to have opposites, such as strife and harmony, represented by a single symbol.

In one very ancient story from Japan, a young man named Urashima had been fishing all alone on the wide sea for three days yet had managed to catch nothing Then he felt a weight in his net and hauled up a many-colored turtle. When he lay down to sleep, the turtle suddenly changed into a beautiful young woman. She explained that she lived in heaven as a star of the Pleiades and had fallen in love with him. Urashima ascended with her to a heavenly mansion where they were married and lived together in happiness for three years. Then, for all the joys of his new life, Urashima began to miss his parents and begged his wife to allow him to visit them once more. She very reluctantly agreed and gave him a box as a parting gift, telling him to grip it firmly if he wanted to return but to never open the lid. On returning home, Urashima found that the village had changed and his parents were long dead. He had failed to realize that a year in heaven was a century on earth. In panic, Urashima seized the box, thoughtlessly opened it, and instantly turned into a very old man, for the box contained all of the years he had spent in the celestial kingdom.

The second avatar of the Hindu Vishnu was as the turtle Kurma, who served as the base of the mountain Mandara, which the immortals used to churn the oceans and bring forth the water of life. According to some Hindu traditions, the world rests on the back of an elephant, which, in turn, is standing on a turtle.

The idea that the world rests on a turtle's back is also found in the mythologies of several Native American tribes, especially of the Eastern woodlands. According to a tale of the Huron Indians, variants of which have been recorded in many other tribes, the goddess Aataentsic, who lived in the clouds, once split the Tree of Life with her ax. Part of the tree fell though a hole in the sky, and Aataentsic, fearing that life might perish, jumped down after it. At that time there was no earth but only water. When Turtle looked up and saw Aataentsic falling, he directed Beaver, Muskrat, Mink, and Otter to dive down and bring up earth from the bottom of the ocean. The animals placed the earth on Turtle's back to provide a cushion, and so Aataentsic settled down on it and the tree took root. The Lenape and other tribes had a similar myth in which the earth was covered by a great flood and human beings sought shelter on the back of a turtle.

In Africa, the turtle is a sort of trickster figure, yet unlike other tricksters, such as the Native American coyote, he is virtually never impetuous. Other tricksters often become victims of their own cleverness and pride, but the turtle is prudent and almost invariably victorious. In one widely told story, a lion captured and tried to devour a turtle. The captive told the king of beasts, "Uncle, if you are wondering how to soften my shield and make it good for eating, just please put me to soak in the river." The lion obliged, and the turtle immediately swam away to hide in the mud (Knappert, p. 244).

This turtle figure was carried from Africa to the New World with the slave trade. When the slaves had to keep their practices and beliefs secret from their masters, they could draw inspiration from the silence of the turtle, as illustrated by the humorous tale "The Talking Turtle," recorded in many versions from Africa and the Caribbean to the United States. According to one version from Alabama, a slave was walking along one morning and saw a turtle by the edge of a pond. "Good morning, turtle," he said, being full of good spirits. "Good morning," replied the turtle. As soon as he could recover enough composure, the man stammered that turtles could not really talk. "You talk too much," said the turtle, and with that the creature slid into the pond. The slave ran home, then returned with his master and found the turtle once again in the sunlight on the edge of the pond. "Good morning, turtle," said the slave. The turtle did not reply. "Good morning," repeated the slave, a bit more insistently, but there was still no answer. "Liar!" shouted the master, and he beat the slave terribly. Later the slave returned to the pond and, finding the turtle in his accustomed place, began to reproach the creature for not having returned his greeting. The turtle responded, "Well, that's what I say about you Negroes; you talk too much anyhow" (Abrams, pp. 274–275).

In *Uncle Remus,* the collection of African-American folktales by Joel Chandler Harris, Turtle is the cleverest of the animals, able to consistently outwit even Brer Rabbit. Turtle is also the most attractive, lacking the malice of the other beasts. In fact, his presence does a lot to soften the nihilism of the stories. One of them began as the animals were at a picnic, and while the females prepared the food, the male animals began to boast. Brer Rabbit said he was the swiftest, Brer Bear claimed to be the strongest, and so on. Brer Terrapin listened calmly until all were finished, then reminded everyone how the tortoise had won a race against the hare in one of Aesop's famous fables. Then Brer Terrapin challenged Brer Bear to a test of strength. Brer Bear took one end of a rope, while Brer Terrapin took the other and slid into the pond. Brer Bear tried to pull Brer Terrapin out of the water, but the rope would not budge. Brer Terrapin had tricked his adversary by tying the rope to a root. When the pulling finally stopped, Brer Terrapin undid the knot and slid out of the water in triumph. The turtle has since become a beloved motif in books for children, in the work of Lewis Carroll, Walt Kelly, and Dr. Seuss, for example.

Selected References

Abrams, Roger D., ed. *Afro-American Folktales: Stories from Black Traditions in the New World.* New York: Pantheon, 1985.

Bierhorst, John. *Mythology of the Lenape.* Tucson: University of Arizona Press, 1995.

Bruchac, Joseph. *Native Plant Stories.* Golden, CO: Fulcrum, 1995.

Harris, Joel Chandler. *Uncle Remus: His Stories and His Sayings.* New York: A. Appleton, 1928.

Knappert, Jan. *African Mythology: An Encyclopedia of Myth and Legend.* London: Diamond Books, 1995.

Oppian. "The Loves of the Tortoise, from *Halieutica.*" Trans. William Diaper. In *Animal Poems.* Ed. John Hollander. New York: Knopf, 1994, p. 158.

Tyler, Royall, ed. and trans. *Japanese Tales.* New York: Pantheon, 1987.

U–V

Unicorn
See Horse; Rhinoceros

Vampire
See Bat

Vulture
See Crow, Raven, and Other Corvids

Wasp

See Bee and Wasp

Weasel

See Beaver, Porcupine, Badger, and Miscellaneous Rodents

Werewolf

See Wolf

Whale

> *Yahweh had arranged that a great fish should be there to swallow Jonah; and Jonah remained in the belly of the fish for three days and three nights. From the belly of the fish he prayed to Yahweh . . .*
>
> —Jonah 2:1–2

The blue whale may be the largest animal ever to have lived, and other varieties of whales are also huge. The whale appears large enough to contain an entire world within its belly. This has made the whale difficult to empathize with or to humanize. In myth and legend, the whale usually appears more as a force of nature than as an individual animal.

Tradition usually equates the creature known as Leviathan in Jewish legend with the whale, though a few people have wondered whether Leviathan could have been some other creature that is now extinct or has retired to the depths of the sea. Jewish tradition relates that on the fifth day of Creation, God made two leviathans, a male and a female. They were so huge that the entire earth could rest on one of their fins. Soon God realized that, should they live to reproduce, they would soon destroy the entire universe, so he killed the female. Then, so that the race would not perish completely, God allowed the male to live until the end of time. And so that Leviathan would not be lonely, God spends the final hours of each day playing with the monster. In the final days of the world, Leviathan will do battle with Behemoth, and both will be killed. A tent for the just will be made from Leviathan's skin, and they will eat a banquet of Leviathan's flesh.

Tradition identifies Leviathan as male, but this is contradicted by the widespread idea of its belly as an enormous womb. The Leviathan killed by Yahweh resembles Tiamat of Babylonian mythology, the primeval goddess-demon from whose body the earth and sky were made. The whale of legend is really androgynous, existing prior to the division between the sexes.

In many Jewish legends, Leviathan was the ruler of the kingdom below the sea. In the story "King Leviathan and the Charitable Boy," recorded by Nathan Ausubel, a young man heard the commandment "Cast thy bread upon the waters. . . ." Not understanding but wishing to do right, he went out every day and threw bread into the sea. A single fish noticed, waited every day for the boy, and ate the bread. The fish grew bigger than all the others in the sea. The smaller fish became afraid, and they complained to King Leviathan. When he learned what had happened, King Leviathan commanded the big fish to bring the young boy. When the boy came to the sea on the following day, the big fish swallowed him, carried him to King Leviathan, and vomited him out. The boy told King Leviathan that he had tried to follow the commandments of God. The Ruler of the Sea took the boy on as a pupil, taught him the Torah, and instructed him in every language of man or beast. The boy finally returned home to become a man of great scholarship and wealth.

In the Book of Jonah from the Old Testament, Yahweh commanded Jonah to preach in the Assyrian capital of Nineveh, which was full of wickedness. Jonah was afraid and took refuge in a ship, but soon there was a terrible storm. Jonah realized that the storm was sent because of him, and so he told the sailors to throw him overboard. When they did, the sea immediately became calm. Jonah was swallowed by a large fish, and he spent three nights in its belly. Finally, the fish vomited him up on the shore. Jonah traveled to Nineveh, where he converted the city and saved it from destruction. The fish was identified as a whale in Matthew (12:40).

One traditional Jewish interpretation of the tale is that the three days spent within the fish represented the exile of the Hebrew people, who should return once again to Zion. In Christian Europe, the jaws of the whale were often used to represent the gate of Hell. The figure of Jonah, swallowed and cast forth, was understood as an anticipation of Jesus Christ, who spends three days in the grave to rise again. An author of late-fourteenth-century England sometimes known as the Pearl Poet retold the biblical story of Jonah in a poem entitled "Patience," in which the author compared the belly of the whale, with its filth and stench, to Hell. Jonah prayed to God, then managed to find a clean niche where he waited for deliverance.

Whales or related animals from the Carta Marina *of* Olaus Magnus, *published in 1539.*

From antiquity through the Renaissance, many tales were told of sailors who would camp and make a fire on the back of a whale, mistaking it for an island. Medieval bestiaries reported that the whale, troubled by the heat, would dive to the bottom of the sea, drowning the mariners. They compared the victims to those foolish people who fail to recognize the work of the Evil One. The depths of the sea, filled with unknown creatures, were equated with Hell, and the whale became the Devil.

But the whale might also be benevolent. The legendary medieval Irish abbot Saint Brendan sailed among wondrous islands with his followers for seven years in a search for the Paradise of Saints. Every year at Easter a whale named Jasconius would appear and let the monks celebrate mass upon its back.

In the tall tales of the fictive Baron Munchausen, first written down by R. E. Raspe in 1785 and later elaborated by several other writers, the baron's ship was swallowed by a whale. Inside the monster, Munchausen found boats from around the world, some of which had been standing at anchor for many years. Under the baron's leadership, a few brave sailors managed to prop open the mouth of the monster with a mast, enabling everyone to escape.

Native Americans of the Northwest coast have long hunted whales in shallow waters using small boats. Biologists no longer classify killer whales as whales at all, but they have traditionally been regarded as such. The killer whale is a common totem of the Haida and related tribes. These Indians tell many stories of a woman who was once gathering mussels, when a killer whale saw her, swam to her, and became her lover. The whale has been central to the cultures of other tribes that have hunted the whale, including the Mahkah in northern Canada, which revived its ancestral whaling traditions during the 1980s and 1990s.

The Taiwanese credit the whale with protecting their island by driving back the ships of foreign invaders. The Japanese maintain that in the twelfth century a governor of the Shichito islands in the southeast named Yoda Emon was saved by a whale after his boat had been destroyed in a storm. In gratitude, the governor forbade whaling in his territory.

Up until the early modern period, the whale was only occasionally glimpsed by Europeans, and then only from a distance or under tense conditions, making it an object of constant rumors and legends. By the eighteenth century, whaling had become a major industry. Whale oil was in great demand for lamps, and the highly constricting corsets worn by ladies were made of whalebone. The hunting was so intense that by the middle of the nineteenth century people already worried that the Atlantic Ocean was close to being depleted of whales.

The epic novel *Moby Dick*, written by Herman Melville in 1851, was intended to record the folkways of whalers before they vanished completely. Ahab, the captain of a whaling ship, had lost a leg to the great white whale named Moby Dick, and he became obsessed with his desire for revenge. He relentlessly pursued his adversary, even after the hull of the ship had been filled with whale meat, until finally Moby Dick killed him and destroyed his ship. The whale here, inspired at least partly by the biblical Leviathan, punished the hubris of Ahab and all of humankind.

As whales were hunted to near extinction in the first half of the twentieth century, the ecology movement adopted the whale as a symbol. "Save the Whales!" was a resonant slogan that seemed to go beyond one creature and embrace the entire natural world. Whale songs, perhaps the most complex melodies produced by any creature in the wild, were recorded not only for scientific study but for entertainment. International restrictions on whaling have now enabled whales to increase their numbers to the point where many species are no longer considered endangered.

Selected References

Ausubel, Nathan. *A Treasury of Jewish Folklore.* New York: Crown, 1948.

Hausman, Gerald. *Meditations with Animals: A Native American Bestiary.* Santa Fe: Bear, 1986.

Melville, Herman. *Moby-Dick, or the Whale.* New York: Penguin, 1992.

O'Meara, John J., trans. *The Voyage of St. Brendan: Journey to the Promised Land.* Atlantic Highlands, NJ: Humanities Press, 1976.

Schochet, Elijah Judah. *Animal Life in Jewish Tradition: Attitudes and Relationships.* New York: KTAV Publishing House, 1984.

Wolf

Homo Homini Lupes est [Man is a wolf to man].

— *Plautus*

More than any other animal, the wolf has been closely associated with martial qualities. It has been continually condemned for rapaciousness and cruelty, yet it has also been praised for fierceness. In early tribal societies the wolf was closely connected with hunting, but later it was often connected with pillage. For herders, it has been a perpetual threat to their flocks. Since military castes are generally an aristocracy, the wolf has generally been identified with nobility as well.

Language contains many traces of a totemic identification of the wolf with several Eurasian tribes in archaic times. The Russian word for "wolf" is pronounced similarly to the German "*volk*" and the English "folk." The very concept of an ethnic group, in many Indo-European languages, may derive from a totemic identification of a tribe with the wolf. Many German names include the root "wolf": Wolf, Wolfgang, Wolfram, Wolfhart, and others. The common French name Luc, the English Luke, is related to "*loup*," the French word for "wolf." Names containing "wolf" are also common among the Cheyenne and other Indian tribes of North America, a remarkable testimony to the surprising universality of animal symbolism. The Native Americans admired the wolf not only for its prowess in hunting but, since Indians retained a tribal organization, its loyalty to the pack.

A totemic identification with the wolf is perhaps most memorably recorded in the story of Romulus and Remus, the founders of Rome who were suckled by a wolf in their infancy. Initially, the wolf was probably not merely their nurse but their mother. Every year on the 15th of February, Romans celebrated the Lupercalia, an archaic festival in her honor, on the Palatine Hill by the cave where the infants had been sheltered.

It is also likely that Romulus and Remus were at one time werewolves—that is, human beings who transformed themselves into lupine form. Legends of werewolves were common among the warrior clans of the ancient world. The *Iliad* mentions a warrior named Dolan who went about in the guise of a wolf until he was finally recognized and killed by the Greeks. Herodotus reported a belief that a nomadic tribe known as the Nueri would change themselves into wolves for a few days every year. Sigmund of the Volsung clan, a hero of Norse and German mythology, would put on a skin at night to become a wolf. Pliny the Elder reported a belief among the Greeks that the Arcadians would select a man from a certain noble family every year and lead him to a marsh. The man would then strip, hang his clothes on a tree, swim to a desolate area, and become a wolf for a period of nine years. The legend probably derived from an initiation ritual of a clan of the wolf. The wolf was sacred to the god Apollo.

As humanity became increasingly settled and urbanized, the reputation of the wolf declined. Ovid tells us in his *Metamorphoses* that Jupiter, the supreme god, once came to King Lycaon in the guise of a simple traveler. As was his practice, the king served up human flesh for his guest. Enraged, Jupiter took on his true form, rose to the sky, and hurled a thunderbolt at the palace. The king fled in terror, and, as he ran, he was changed into a wolf.

Even Herodotus and Pliny, who were often credulous, did not believe reports of people changing into wolves. By the time of Christ the educated people of Greece and Rome generally dismissed stories of werewolves. Such tales appealed, however, to a growing taste for horror. Perhaps the most famous werewolf tale of all is in the *Satyricon* of Petronius, written in the middle of the first century A.D. The freedman Niceros told how a young soldier had accompanied him to a farm at night and they stopped for a while by a cemetery, where the companion slipped away. After waiting nervously for a while, Niceros looked around and caught sight of the soldier, who was taking off his clothes and urinating in a circle around them. After completing this ritual, the companion turned into a wolf, howled, and ran away. Niceros hurried to the farmhouse, where he learned that a wolf had broken into the pasture and attacked the sheep, but one of the farmhands had stabbed the culprit in the neck with a spear. On returning home, Niceros found the soldier bleeding profusely from the neck, and he knew that his companion was a werewolf. In its broad outlines, the story is like many that were told of werewolves up through the modern period: a wolf is wounded and a person is later found bleeding from the same part of the body.

Norse mythology shows a highly ambivalent attitude toward the wolf. Two wolves accompanied Odin, the god of magic, but he was destined to fall prey to the great wolf Fenris when gods battled giants at the end of the world. This monster had been sired by Loki, the god of fire, and he grew so strong that the gods themselves were terrified. No ordinary fetter would hold Fenris, so the gods summoned dwarves to fashion a chain from the footfalls of a cat, the roots of a mountain, and other ingredients as elusive as the restraints of civilization. Though the fetter appeared as soft as a silken string, Fenris refused to let himself be bound with it unless a god placed one hand in his mouth as a pledge. Only Tyr, god of battles, had the courage to

do this. Realizing that he had indeed been captured, Fenris bit off Tyr's hand. The wolf would finally be able to break the chain as the final days of the world approached.

The ancient Hebrews were primarily a tribe of herders, and wolves were a constant threat to their sheep. In the Bible, wolves were often identified with either invading armies or with Hebrews who had become greedy and corrupt. Reproaching his nation, the prophet Ezekiel said, "Her leaders in the city are like wolves tearing their prey, shedding blood . . . " (21:27). Jesus told his disciples, "I am sending you out like sheep among the wolves . . . " (Matt. 10:16).

Saint Francis tamed a wolf, Gubbio, who later accompanied him, a feat Christians often interpreted as the triumph of spirituality over appetite. During the Middle Ages, bounties were placed on wolves, sometimes in the same amounts as those for brigands and highwaymen. Wolves were hunted to extinction in England during the fifteenth century, in Scotland during the sixteenth, and in Ireland during the eighteenth. The last wolves in Germany were shot around the middle of the nineteenth century. Wolves have remained continuously in mountainous regions of France, Spain, and Italy, as well as in the forests of Eastern Europe. With the growing fear of witchcraft in the Renaissance, people began to regard wolves not simply as pests but as agents of the Devil.

In the *Malleus Maleficarum* or "Witches' Hammer," a manual for witch finders published in 1484, authors Heinrich Kramer and James Sprenger stated that wolves that show "such astuteness that no skill and strength can capture them" must be either devils in disguise or scourges of God" (p. 65). Wolves were regarded as a form in which witches went about at night. Particularly in France, suspected werewolves were often brought to trial and executed. Certain physical features, such as eyebrows that grew together, were considered signs of a secret identity as a werewolf, and any unexplained wound or scar might arouse suspicion of clandestine adventures in lupine form.

The wolf's reputation for rapacity extended across Eurasia, and stories of werewolves were also common in Eastern Europe. A good example is a tale recorded by Edmund Veckenstedt in Lithuania of a peasant who had gone to the stable each morning, only to find the mangled bodies of his horses with their necks bitten through. One night he stayed up to watch the stable, and his neighbor approached carrying a bundle of sticks. The intruder threw the sticks on the ground and began to roll over them. After passing the first stick, his head became that of a wolf, and with every subsequent pass, another part of his body changed, until finally he was entirely a wolf. In this form, the neighbor raided the stable, but while he was gone the peasant quickly took one stick away. After his predations were finished, the wolf rolled over the sticks once more and changed back into a man, but the transformation was not complete. The peasant accused his neighbor in town the next morning, and a physical examination showed that the culprit retained the tail of a wolf.

But the most famous literary product of this period is the story of Little Red Riding Hood, who is lured away from the path to her grandmother's house by a wolf. Early versions of the story, including the version in *Stories of Mother Goose* by Charles Perrault (first published in 1697), are all simple warning tales. Perrault ended his tale as the wolf, having already devoured the grandmother, ate the little girl. He concluded with the moral:

Wolves may lurk in every guise.
Handsome they may be and kind,
Gay and charming—never mind!
Now, as then, 'tis simple truth—
Sweetest tongue has sharpest tooth! (Perrault, p. 29)

Perrault clearly wanted to drive the lesson home as emphatically as possible, but many people could not bear the harshness of the ending. In the somewhat convoluted version from the collection of fairy tales published by the Grimm brothers (tale no. 26 in the final edition of 1857), a woodsman rescued Little Red Riding Hood and her grandmother from the belly of the wolf.

In the heavily populated regions of northwest Europe, wolves were less of a threat, and a more complex, if not always more favorable, view of them emerged. As the ancient tradition of the beast fable was developed in medieval Europe, it was increasingly adapted to social commentary, and various sorts of animals were used to represent different classes. The wolf was increasingly used for satiric portraits of monks. The relatively long hair covering the heads and bodies of wolves is a bit like the robe and cowl of a monk. Even more significant, monks and wolves shared a reputation for greed. Finally, in the middle of the twelfth century, an unknown Flemish author wrote a humorous epic about the wolf-monk entitled *Ysengrimus*. The wolf-monk, Ysengrim, ingenuously tried to reconcile his ravenous appetite for sheep with monastic law, and he claimed to practice a "religion of the stomach." He matched wits with the peasants and with his companion the fox until finally he was killed by a clan of swine (Ziolkowski, pp. 210–234).

Ysengrim soon became a generic name for the wolf of folklore, which played a prominent role in the cycle of Renard the fox. No longer a monk, Ysengrim was usually a naive noble while Renard was a cunning, unscrupulous peasant. Ysengrim was constantly beaten, cuckolded, and maimed, and the stories about him left readers torn between frustration, laughter, and pity. He represented the aristocratic order that was slowly but inexorably starting to give way to the emerging bourgeoisie.

Aristocratic houses had often adopted the wolf as their symbol in heraldry; as regimes became increasingly democratic, the wolf was blamed for the cruelty and intemperance of royalty and the nobility. This was particularly so in the United States, where the campaign to eliminate predators such as the wolf became a moral crusade. By the 1920s the grey wolf, which once had probably numbered in the millions, was almost completely extinct in the United States.

But the disappearance of the wolf created a wave of nostalgia. At the end of the nineteenth century, Rudyard Kipling, known as "the poet of the British Empire," wrote *The Jungle Books*, a collection of animal stories centered mostly on an Indian boy named Mowgli who was raised by wolves. Like Britain, the wolves have both a king and a parliament, but the "law of the jungle" that they follow is sterner than that of a modern republic. The den of wolves is essentially a military school, which endeavored to make young boys from the aristocracy into men.

As World War I began to approach, ever more people felt admiration for the martial qualities of the wolves. German authors such as Hermann Hesse and Hermann Löns wrote stories in which the wolf appears as a representative of a natural order, heroically resisting the encroachments of civilization. In a story entitled "Lobo, the King of the Currumpaw" (1900), the Canadian-American author Ernest Seton-Thompson celebrated a wolf named Lobo as a romantic outlaw.

The regime in Nazi Germany, seeking to cultivate the fierceness and even the cruelty that had been often associated with wolves, made the wolf into a sort of cult. Adolf Hitler adopted the nickname "little wolf," and he gave his various headquarters names like Wolf's Lair, Wolf's Gulch, and Werewolf. He once explained that people cheered him rapturously because "a wolf is born." On a more practical level, the Nazis introduced the first legislation for the protection of wolves.

The United States and other countries, however, were not very far behind. Aldo Leopold in his essay "Thinking Like a Mountain" (1948) tells how he, as a young man, had never passed up an opportunity to kill a wolf. One day he shot an old wolf and her pups on a mountainside. The passage in which he realized the error of his ways is perhaps the most famous in all of American nature writing:

> We reached the old wolf in time to watch a fierce green fire dying in her eyes. I realized then, and have known ever since, that there was something new to me in those eyes—something known only to her and to the mountain. I was young then, and full of trigger-itch; I thought that because fewer wolves meant more deer, that no wolves would mean a hunters' paradise. But after seeing the green fire die, I sensed that neither the wolf nor the mountain agreed with such a view. (p. 130)

At about that time, conservationists under Leopold's leadership began to defend wolves as an integral part of the environment.

With government protection, the population of wolves in America began to rebound in the latter half of the twentieth century. In 1963 naturalist Farley Mowat published a fictionalized account of his sojourn in the wilds of Alaska entitled *Never Cry Wolf*. He wrote about a pair of alpha wolves named George and Angela. The book quickly became a best-seller and established a popular image of wolves as living an ideal of family life. Mowat's praise of the marital fidelity of wolves resonated in a society where people were becoming increasingly concerned about divorce. In the 1990s, Clarissa Pinkola Estés published her best-selling *Women Who Run with the Wolves,* in which she used the wolf to symbolize the "wild woman archetype"—that is, the female who, though often nurturing husband and children, retains a primal connection with the natural world.

Today, in America and much of the world, a craze for wolves continues, and they constantly are seen on posters and in jewelry. Nevertheless, the old ambivalence toward wolves remains, and the old hatred of them can erupt unexpectedly. Plans to reintroduce wolves in Yellowstone National Park were implemented in the 1990s only over vehement opposition from ranchers.

Selected References

Delort, Robert. *Les animaux ont une histoire.* Paris: Éditions du Seuil, 1984.

Estés, Clarissa Pinkola. *Women Who Run with the Wolves: Myths and Stories of the Wild Woman Archetype.* New York: Ballantine Books, 1992.

Grimm, Jacob and Wilhelm. *The Complete Grimm's Fairy Tales.* Trans. Margaret Hunt and James Stern. New York: Pantheon, 1972.

Kipling, Rudyard. *The Two Jungle Books.* Garden City, NJ: Sun Dial Press, 1895.

Kramer, Heinrich and James Sprenger. *The Malleus Maleficarum.* Trans. Montague Summers. New York: Dover, 1971.

Leopold, Aldo. "Thinking Like a Mountain." In *A Sand County Almanac: And Selected Sketches from Here and There.* New York: Oxford University Press, 1949, pp. 129–133.

Lopez, Barry Holstun. *Of Wolves and Men.* New York: Charles Scribner's Sons, 1978.

Mowat, Farley. *Never Cry Wolf.* Boston: Little, Brown, 1963.

Perrault, Charles. *Perrault's Fairy Tales.* Trans. A. E. Johnson. New York: Dover, 1969.

Pliny the Elder. *Natural History: A Selection.* Ed. and trans. John F. Healey. New York: Penguin, 1991.

Sax, Boria. *Animals in the Third Reich: Pets, Scapegoats, and the Holocaust.* New York: Continuum, 2000.

Seton-Thompson, Ernest. *Wild Animals I Have Known.* New York: Charles Scribner's Sons, 1990.

Veckenstedt, Edmund, ed. *Mythen, Sagen und Legenden der Zamiaten* (2 vols.). Heidelberg: Carl Winter's Universitätsbuchhandlung, 1883.

Ziolkowski, Jan M. *Talking Animals: Medieval Latin Beast Poetry, 750–1150.* Philadelphia: University of Pennsylvania Press, 1993.

Worm

I am a czar—a slave; I am a worm—a god.
—Gavil Derzhavin

Through most of history, people generally have not distinguished sharply among earthworms, eels, and snakes. Up through much of the nineteenth century, the words "worm" and *"wurm"* were sometimes used, in English and other Germanic languages, to designate a snake. The earthworm, however, has never had the satanic glamour of other serpents. With facial features that are difficult to see, earthworms are hard to distinguish from one another. In consequence, they are seldom thought of as individuals, and even in mythology and folklore they rarely speak.

Worms have been thought of since ancient times mostly for their presence in moist, fertile earth. In antiquity it was believed that worms were generated spontaneously from dirt, in part because they would appear after rainfall. This primeval character was shown in an incantation, from Mesopotamia in the second millennium B.C., entitled "The Worm and the Toothache":

> After Anu [god of the sky] had created heaven,
> Heaven had created the earth,
> The earth had created the rivers,
> The rivers had created the canals,
> The canals had created the marsh,
> And the marsh had created the worm—
> The worm went, weeping before Shamash [god of the sun],
> His tears flowing before Ea [god of deep water]:
> What wilt thou give me for my food? (Pritchard, pp. 79–76)

The gods first offered the worm a fig, but the annelid refused and asked to be placed in the gums of a person.

In literature, a worm has usually been a symbol of humble status. A psalmist, for example, has written, "Yet here am I, now more worm than man/scorn of mankind, jest of the people ... " (Psalms 22:6). The book of Isaiah concluded with an eschatological prophecy that God would make the heavens and earth anew. In the final words, God told the prophet how all people will come to worship:

> And on their way out they will see
> the corpses of men
> who have rebelled against me.
> Their worms will not die

nor their fire go out;
they will be loathsome to all mankind. (Isaiah 66:24)

Worms eat corpses, so to live on as part of a worm was to be the destiny of all who failed to transcend the body.

In the late Middle Ages and Renaissance, Europeans became increasingly obsessed with physical decay, and worms symbolized the corruption of the body after death. Worms were often painted crawling in and out of a decaying corpse. The following lines from William Shakespeare's *Hamlet* showed a noteworthy awareness of ecological cycles:

> *Hamlet:* A man may fish with the worm that hath eat
> of a king, and eat of the fish that hath fed of the worm.
> *King:* What dost thou mean by this?
> *Hamlet:* Nothing but to show how a king may go a
> progress through the guts of a beggar. (4.2)

The worm, the most humble of animals, was always triumphant in the end, showing the ultimate equality of all living things.

Just as serpents are traditionally associated with moral corruption, so worms are often connected with physical decay. Their habit of burrowing inside a fruit or flower has often impressed people as a botanical equivalent of demonic possession, and it can seem vaguely sexual. This is apparent in "The Sick Rose," written by William Blake in the last decade of the nineteenth century:

> O Rose, thou art sick.
> The invisible worm
> That flies in the night
> In the howling storm
> Has found out thy bed
> Of crimson joy
> And his dark secret love
> Does thy life destroy. (p. 40)

But the connection of worms with the earth could be restful as well as disturbing.

The very last study written by Charles Darwin before his death was entitled *The Formation of Vegetable Mould through the Action of Earthworms*. Some scientists have regretted that the founder of evolutionary theory should have turned to such a specialized theme in the end, but the choice reflected his desire for bucolic peace. Darwin wished to show that earthworms, by tradition the lowest of creatures, are an essential part of natural cycles. They improve the fertility of the soil and so are essential for the continued prosperity of other creatures, including humankind. With the growing ecological awareness in the latter twentieth century, earthworms have increasingly come to symbolize the ultimate unity of all life. This is even apparent in the science of physics, where discontinuities in time and space are now sometimes referred to as wormholes.

Selected References

Anonymous. "The Worm and the Toothache." In *The Ancient Near East: An Anthology of Texts and Pictures*. Ed. James B. Pritchard, trans. W. F. Albright et al. Princeton, NJ: Princeton University Press, 1958, p. 70.

Blake, William. "The Sick Rose." In *The Norton Anthology of English Literature* (2 vols.). 5th ed. Ed. H. Abrams. New York: W. W. Norton, 1986, vol. 2, p. 40.

Worster, Donald. *The Wealth of Nature: Environmental History and the Ecological Imagination*. 2nd ed. New York: Cambridge University Press, 1995.

Wren and English Robin

Call for the robin redbreast and the wren,
Since o'er shady groves they hover,
And with leaves and flowers do cover
The friendless bodies of unburied men.
—John Webster, *The White Devil* (act 5, scene 4)

Animals gain special attention from us when they have some characteristic that is either unique or extreme, and with the wren and robin this feature is their smallness. The wren, which is grayish russet-brown, is associated with Christmas, while the robin, which is more brightly colored, is associated with Easter. Their connection in folklore is so close that the robin and wren have often been erroneously believed to be the male and female of a single species. In Britain people say, "The robin and wren are God's cock and hen" (Cooper, p. 194). According to a French legend, the wren fetched fire from Heaven, singeing its wings, then passed the brand to the robin, which burned its breast.

In *Lark Rise to Candleford*, her account of growing up in rural England during the nineteenth century, Flora Thompson tells how boys would regularly take eggs from the nests of birds for food, decoration, and sport. The wren and robin, together with only a few other birds, were spared because, to quote a saying:

The robin and the wrens
Be God Almighty's friends. (p. 153)

But the wren has been viewed with more ambivalence than its little cousin.

The wren is known throughout Europe as the "king of birds." In Latin, it is known as *"regulus,"* in Greek as" *basiliskos,"* and in Old German as *"kunigli,"* all of which mean "monarch." The Roman author Suetonius claimed in his history of the deified Julius Caesar that the assassination of the dictator was foretold by the fate of a wren. Shortly before the dictator was killed, a wren, pursued by raptors and bearing a sprig of laurel, flew into the Hall of Pompey, named after Caesar's former rival, where it was overtaken and torn to pieces.

The status of the wren as king may seem paradoxical, since people usually associate greatness with size. As might be expected, veneration of the wren generally appealed to common people rather than to elites, which is probably why the cult has been far more prominent in folklore than in literary culture. Nevertheless, archeologist Edmund Gordon believed that the wren was celebrated in an animal proverb, from the early second millennium, from Sumer, the oldest urban culture. When the elephant boasted about his size, the wren answered him by saying, "But I, in my own small way, was created just as you . . . " (p. 10).

The wren seems to proclaim this uniqueness with a remarkably loud, melodious song, which will usually capture the attention of a person strolling though a meadow long before the bird itself is seen. The best-known version of the story explaining how the wren became king of birds is by the Brothers Grimm (tale no. 171). The birds gathered to select a king and decided that the crown would be awarded to whichever could fly the highest. The eagle flew far above all the other birds and descended to claim his prize. The wren suddenly piped up that the crown was his. He had lain unnoticed on the back of the eagle until the large bird began to descend, whereupon the wren took off and flew so high that he could see God himself. Other birds objected that the contest had been won through trickery and so the result was invalid. The assembly decided that the crown could go to whoever burrowed most deeply in the earth. While other birds such as the rooster and duck began to dig, the wren simply found a mouse hole and descended. Though birds continued to object, the wren, to this day, slips in and out of hedges and proclaims, "I am king."

The story shows both the reverence and the ambivalence with which people have traditionally regarded the wren. In much of Europe, especially the British Isles, the wren is never killed throughout most of the year but is ceremoniously hunted on Saint Stephen's Day, December 26. The body of the slain wren is paraded though the streets on a pole in a colorful procession, to the accompaniment of music and song. Many legends are invoked to explain the ceremony. One legend held that the call of a wren betrayed Saint Stephen to his persecutors. According to an Irish legend, the Gaelic warriors were once planning a surprise attack on the troops of Oliver Cromwell, but wrens alerted the enemy by beating on drums.

Still another legend, this one from the Isle of Man, related that there once lived a mermaid whose beautiful form and sweet song were irresistible to men. She would gradually lure them into ever-deeper waters until they finally drowned. Finally, a knight came along who was able to withstand her enchantment. He was about to kill the mermaid, but she escaped by taking the form of a wren. From that time on she was compelled to assume the form of a wren one day every year. People would kill the birds without mercy on that day, in hope of finally putting an end to the sorceress, and the feathers of the wrens were kept for one year as a charm against shipwreck. The fact that there are so many explanations for this ceremonial hunt suggests that it goes back very far, perhaps to Neolithic times, and its original significance has been lost.

In western France, a similar ceremony was sometimes performed with the robin on Candlemass Day. The body of a robin was pierced with the branch of a hazel tree, which was then set aflame. The robin of folklore, as well as the wren, has been intimately connected with death and resurrection. Most of the legends about the robin center on the bright red color of its breast. According to one tale, the robin tried to puck the thorns from the crown of Christ, whereupon blood fell on its breast. According to a legend from the Hebrides, the fire that warmed the Holy Family in the stable was about to go out, so the robin fanned the flames with its wings, thus burning its breast.

The robin traditionally attended to the bodies of those who had been denied a proper funeral. In the anonymous British ballad "The Children in the Wood," an abandoned boy and girl perished in a deep forest:

> No burial these pretty babes
>   Of any man receives,
> Till robin-red-breast painfully
>   Did cover them with leaves. (Anonymous, p. 17)

But, for all the associations with martyrdom and death, the robin, like the wren, was generally thought of with joy as a herald of the spring. In the children's classic *The Secret Garden* by Frances Hodgson Burnett, a cheerful robin led the heroine to the door of a wall surrounding an abandoned garden that was filled with mystery and wonder. Perhaps no other animals have been as symbolically linked with the seasonal rhythms of traditional rural life as the wren and robin. Today their use, especially on greeting cards, is increasingly nostalgic.

Selected References

Anonymous. "Children in the Wood." In *The Book of British Ballads.* Ed. S. C. Hall. London: George Routledge and Sons, 1879, pp. 13–17.

Burnett, Frances Hodgson *The Secret Garden.* New York: Barnes and Noble Books, 1990.

Cooper, J. C. *Symbolic and Mythological Animals.* London: Harper-Collins/ The Aquarian Press, 1992.

Gordon, Edmund I. "Sumerian Animal Proverbs: 'Collection Five.'" *Journal of Cuneiform Studies* 12 (1958): 1–6.

Grimm, Jacob and Wilhelm. *The Complete Fairy Tales of the Brothers Grimm.* Trans. Jack Zipes. New York: Bantam Books, 1987.

Gubernatis, Angelo De. *Zoological Mythology or the Legends of Animals* (2 vols.). Chicago: Singing Tree Press, 1968.

Lawrence, Elizabeth Atwood. *Hunting the Wren: Transformation of Bird to Symbol.* Knoxville: University of Tennessee Press, 1997.

O'Sullivan, Patrick. *Irish Superstitions and Legends of Animals and Birds.* Dublin: Mercier Press, 1991.

Pritchard, James B., ed. *The Ancient Near East: An Anthology of Texts and Pictures.* Princeton: Princeton University Press, 1958.

Rappoport, Angelo S. *The Sea: Myths and Legends.* London: Senate, 1995.

Suetonius. *Suetonius* (2 vols.). Trans. J. C. Rolfe. Cambridge: Harvard University Press, 1998.

Thompson, Flora. *Lark Rise to Candleford: A Trilogy.* New York: Penguin, 1973.

Warner, Rex. *Encyclopedia of World Mythology.* New York: Galahad Books, 1975.

Androcles, 175–176
Androgyny, 228
Andromeda, 70
Animal Farm, xvii, 199
Animals
  classification, ix–x, xviii
  demonic, xv, 22–23
  divine, xiii–xv, 102
  and ecology, xx
  exploitation, xvii, xix
  languages, xx
  marriages with humans, xii–xiii
  metamorphosed, xii–xiii
  and myth, xx
  naming, ix, x
  political, xvii–xviii
  satiric, xvi
  as traditions, xi, xx
Animals of the Soul, 50
Anthony, Mark, 176
Anthony, Saint, xiv, 38
  and pigs, 197
Antigone, 88
Ants, **1–5**, *2, 3, 4*
Antz, 5
Anubis, 90, 117–118
"Anzu," 102
Aoife, 251
Ape-men, 13
Apep, 228
Apes, xvii, xviii–xix, **6–14**, *9*
Aphrodite, 144, 217
  and doves, 96
  emergence of, 244
  and scallop shell, 244
  and sparrows, 235
Apikunni, 30
Apis, xiv, 47, 86
Apollo, 49
  as crow, 73
  and horses, 158
  as Lord of the Dolphin, 219–220
  and snake, 228
  and swans, 250
  and turtles, 257
  and wolves, 268
Apollodorus, 80
  and geese, 250
  on Trojan Horse, 158
Apollonius of Rhodes, 95
  on centaurs, 157
"Apology," 114
"Apology for Raymond Sebond," xviii, 4, 12, 36, 58
Apuleius, Lucius, 2, 17, 52, 189, 217
Arabian Nights Entertainments, 10, 108

Arabs
  and crocodiles, 71
  and elephants, 108
Arachne, xiii, 237–238
Arbiter, Petronius, 198
Arcas, 25
Archilochus, 147
Ares, 82
Argos, 188
Ariadne, 46
Arion, 220–221
Aristophanes
  on crows, 73
  on frogs, 125
  on larks, 81
  on wasps, 38
Aristotle, ix
  on bees, 35
  on hedgehogs, 148
Ark, *xiii*
Artemis, 25, 26
  as cat, 58
  and does, 143–144
  and dogs, 86
Arthur, King, 26
Arthurian tales
  and salmon, 212
  and stags, 144
Asclepius, 66, 89, 157, 215
  and snakes, 230
Ashanti, 109, 238
Ashurnasirpal II, 102
Aspares, 250
Asses, x, **14–20**, *15, 16, 19*
Assurbanipal, xvi
Assyrians, xvi
  and doves, 96
  and eagles, 102
Astarte, 58
  and doves, 96
Atargatis, 211
Athena, xiv, 159
  and Arachne, 237–238
  and owls, 189
  and snakes, 228
Attar, Farid Ud-Din, 80
Attis, 47
Aubry, 92
Audhumbla, 48
Augustus, Emperor, 144
Ausubel, Nathan, 264
Avianus, 252
Aztec mythology
  and deer, 146
  and dogs, 87, 88
  and hummingbirds, 187
  and owls, 191

and snakes, 229

Baalam, 16
Baba Yaga, 160–161
Babe the pig, 200
Baboons, xiv
Babrius, 175
   and swallows, 248
Babylon, ancient, xx
   and boars, 195
   and dogs, 88–89
   and eagles, 102
   and foxes, 117
   and lions, 174
   and mermaids and mermen, 219
   and owls, 189
   and scorpions, 215
   and snakes, 228
Badgers, **29–34**
Bambi (film), 146, 181
Bambi: A Life in the Woods, 146
Barbary apes, 10–11
Barclay, Margaret, 91
Barrie, James M., 71
Barrymore, Ethel, 207
Basilisks, 230
Bast and Bastet, 58
"The Bat," 21
Bathala, 9
Batrachyomachy, xvi
Bats, **21–23**
"The Battle of the Books," 242
"The Battle of the Frogs and Mice," 125
"The Bear," 28
Bears, xii, xvi, xvii, **23–29**, *25*
Beaver War, 30
Beavers, xii, xviii, **29–34**, *31*
Bede, 236
Beelzebub, 114–115
Bees, **34–41**, *35, 37*
Beetles, **41–43**, *42*
Behemoth, 155–156
Benedict, Saint, 97
Bennu bird, 150
Beowulf, 82
Berlin, Isaiah, 147–148
Bewick, Thomas, 178
Bible. *See* Judeo-Christian tradition
Birds, xiv, xx. *See also* Cocks, Corvids,
   Hens, Musical birds
The Birds, 73, 81
Black Beauty, 163
"The Black Cat," 60–61
Black Panthers (African-American
   group), 180
Black Witch of Fraddan, 60
Blackfoot, 30

Blake, William
   on flies, 114
   and hippopotamuses, 155–156
   on tigers, 178–179
   on worms, 275
"Blissful Longing," 54–55
Blossom, 187
Blue jays, 72
Boille, Jean, 60
Bolshevik Russia, xvii
Bondt, Jacob de, 11
The Book of the Dun Cow, 212–213
al-Borak, xv, 160
Bosch, Hieronymus, 126
Bottom, 18, *19*
Boudicca, Queen, 138
Brahma, 105, 188
   as boar, 195
Brendan, Saint, 265
Brer Bear, 259
Brer Fox, *136*, 139
Brer Rabbit, xvi, *136*, 139, 259
Brer Terrapin, 259
Brothers Grimm. *See* Grimm brothers
Brown, Joseph E., 50
Browning, Robert, 201, 204–205
Bryant, William Cullen, 149–150
Buddha, 6–8
   and dragon, 228
Buddhism, xiii
   and cats, 62
   and cicadas, 132
   and dogs, 87
   and elephants, 106
   and hares, 136
   and monkeys, 6–8
   and rats, 205
Buffalo, 50
Bullfights, 47, 51
Bulls, xiii–xiv, xix, **44–52**, *45, 49*
Bunny, Bugs, 140
Burma, 53
Burnett, Frances Hodgson, 279
Buto, 228
Butterflies, xx, **52–56**, *53*
Byzantine Empire, 102
   and hedgehogs, 148
"Byzantium," 219

Cadmus, 229
Cáer, 251
Caesar, Julius, 108
   on hares, 138
   and stags, 142
   and wren, 277
Cain and Abel, 223, *224*
Cairan, Saint, 142

Caligula, 159
The Call of the Toad, 127
Callisto, 25
Calvino, Italo, 197
Cambrensis, Giraldus, 252
Cambyses, 47, 86
Camel cigarettes, 19–20
Camel, Joe, xix, 20
Camels, **14–20**
Campbell, Joseph, 212
Cannic, Saint, 142
Canterbury Tales, 15
Canus, 158
Captain Hook, 71
Capybaras, 29
Caracalla, 176
Caras, Roger, 222
Carp, **211–214**
Carroll, Lewis, 68, 140, 259
Cassius, Dio, 138
Castor, 250
"The Cat Maiden," *58*, 59
Çatal Hüyük, xiii, 44, 174
Caterpillars, 52, 238
Catherine the Great, 161
Cats, xiv, xv, xvii–xviii, **57–64**, *65*
    Churchill on, 193
    and mice, 203
    See also Jaguars, Lions, Panthers, Tigers
Cattle. *See* Bulls, Cows
"The Cattle Raid of Cooley," 50
Catullus, 235
Cavalieri, Paola, 13
Cave paintings, xiii–xiv
    of bulls and cows, 44
    of great cats, 173–174
Celtic mythology
    and corvids, 74
    and deer, 143, 145
    and dogs, 87
    and pigs, 195–196
    and salmon, 212
    and snakes, 228
Centaurs, xv, 157–158
Cerberus, 87
Cernunnos, 143
Ceyx, 217–218
Chang Kwo-lao, 18
Chang-O, 136–137
Chapman, George, 164
Charbonneau-Lassay, Louis, 42
Charlemagne, 108
    and stags, 142, 144–145
Charles V, Emperor of Spain, 51
Charlotte's Web, 200, 242–243
Chaucer, Geoffrey, 15, 67
    on eagles, 103

and foxes, 120
"Che cos' è la poesia?" 147, 149
Cherokee Indians, 191
Cheyenne Indians, 267
Chickens. *See* Cocks, Hens
"The Children in the Wood," 278
China
    and badgers, 32
    and bats, 22
    and boars and pigs, 197–198
    and carp, 213
    and cicadas, 132
    and cocks, 65
    and cranes, 152
    and crows, 75
    and dogs, 90
    and dragons, 233
    and ducks, *251*
    and fireflies, 114
    and foxes, 120–121
    and hares, 135, 136–137
    and hedgehogs, 148
    and horses, 160
    and lions, 174, 176
    and owls, 191
    and oxen, 47
    and peacocks, 188
    and the Phoenix, 151
    and scorpions, 216
    and serpents, 233–234
    and sheep and goats, 227
    and snakes, 230, 231
    and spiders, 240
    and tigers, 177
    and toads, 126
    and turtles, 256, 257
Chiron, 157
Christianity
    and animal sacrifice, 60
    and asses, 17
    and cats, 60, 62
    and the crowing cock, 65, 66–67
    and dolpins, 220
    and doves, 95–97
    and eagles, 103
    and fish, 211, 213
    and frogs, 124
    and octopuses, 245
    and parrots, 187
    and peacocks, 188
    and pigs, 196–197
    and scorpions, 216
    and sheep, 225–226
    and sparrows, 235, 236
    and swallows, 248
    and turtles, 256
    See also Jesus, Judeo-Christian

Goldsmith, Oliver, 11, 30
Goodall, Jane, 13
"The Goose Girl," 162
Gordon, Edmund, 277
Gowdie, Isobel, xv, 138
Graham, Alistair, 71
Graham, Kenneth, 32
Grandville, J. J., xvi
Grass, Günter, 93, 127
Grasshoppers, xviii, 1–2, 4, **129–133**
Graves, Robert, 59
The Great Ape Project, 13
Great English Sparrow War, 236
Greece, ancient, xiv–xv, xx
   and ants, 2
   and asses, 16
   bull sacrifices, 45
   and cattle, 47, 48–49
   and cocks and hens, 64–65
   and crocodiles, 70
   and crows, 73
   and deer, 143–144
   and dogs, 89
   and dolphins, 219
   and doves, 95, 97, 97
   and frogs, 124–125
   and geese, 252
   and grasshoppers, 131
   and horses, 158, 159
   and lions, 175
   and monkeys, 8
   and pigs, 195
   and rams, 223
   and scorpions, 215–216
   and snakes, 228, 230, 232
   and swans, 250
   and turtles, 256–257
   and werewolves, 267–268
   and woodpeckers, 82
Green Knight, 27
Griffins, 102, 186, 208
Grimm brothers, xii, 18
   on doves, 97–98
   and fish, 213
   on frogs, 127
   on hedgehogs, 148–149
   on horses, 162
   and Little Red Riding Hood, 270–271
   and Lohengrin, 251
   and Pied Piper, 204–205
   on storks, 153
   and wrens, 277
Grimm, Jacob, 82, 250
Groundhogs, 33
Gryllus, 195
Gubernatis, Angelo De, 232
Guinefort, 92

Gula, 88–89
Gulliver's Travels, 11–12, 163

Haida, 32
   and ravens, 76
   and salmon, 213
   and whales, 265
Hamburgers, 51
Hamlet, 275
Ha-Nakdan, Berechiah ben Natronai, 120
Hannibal, 106
Hanno, 9–10
"Hans My Hedgehog," 148
Hanuman, xiv, 8
al Haq, Mohammed, 119
Hardy, Thomas, 81–82
Hares, xii, xv, **135–140**
   and elephants, 109
Harris, Joel Chandler, 139, 259
Harts, **141–147**
Hathor, *xiv*, 48, 174
Hatto, Bishop, 205
Hausa, 238
Hausman, Gerald, 211
Hawks, **111–113**
   and cuckoos, 79
Hearn, Lafcadio, 53, 240, 253
Hebe, 64–65
Hebrews, xv
   and asses, 16
   and bears, 25
   and bulls, 44–45, 47, 47
   and dogs, 90–91
   and doves and pigeons, 95
   and frogs, 124
   and lions, 175
   and owls, 189
   and pigs, 196
   and plague, 206
   and scapegoats, 225
   and scorpions, 214
   and serpents, 231
   and sheep, 224–225
   and whales, 263–265
   and wolves, 269
   See also Judaism, Judeo-Christian tradition
Hecate, 86
Hecht, Anthony, 255
Hedgehogs, **147–149**
Heket, 123–124
Helen of Troy, 158, 250
Helle, 224
Henry V, 247
Hens, **64–68**, *65*
Hera, 48, 79, 157

ABOUT THE AUTHOR

Boria Sax holds a doctorate in German and Intellectual History from the State University of New York–Buffalo, and he currently works as coordinator of Learning Services at Mercy College in Dobbs Ferry, New York. He has been a consultant to many human rights organizations, including Amnesty International, Helsinki Watch, and the International League. In addition, he is founder and president of the nonprofit organization Nature in Legend and Story (NILAS, Inc.), which is dedicated to promoting "understanding of traditional bonds between human beings and the natural world." He has given guest lectures at the National Zoo, the Staten Island Zoo, the Rockwell Museum, Duke University, the New York Botanical Garden, and many other educational institutions. His previous books include *The Frog King* (1990), *The Serpent and the Swan* (1998), and *Animals in the Third Reich* (2000).